Building Virtual Reality with Unity and SteamVR

Building Virtual Reality with Unity and SteamVR

Jeff W. Murray

CRC Press
Taylor & Francis Group
Boca Raton London New York

CRC Press is an imprint of the
Taylor & Francis Group, an **informa** business

AN A K PETERS BOOK

CRC Press
Taylor & Francis Group
6000 Broken Sound Parkway NW, Suite 300
Boca Raton, FL 33487-2742

Printed on acid-free paper

International Standard Book Number-13: 978-1-138-03351-1 (Paperback)
                                      978-1-138-05124-9 (Hardback)

Visit the Taylor & Francis Web site at
http://www.taylorandfrancis.com

and the CRC Press Web site at
http://www.crcpress.com

Printed and bound in the United States of America by Sheridan

It is my hope that, in the future, VR will bring families and friends closer together and keep them close. This book is dedicated to all of my family. To my parents. To uncles and aunties, cousins and... well, also to the cat. Cat, be nice to the boys.

Contents

Acknowledgments

M Y WIFE IS AMAZING. My kids are also amazing. When I hit my least motivated moments, they always inspire me to keep going. There are no words to describe how amazing it is to have such awesome people in my life.

I would like to extend special thanks to the people who believed in my work and helped me with their awesome support: Michael Zucconi—senior public relations manager at HTC, and thank you sincerely to the entire HTC Vive team. Thank you to Leap Motion. Thanks to the entire OSVR team. Many thanks to Haoyang Liu and Dr. Tristan Dai of Noitom as well as the entire Noitom and Perception Neuron teams in Beijing and Miami. In my research, there were countless sources but I would like to call out Alexander Kondratskiy for sharing his research and findings on his excellent blog, Dan Hurd and Evan Reidland for sharing info on *Lucky's Tale*, and thank you to Columbia University researchers for sharing some of their extensive work on motion sickness.

Thank you Brian Robbins for getting me started in writing books, thanks Richard Bang of Freekstorm for the SteamVR skybox trick, Hello Games for *No Man's Sky* (the game I dreamt of playing since I was a kid), Tami Quiring, Nadeem Rasool, Dwayne Dibley, Liz and Pete Smyth, Isaac and Aiden, Jonah and Simona, Mike Desjardins, Jillian Mood, Christian Boutin, David Helgason, James Gamble, The Oliver Twins, Jeevan Aurol, Rick King, Byron Atkinson-Jones, Aldis Sipolins, Ric Lumb, the whole team at CRC Press/AK Peters, including Jessica Vega and Robert Sims, everyone at Nova Techset, especially Ragesh K.

Thank *you* for buying this book. I wish I could tell you how awesome it is to know that someone else is reading this. The potential for VR goes beyond anything we have seen in a long time—it transcends format, convention, and politics. The virtual world is free from restriction, open to new ideas, and it is already fast developing new perspectives and journeys for all of us. I truly cannot wait to see what you create and I sincerely hope this book helps you to get up and running. Get in there, create new universes, and feel free to let me know when I can come visit them.

Jeff W. Murray

Author

Jeff W. Murray is the author of *Game Development for iOS with Unity3D* (2012) and *C# Game Programming Cookbook for Unity 3D* (2014), also published by CRC Press. In his game development career spanning over 14 years, he has worked with some of the world's largest brands as a programmer, game designer, and director. He has worked with the Unity engine since its initial public release, on projects ranging from hit mobile games to medical simulations. Murray currently works in VR research and development for IBM Research.

Introduction

IN 2017, WE STAND at the gates of a new technological landscape. As we look out at the real estate trying to figure out just how and what to build there, it is clear that there is still a lot to discover. There are few rules. In the virtual world there are no politics, no corporations, and no borders to what we can experience or what we can build for others to experience. Where this goes from here is up to us. We are only just learning how people react to virtual reality (VR), what the possibilities are, a seemingly endless number of possibilities in entertainment, learning, rehabilitation, experience, and development. Even the very basics of interfaces: how our fellow cybernauts interact with the virtual world, is still undecided. What feels natural in the virtual world? How do we move around, touch things, feel objects, and manipulate the environment? The number of people with access to the tools to create virtual content has also never been so wide-ranging and we have more people than ever coming up with new and exciting additions to our virtual experiences. In the race to provide technology to accommodate this new experience, hardware manufacturers are running as fast as they can to make VR better, stronger, and faster. No matter how quickly we run to keep up, the technology does not stop evolving and changing. Technology will keep moving. We will never stop learning. New technology appears all the time and, when you reach the end of this book, it will be up to you to get involved and to potentially start shaping VR's future. Do not be afraid to throw out convention and try out alternative ways of doing things that are different to the ways we have interacted with games or simulations in the past. You are a visionary who could help shape the VR landscape of tomorrow. The virtual experiences of the future will be built upon the experiences of today, so experiment and create amazing new things! Remember to have fun, look after yourself, and be nice to each other.

Prerequisites

Your set up costs will be a development PC and whatever cool hardware tech you want to plug into it. Along with your chosen VR devices, let us take a quick look at what else you will be needing:

Unity (available from the Unity store at http://www.unity3d.com): Unity and the required SDKs can be downloaded free of charge with no catches. Unity Personal boasts that it is a fully-featured version of Unity with just a few caveats. You can do everything in this book with Unity Personal, just as long as you have a VR headset to test with. If there is any sort of question as to whether or not you need a paid version of Unity, you can always try out the free Personal edition to get used to it and see how it all goes before you put any money into it.

Steam client: The Steam client is a free download that gives you access to Valve Software's library and a store full of games. Essentially, Steam is an application that allows you to download and buy things, but in the context of this book Steam is the application that you use to download and run SteamVR with.

SteamVR: SteamVR is a system based on Open Source Virtual Reality libraries. It provides a platform for VR. SteamVR runs as a part of the Steam client. Unity will communicate with your VR hardware through the SteamVR system.

C# programming knowledge: Again, to reiterate this very important point: this is *not* a book about learning how to program. I will be explaining how all of the code works, but you will need to know some C# and there are a number of other books out there for that specific purpose. Programming is a vast subject and it makes no sense to try to teach you both this and VR development at the same time. This book is about making VR experiences, not about learning to program. I will do my best to explain everything as well as I can, of course!

WHO IS THIS BOOK FOR?

Unity have done an amazing job with their own guides and tutorials, so if you have never used the engine before I would highly recommend taking a look at the Unity documentation and following their guides for basic use of the editor. There is a basic crash course in this book, but I do not go into detail. I will do everything I can to outline processes, keyboard shortcuts, and where to click to make the right things happen, but this is not a book to teach Unity.

This is also not a book about programming and it is not a book about the right or wrong ways to write code. We assume that the reader has some experience of the C# programming language but may be completely new to VR or VR-focussed development. I also feel it is important to note that I am a self-taught programmer and I understand that there may well be better ways to do things. This is a book about concepts and it is inevitable that there will be better methods for achieving some of the same goals. Techniques and concepts offered in this book are there to provide a solid foundation, not to be the final word on any subject. Use the concepts, make them your own, and do things the way you want to do them. Most of all, try to have fun doing it.

CHAPTER 1

A Brief Introduction to the Virtual World

W<small>E ARE THE CLOSEST</small> we have ever been to experiencing "true" virtual reality (VR). Sure, we have had flashes of VR in the past but nothing can compare to the current generation in both terms of experience or technology. The amount of telepresence (the feeling of actually being there) we can achieve today is higher than ever before and we are interacting with VR in completely new ways. The temptation to rely on aspects from traditional simulation or game development is natural, but it is time to throw out the rulebook. You are standing at the forefront of an entirely new form of entertainment where the rules have not yet been written. This chapter looks at VR from a bird's-eye view; we will look into how we got to the consumer VR technology we have today, what the challenges are, what is possible, and a little about what it means to be a VR developer in the current generation, and how we can go about planning and designing for it.

This chapter is not an in-depth examination of the subjects—some of these sections would probably make good books of their own—but this chapter is intended to give you a good virtual grounding before we cross over to the virtual world later in this book.

HOW LONG HAVE WE BEEN VIRTUAL?

The term has been with us for a lot longer than you might expect. One of the earliest uses, most likely the first, was by the writer Antonin Artaud in his collection of essays "The Theatre and its Double" published in 1938 (Artaud, 1958). Artaud referred to "The Virtual Reality of Theatre" which looks at the theater and the relationships between the actors and reality. Although Artaud was not talking about VR in any sense as we know it, I do feel that there are some interesting parallels between VR and the theater in terms of the presence and dramatic use of space. Artaud believed that the theater was a place where people would go to find a sense of humanity, a connection to the emotional beyond, and other media. In a way, he attempted to describe how theater created a sense of presence for the theatergoer through emotional and psychological connection to the stage and its performers. In the virtual world, our visitors need to feel a connection or a presence in perhaps a similar way to what Artaud described. An emotional and psychological investment by our VR visitors helps them to connect and immerse with the virtual world.

When the work is done to connect a user with the psychological and emotional content, we also have to understand the environment around us, to find context for how the virtual universe works, and how we are supposed to interact with it. The lighting, the way things move, colors, the world scale—the entire stage has a massive impact on how our virtual visitors feel and the depth of experience they are likely to have. Just as a stage play might guide the audience through a story with both visual and nonvisual cues, the virtual visitor will look to more than the most obvious places to define their virtual experience.

BEFORE THE HEADSET

One of the first VR simulations was a device known as a Link Trainer. It was essentially a flight simulator using motors and mechanical devices to simulate the types of conditions a pilot might experience in the air. It was intended to help train pilots to know how to compensate for various conditions and control an aircraft safely without having to risk a real aircraft. The fact that this device was around and working in 1929 blows my mind!

Science fiction writers have dreamed for a long time about entering a simulated world but it is only now that we are actually getting close to achieving something so realistic as to be truly meaningful. Back when VR first appeared in popular culture, the virtual world had no real grounding in reality because the technology it might one day require was completely unknown. In the 1935 short story *Pygmalion's Spectacles*, the science fiction writer Stanley G. Weinbaum told of a pair of goggles that would provide holographic recordings for the wearer (Weinbaum, 1949). It would be a long time before anything even close to that prediction would make it to fruition, but the idea of being able to travel to other worlds through a headset or viewer had truly been born.

THE BIRTH OF THE HEAD-MOUNTED DISPLAY

Around 4 years after Stanley G. Weinbaum penned *Pygmalion's Spectacles*, something called the View-Master Stereoscope appeared. It was a device for viewing photographs based on the principle of showing a different image to each eye to form a stereoscopic 3D picture. One interesting point about the View-Master is its equivalent similarities to today's Google Cardboard, taking people to locations that they may not be able to visit in the real world—virtual tourism. That was not the only use for View-Master, however, as the US military saw the potential in the 1940s, ordering around 100,000 viewers (Sell, Sell and Van Pelt, 2000).

The View-Master is still going strong, albeit in a few different forms. Mattel makes the regular View-Master binocular-type viewers and now a View-Master Virtual Reality smartphone-based headset mostly intended for educational and educational leisure use.

Though unrelated directly to the head-mounted display (HMD), Morton Heilig's Sensorama is widely regarded as the next milestone in VR after the View-Master. It was essentially a 3D cinema unit about the same size as an arcade cabinet. Patented in 1962, Sensorama featured stereo speakers, a stereoscopic 3D screen, a vibrating seat and—hard to believe though it may be—fans with smell generators so that viewers could even smell the action. Its inventor Morton Heilig was a filmmaker. He made all of the short films for Sensorama and he tried to make movies that would give the viewer a feeling of being inside them. In one movie, the viewer would have the viewpoint as if they were on a bicycle ride through Brooklyn, New York. The Sensorama would blow air into their face and make smells that were akin to the city. The 3D speakers roared out the sounds of the streets as the vibrating chair shook to simulate the feeling of the bumps in the road as they are hit by the wheels. Sensorama took its viewers and attempted to make them feel a telepresence inside the actual experience, rather than merely looking at it. Regardless of whether or not it was a success, the goal was very similar to what we would like our virtual worlds to do today. Sadly, Heilig's invention failed to sell and with no investment, it never got any further than the prototype stages.

This is the point where we come back to HMD. After Sensorama, Morton Heilig went on to work on something known as the Telesphere

Mask—the first HMD. Its television screen was capable of stereoscopic 3D but the device had no motion tracking because, at that stage, there was just no need for it. Telesphere Mask was used only for noninteractive film, but it remains to be the first example of a head-mounted display, representing a major step toward VR.

A year later, two engineers took HMD concept and introduced motion tracking, with their system called Headsight.

Headsight was the brainchild of Philco Corporation. It featured a magnetic tracking system and would show images on its cathode-ray tube (CRT) screen, live-fed from a closed-circuit television camera. The camera would move around based on the tracked position of the headset, which made the invention an interesting prospect for the military as it could be used as a remote viewer in situations where sending in a human might be too dangerous.

For the next major jump in tech, we skip forward to 1968 when Ivan Sutherland and his student Bob Sproull created The Sword of Damocles. I love the name. The Sword of Damocles refers to an ancient Greek anecdote, where Damocles trades place with a king only to discover that being a king is a much more dangerous and difficult job than he anticipated. The phrase is also used to express the ever-present danger those in power have to live with, such as a queen who fears someone else might like to forcibly take the throne from her, or perhaps the leader of a criminal gang who fears takeover from another criminal.

You can find the phrase "Sword of Damocles" in all kinds of literature, ranging from Shakespeare to videogames and movies.

Sutherland and Sproull created Sword of Damocles as the first VR system to take HMD and connect it to a computer to create the images. Though technology would only allow for simple (by today's standards) wireframe graphics, I am sure that in 1968 entering this virtual world must have been a pretty amazing and perhaps humbling experience. Given its name, I think its creators may have thought the same.

The military and medical fields continued to study applications of VR over the years, but it was generally too expensive to be accessible outside of organizations with deep pockets. From the mid-1980s, public interest in VR started to grow and hardware makers began to look at the possibilities of delivering VR entertainment experiences. Despite growing interest, it was not until 1987 that the term VR was actually used to describe these types of experiences, despite Artaud having used the term nearly 50 years prior. Jaron Lanier, whose company VPL research developed VR gear, is credited as popularizing the term VR as an all-encompassing term for the field he was working in.

VR arcade machines began to appear in the late 1980s and early 1990s but the machines were just too expensive for the mass market, costing in excess of $50,000 each. Despite the advancements throughout the 1970s and 1980s, costs associated with VR kept it outside of the reach of the general public. Consumer VR was almost unfeasible right up until the 1990s when, at last, capable technology finally began to become affordable.

THE ROAD TO CONSUMER VIRTUAL REALITY

One name you might be surprised to read about here is Sega. In 1993, the company was riding high from game console success when announced something called SegaVR. SegaVR was intended to be HMD add-on for the Sega Genesis game console. Launch titles included *Virtua Racing* and *Matrix Runner*, though it never came to be. After technical difficulties and reports of headaches and nausea during playtesting, SegaVR never launched. It was cancelled in 1994 before consumers even had a chance to try it for themselves, 1995 was a milestone for this new affordable consumer VR market, seeing the arrival of the Nintendo Virtual Boy and the Forte VFX1.

People often mention the Nintendo Virtual Boy as having a key place in the advancement of VR. I think the only thing that the Virtual Boy did was to highlight the problems in getting a wary public to hand over their hard-earned cash for unproven technology. It was affordable, futuristic, and had some great launch titles, but it failed to reach sales targets. The media savagely attacked it, reporting on a wide scale that people were experiencing headaches. Perhaps it was the low quality, monochromatic display, the uncomfortable position you needed to be in to play or the fact that it was, in-fact, a moving GameBoy built into a modernized version of a View-Master. The technology was not good enough and interest alone in VR was already starting to wane as a result. Even in true VR experiences of the time, the types of display technology used back then were CRT displays with low refresh rates. Viewers would see a lot of ghosting when they moved their heads. The lens was difficult to adjust and HMDs from the 1990s were also uncomfortable and bulky. Some weighed as much as five pounds or more. Add the pull from the heavy cables into the equation and it did not take too long for the viewer's neck to get tired and start to ache. Low processor speeds, lenses that caused eye strain and headaches, slow head tracking, and the widespread nausea and sickness were no doubt the biggest contributors to the steady decline of VR in the latter half of the decade.

HOME PC VR

Often overlooked, the VFX1 came about in 1995 and was made by Forte Technologies. It cost around $695 and its HMD was an impressive bit of kit that could play PC games like *Quake*, *DOOM*, *Decent*, and *Magic Carpet* on a regular IBM PC 386.

The VFX1 was feature-rich. It had built-in headphones, a microphone, and head movement tracking on three axes. Its display may have been far from where we are today, but at the time it was spectacular with its 256 color graphics rendering out to dual 0.7" 263 × 230 LCD displays at 60 Hz. Before you go comparing those numbers to something like the current generation of Oculus Rift rendering 120 Hz 2160 × 1200 on OLED screens, remember that games at that time were rendering around these kinds of resolutions anyway so a higher resolution display would have been an expensive waste of money. At the time, the VFX1 was an amazing, if a little costly, home VR system. It without question is the closest to the headsets we have today, but for whatever reason it just did not sell. Likely, it was the lack of capable computers in the home that reduced its market below Forte's expectations. There were less home computers, the very latest high-end systems running processors at around 133 MHz, which does not even begin to compare to todays 3+GHz processors. By late 1995, 3DFX had only just introduced the first home PC 3D graphics acceleration card, the Voodoo (3Dfx Interactive, 1995). Most home PCS were low spec and slow rendering. Display systems, too, were far from ideal for headset use. A new PC with a Pentium Pro processor could cost well in excess of $1000 and you still needed to pay another $700 on top of that for a headset. Neither the VFX1 nor its predecessor the VFX2 was popular enough to keep their makers in the business.

CONSUMER VR REBIRTH

VR had been riding high in the public eye throughout the 1990s. The VR scene had been trendy for a while, making appearances in hit Hollywood movies and defining a generation with its imagery, but by the year 2000 the market had fizzled out almost entirely. The technology had not been capable of providing what the public demanded of it, to create experiences that were comfortable enough for regular people to actually want to be a part of. There were a few arcade machines still around, but most hardware manufacturers had written VR off as a bad business decision. It would take another wave of technological advancement, in another field entirely, that would allow VR to make its triumphant return to our homes. Fast forward to 2012. The crowdfunding website Kickstarter was all the rage as it allows inventors, content creators, and business people to look to their fans and audience for funding. Crowdfunding was the buzzword of the day and a promising young startup named Oculus was about to smash past their funding goals and restart the virtual fire. Their system, the Rift, promised a new and exciting VR that was bigger and brighter than ever before. Its creators raised over 2 million USD. With the technology in place, consumers lined up to step into more life-like experiences, lower latency, and affordable VR in their own homes.

VR has come a long way since the days of wireframe-only graphics on low resolution displays at low frame-rates. Today, it's possible to play an almost photo realistic videogame at 120 frames per second through a headset running at a higher quality than some desktop computer monitors. How did this all happen, though? And why was not today's technology possible sooner?

Palmer Luckey, founder of Oculus VR, accredits the jump in technology to the mobile phone manufacturers. The first prototype of his headset was made from a mobile phone screen wired up to aftermarket components hacked and taped together. All of the tech, and access to it, happened at the right time. All it took was one clever engineer to put it together in the right way. The miniaturization, affordability, and improvements in screen technology, gyrometers, infra-red tracking hardware, and mobile camera technology were huge contributors to the birth of this generation of VR devices.

There are many different headsets on the market, taking different approaches. You can buy cardboard VR for less than $50 that you can use simply by slotting in a mobile phone. The HTC Vive offers a standing up, moving around, room-scale experience that you can now convert to a wireless headset with an add-on. The hardware is now more than capable of delivering on the experience and it looks like demand is booming, too, with over 1.3 million headsets shipped in 2016 and VR market projections up to 4.6 billion USD in 2017 (Statista, 2016).

The technology is moving fast, changing and evolving constantly as we try to solve some of its problems and make better VR experiences. VR headsets are not just two screens in your face.

WHAT DOES NOT WORK ABOUT VR?

The level of technology capable of making VR is so new that we are only just starting to discover and solve the problems. Despite our efforts to make everything work, it may even turn out that some of VR's biggest issues turn out to be unsolvable with the tech we currently have available.

Latency

The term "latency," in reference to VR technology, usually refers to something called motion to photon latency. In layman's terms, this is the delay between the speeds at which the screen updates versus the speed that the person viewing the screen moves their head at.

The mind has no problem at all making sense of things at over 100 milliseconds of latency time, but it makes for an uncomfortable experience. The brain is not easily fooled into believing that an image is reality. It takes just the tiniest difference between how quickly you turn your head and what you see in the display for it to become a major contributor to an uncomfortable experience.

Many believe that an acceptable latency rate is below approximately 20 milliseconds. The lower we can get this number, however, the better. Current generation devices deliver between 10 and 20 ms; but this number is only made possible with optimization techniques to do some clever estimations or "cheats" to update the display quicker.

Latency gets better with each generation of devices but we still have to use "cheats" to reach the acceptable levels of latency. To solve the problem properly, experts such as John Carmack and Michael Abrash believe that we may have to go back to the drawing board to fundamentally redesign how our display systems work.

Due to the delay between the computers running the simulation and the ones doing the calculations, even measuring latency is problematic at this level. To measure VR latency, developers have been known to use high speed video to capture both the motion and the simulation, and the two videos are compared by stepping frame by frame through the video.

Juddering and Smearing

Computer graphics cards render with frames, normally at a rate so fast that our eyes do not see any sort of break or discrepancy between updates. The problem with VR is that we are building an interface that needs to work extremely closely in sync with the physical body. The display is trying to "trick" the brain into believing that it is seeing something unreal.

Whereas a monitor only renders a very limited field of view, HMDs aim to surround the viewer with a wide field of view intended to replace real-life vision. It may not seem like it, but the speed at which you can turn your head and move your eye in the same direction can actually bring up perceptual problems caused by the eyes seeing in-between those frame updates. Having the wider field of view means that your eyes need to travel longer distances than they might with a traditional monitor, which is why it becomes more of an issue with HMD displays.

Frames are updated at a fixed rate, at fixed intervals in time, whereas the real-world updates smoothly and consistently. When the eyes move faster than the display, there is no built-in system for our brains to fill in the gaps between frames. There are several hacks we can employ to reduce the effects, or to hide them, but they too have side-effects which need to be addressed. It may be that the only real solution is to raise the frame rate higher than is possible with current graphics rendering technology.

The Screen Door Effect

The screen door effect is a term referring to visible lines between pixels on a screen. It gets its name because the effect is as though you are looking out through a screen door. In a VR headset, the screen door effect is caused by the magnification that the lens needs to perform to give you the required field of view and required focus on the little screen inside the headset. Small screen technology is consistently improving, but it is unlikely that the screen door effect can be completely solved any time soon because of the sheer size of resolution required to be able to eradicate it. Not only would rendering at much higher resolutions demand more power from the computer doing the heavy lifting, but it would require expensive screen technology that just is not out there yet. Thankfully, once you get into VR and start engaging in some good VR content, the screen door effect becomes less and less of an issue. It's there, we know it is, but the content usually takes your mind off it enough to just enjoy the experience.

At the time of writing, Razer's HDK2 headset is the only HMD to include I.Q.E. (image quality enhancement) technology that is said to significantly reduce the screen door effect. Although it may not be possible to completely eradicate, technologies like this could help to make the effect less noticeable to the viewer.

VR Sickness

Motion sickness symptoms have plagued the VR industry since the begin-ning and despite numerous questionable claims that it has been solved, even NASA have not found a fix-all solution. There are several theories as to why people get sick in VR and by following those leads we can, in some circumstances, reduce it, but with no conclusive evidence as to its cause, it remains a stubborn problem for VR developers. In Chapter 12, we will look at some ways to lessen the impact of motion sickness by looking at some of the most common problems and solutions that have worked in some situations. We may not be able to cure it, but there are certain tools you can provide your viewers to try to lessen its grip on them. The more options you can give, the better, as no two people appear to be affected by VR sickness in the exact same way.

What Sorts of Experiences Can We Expect?

After Rift was successfully funded by Kickstarter, its low-cost development kits (given as one of the perks to backers who paid over a certain amount) gave small developers and smaller studios an opportunity to buy into cut-ting edge VR technology. After the company was acquired by Facebook, they appeared to move away from their earlier developer-centric approach and looked more toward a consumer focus. As Rift slowly found some stable ground, HTC was already integrating the Vive into gaming com-munities and innovating far beyond what a sit down VR experience could deliver.

Though a little late to the room-scale market, Rift now offers tracked controllers and room-scale support via the purchase of additional tracking cameras and controllers. Touch is the equivalent of Vive's wand-like con-trollers, tracked around the play area by two or more cameras connected to a PC via USB cables. The recommended play area sizes are significantly smaller than the Vive (Lang, 2016) with a two-camera Rift set up offering coverage for a 5 ft by 5 ft area, but the purchase of more tracking cameras can open up the play space beyond 10 ft. I will not be covering Touch in this book, but we will look at Vive wand controllers in detail, in Chapter 9.

Development Kit 1

The Rift began with a Kickstarter crowdfunding campaign on August 1, 2012. The first wave of HMDs was given as rewards to backers who pledged $300 or more to the fundraising. This was a game-changer for VR. A real VR experience in your own home for less than the price of a new PC!

The first demos and games had incredible novelty value, since most users had never experienced anything like it before, and videos of people experiencing VR for the first time soon flooded video sharing sites like YouTube. My own DK1 demo ParrotCoaster was featured on several news sites, including BBC News showing viewer's reactions to the nauseous feelings they experienced as they encountered the new sensations of a virtual rollercoaster. The comedic reactions of VR-goers shared across the numerous social networks no doubt helped the adoption of VR by the general public. Despite the DK1 only being available to developers, the public's renewed interest in VR was obvious. Television, magazines, news coverage; VR was a hot topic in the public eye once again, for the first time in 20 years.

On the one hand, it was an innovative and experimental time for VR, yet on the other hand most developers (including myself) were falling into the trap of trying too hard to recreate reality rather than creating a new one. The first wave of new VR experiences was mostly first-person viewpoints where the view through HMD would represent the view of the player character inside in the simulation, and the gold rush to add VR to anything and everything meant that only a limited number of developers actually stood out.

As well as experiences built from the ground up for VR, we began to see third-party modifiers to existing games that would enable games such as *Minecraft, Mirror's Edge,* and *Skyrim* to work even though they were never designed for that purpose. It was great to be able to get inside their worlds and look around, but many were simply too hard to navigate or just not compatible with the new technology. They could display in VR without too much trouble, but user interfaces, game design, and game interactions were not suited to the medium. Problems included the difficulty of using the keyboard when you cannot see the keys, or clicking on a button that is barely within your visible range of vision. The DK1 display was also quite poor, displaying at a relatively low resolution, much lower than the average desktop display, making it impossible for situations where a lot of user interface text was called for. Most games on-screen text would usually be too small to be read. It was not just the interfaces that caused problems, though. Several unsupported third-party systems had been developed to provide support for major AAA games like *Skyrim* and *Mirror's Edge*, but as these games were not designed for VR there were problems with the interfaces or, such as in cases like *Mirror's Edge*, the camera systems, which were not designed to be VR-friendly.

Mirror's Edge has players hurtling across the tops of buildings doing some extreme Parkour moves over, under, and around obstacles in first person. Limitations of the DK1 technology and the fact that most design choices had been based on desktop monitors, rather than HMDs, many of these early major game experiences left many players feeling extremely sick and unable to play for more than minutes at a time. Note that there were some people that got along with all of these things just fine, with no nausea or sickness at all, but it was the majority of badly affected users who felt like VR just was not for them. Many DK1 owners stepped away from VR altogether, opting to wait and see if the sickness would be lessened or eradicated in future versions, though some developers signed straight up for the next round.

Development Kit 2

The second Rift development kit, known as the DK2 (Development Kit 2) launched in July 2014 and was leaps and bounds ahead of its predecessor. Gone was the 640×800 pixels per eye display, now upgraded to 1200×1080. One of the biggest and most significant changes was the upgrade from an LCD (liquid crystal display) to Low-Persistence OLED (organic light-emitting diode) display. The motion response speed of LCD meant all kinds of problems with image smearing and juddering on the DK1, whereas OLED offers a much faster response time. The low persistence meant that pixels would be updated faster and be lit for a shorter time, which in turn reduces smearing and judder. As well as significant visual improvement, this meant VR sickness sufferers were affected much less with the DK2 than with its predecessor. Perhaps naively, it was actually said that switching to a low-persistence OLED display would solve the VR sickness problem altogether. Of course, we now know that this was not the case and despite it helping reduce the impact of VR sickness, it still exists and is most likely caused by more than just one single aspect or element of the VR experience.

The DK2 also boasted positional tracking, which meant viewers could now lean in or look around objects in the virtual world. This new feature alone opened up the latest wave of VR experiences to a host of original possibilities.

It was during the time of DK2 that VR really started gaining traction in the games industry, with more and more of the larger game development companies adding native VR support to their games.

Consumer VR: Rift CV1 and the HTC Vive

As VR matures, we are already seeing experiences that move away from replicating reality and closer to becoming entirely new forms of entertainment. One such evolving form is "virtual reality movies." VR movies are stories that take place around the viewer. The best way I can describe the experience is to imagine that the actors are performing around you and although you cannot move, you can look anywhere you like. At the time of writing, there are more than four VR movies on the official store. One of them, Henry, tells the story of a small hedgehog who likes to hug. He exists in a wonderful cartoon world which looks like it could easily have come straight out of a big budget movie such as *Toy Story* or *Cars*. Henry does not have many friends because when Henry hugs, they get hurt by his spikes. In this story, Henry makes a birthday wish that comes true and some balloon animals come to life. There are so many elements that work together to make the movie work including lighting, the scale of the world, its sound effects and voiceover storytelling; all working together to create not just an ambience but a real sense that you are inside Henry's little house. With the correct lighting, environment, sounds, and use of space you can do more than just show people a new world; you can make them feel like they are actually inside of it. Henry demonstrates that it is not simply realism or realistic imagery which brings the viewer into the virtual world, but in fact the overall creation of a presence in the space.

Independent movie makers are finding VR can be a great place for storytelling.

Offered as part of the CV1 package was *Lucky's Tale*. On the surface, this game looks like a regular 3D platform game with a cute little fox named Lucky leading the way. His friend, Piggy, has been captured by some sort of giant tentacle monster. It is the player's job to traverse the numerous levels and go and save Piggy by controlling Lucky in third person. That is, the camera follows Lucky around rather than showing his point-of-view.

CAN I GO INSIDE THE COMPUTER, LIKE TRON? THE COMPLICATIONS AND CHALLENGES VR IS FACING

Hollywood has painted a rather unrealistic view of the virtual world. Most movie representations show it as a technology that can take over all of the senses to make the experience almost indistinguishable from reality. The photorealistic images, sounds, and methods of moving around and interacting with the world are lifelike, perfect reproductions of their real-world counterparts. At the time of writing, it is not even possible to reliably use our bodies in the virtual world let alone get a sense of taste or smell. There are old problems to solve, new problems to solve, and seemingly endless ways we can interact in the virtual world or ways that the virtual world can interact with the viewer. As the technology evolves, so does a language for using VR.

Motion Tracking and Motion Capture for Input

Camera-based tracking is not new to the games industry and developers are keen to reuse existing technology in the virtual world. Microsoft's Kinect camera has been used to try to achieve full body tracking, but with limited results. One problem is that the camera only sees from a single angle, which may be remedied by using multiple cameras combined to build up a full picture of the subject to be tracked. The first-generation Kinect device produced rather low-quality video images of the subject though significant improvements have been made in the latest model. That said, camera tracking is always tricky because of lighting and environmental lighting can have a major effect on the quality of tracking that can be achieved. Some types of lighting setups can cause it to fail completely, while others provide an almost perfect tracking rate. Although this is fine in controlled environments (studios etc.) in order to solve the problem properly, the winning consumer solution is going to need to work regardless of the lighting in the environment it is set up in.

The Perception Neuron is a motion capture suit made by Noitom. Rather than taking the traditional approach of using cameras for motion capture, the Neuron uses something called IMU (inertial measurement units). The suit has a number of inertial trackers connected to a small hub on the back, which sends positional information to the computer via either USB or WI-FI connection. As well as a capture device for animation and movement study, the Perception Neuron is being used increasingly in VR simulations. By providing full-body motion capture, Neuron makes an interesting way to interact, in an intuitive way, with the virtual world.

Leap Motion is a company founded in 2010 by Michael Buckwald that focuses primarily on a camera-based hand tracking technology. Initially, Leap Motion was intended to be used as an alternative to the computer mouse. Rather than using the mouse to move the pointer around the screen, Leap Motion allows users to use hands and fingers to point at the screen and use gestures. Growing alongside the current wave of VR, it was perhaps inevitable that the two would meet. It was not long before the VR community began using Leap Motion with HMD. Earliest attempts to use Leap Motion for VR were complicated because the ideal angle for the Leap device was for it to be on a desk, facing directly upward, as it was originally designed to be used. With VR, the Leap Motion device worked better when it was fitted against the front of HMD looking forward. This change of angle called for a different approach. Currently in Beta, Leap Motion now offers software named Orion, which is its custom hand recognition system made specifically for VR HMDs. With a small mounting plate (or a little tape or tack to attach the Leap device to the front of the display) the user's hands and fingers are tracked by Leap Motion and represented in the virtual world by 3D modeled hands and fingers.

Haptic Feedback

Tracking the physical body will help a great deal in making VR feel more real, but what about touching, feeling, or being affected physically by the virtual world? We call this haptic feedback. Many regular game controllers give you haptic feedback in the form of vibration from the controller. You might have felt this on Playstation or Xbox controllers. The HTC Vive controllers also have a vibration feature that can be used to make the virtual world feel a little more solid. For example, I was recently playing a game where the player holds a sword and a shield. The sword was controlled by the right controller and the shield on the left. If I tried to put the sword through the shield, there was nothing that the game could do to stop me but it did provide a little vibration whenever the two objects collided with each other. This tiny bit of feedback served to highlight what was happening and it made the objects feel like they had some kind of physical presence rather than just being images of the objects I was looking at.

Outside of controller feedback, one technologically ambitious feedback systems is called the TeslaSuit. The TeslaSuit sends pulses, of varying amplitude, frequency, and pulse ranges, to electrodes. The electrodes stimulate the wearer's skin, muscles, and nerve endings to create feedback. Essentially, it's a suit that zaps you with electricity whenever the computer tells it to. Its modular design allows for expansion, such as a motion capture module that may be able solve the problem of full-body motion tracking. At the time of writing, however, this technology is very much still under development and its final capabilities have yet to be finalized.

Other haptic feedback systems tend to be more focused on particular parts of the body, solving problems such as fingers and hand touching with a glove rather than tackling the entire body in a single suit. The Phantom Omni® Haptic Device provides what looks like a stylus attached to a robot arm. You move the stylus around and the robot arm feeds back as though the stylus is touching whatever is happening in the virtual world. This has amazing uses in medical training and simulation as well as potentially providing a haptic method of interacting with the computer-generated environment.

Eye Tracking

Aside from what our bodies are doing in VR there is also a need to find out what it is viewers are looking at. Companies such as Fove, Tobii Tech, and SMI believe that eye tracking has an important place in their future. With eye tracking, the computer detects where in the headset the viewer is looking and feeds that information back into the simulation for processing. This type of technology would be particularly helpful in virtual worlds where face-to-face meetings are important, or for advanced interactions with non-player characters. For example, one such interaction might be having an avatar that could look back at you when you look at their face, or perhaps an avatar that would focus on the same background object as the viewer and comment on it. Eye tracking also has potentially game-changing implications for people with physical disabilities, by making it possible to control and interact just by looking.

Space and Movement

The Vive represented a huge leap forward for moving around in a physical space. Room-scale VR is the freedom to literally walk around a real-world space and have the hardware track your position in it, and represent your position in the VR simulation. The range is impressive and you can track a viewer in a large room, but in the quest for more freedom of movement, the search is on for solutions to tracking much larger spaces.

The Vive uses sensors built into the headset to detect laser beams. The base station casts out a sweep of beams that cover the room and the Vive's many built-in sensors detect them. Based on which sensors are hit, angles and so forth, it is possible to discover the headsets position and rotation. Other headsets use a camera-based approach, with a number of infra-red LEDs on the headset are picked up by one or more cameras. The positions of the lights, as they are detected by the camera, are then used to calculate the headset position and rotation in the space. Both approaches have their advantages and disadvantages and both approaches present huge challenges to overcome to be able to expand the play area space. Accurate detection calls for crystal clear detection, which has the real danger of driving up the prices beyond affordability. Using the current approach to positional tracking, a balance must be found between range and cost. At the moment, warehouse-sized tracking is priced beyond that of the average home-user. A large-scale tracking system can cost in excess of $15,000.

Eventually, I expect headsets to either include mobile devices inside them or to be driven by mobile computers. Until mobile technology reaches the same level as high-end desktop gaming computers, in large-scale environments we hit the problem of running cables safely and efficiently. USB cables in particular have limits on how long they can be without needing to be boosted. To avoid having to trail cables from computers to headsets, one solution is the wearable computer. Backpack computers are just that; computers, similar in size and weight to laptops, made specifically to be carried as a backpack. They are perfect for large-scale VR simulations and there are already plans to open laser tag-like VR experiences to the public using this type of technology in the very near future.

If you do not have a large warehouse but you still want to move around realistically in VR, the answer may be something called a motion platform. Wearing special shoes, the user's feet slide around on a platform. The motion platform detects the movement and uses that data to move them around in the virtual world.

Making Content Inside VR

There are several different drag and drop systems in development for creating different types of content in VR, from simple 3D model viewers to full-scale game production.

EditorVR is Unity's currently experimental system that will enable Unity developers to work directly inside VR rather than having to put on the headset, preview, take off the headset for editing and so on. This type of workflow suits VR development, but there are a lot of challenges still to overcome to make it easy to use, intuitive, and to ensure that developers do not suffer any excessive fatigue.

An associate project of EditorVR is Unity's Carte Blanche. Carte Blanche is a vision for an editor based in VR that can provide VR-in-VR authoring tools for nontechnical users. A drag and drop system is proposed, taking full advantage of motion controllers to track gestures and hand movements. It is still a way off and still in early conceptual stages, but Carte Blanche offers a glimpse at how content generation might work in the VR of the future.

DESIGNING AND DEVELOPING FOR VIRTUAL REALITY

If you already have a game design document, or plans on how you intend to implement all of the interactivity in your virtual world, there is a very good chance that the final working systems will end up quite different from those original ideas. Testing and iteration are going to be at the very center of your production process and what feels right will triumph over anything that may have seemed right on paper. Preplanning may seem like a difficult task in VR design, but we can look to traditional software and game design for a few clues on how to deal with a project that will most likely change dramatically, evolving as its development progresses. This is not a problem specific to VR. Designing software of any kind is a learning process and no-one really understands fully what will be involved or what will crop up to block the road ahead. In software development of all kinds, debugging is the process of solving and removing unsuspected negative issues. The hardware, operating systems, middleware, network connections, and so on, combined with the human element of creativity, varying approaches to thought and problem solving—there are a huge number of unpredictable factors that can and will come into play.

At this point, I refuse to get into an argument as to different approaches to project management and which one is better than the other. The argument goes on forever. Ask two producers in videogames which production process is best for videogames and you will likely get two answers. What I do want to look at are a few ways to manage the process without going too far down any particular project management method.

Plan: Any Sort of Plan Will Do

When the project is a single developer, having a plan can be a good bonus and a great way to keep things on target and moving forward in the right direction. Personally, when I work alone I like to use to-do lists for everything. I start out with an outline, then bullet-point it out into more detail, and continue to break it down until I can see all of the systems I need to build. I can see the approximate scope of the project and I can at the very least begin to think about any areas that may cause problems before I hit them. At this stage, nothing is particularly detailed—just a list of jobs, really. I can break them down as much as I want, or leave them at a bird's-eye view of a particular area. When motivation dips and the going gets tough, one huge advantage is that I can break down my task lists further and further just so that I can have something to check off the list on any particular day. Having an item to check off, no matter how small, feels like progress and progress is good!

Working on projects that have more than one person working on them will flow much better if everyone involved has an idea of what they are supposed to be working on—or, at the very least, which direction they are supposed to be running in.

When you have some idea of the systems required for your project, the main advantage is that you know right from the beginning where your strengths and weaknesses are. By breaking down the tasks which seem to be the most intimidating, each one can be split into manageable pieces or you can spend more time working out how to construct them.

Get Your Main Interactions in Place Early

The interactions your users will use most are the most important. Develop those first, then develop everything else around them. For example, if your project calls for the use of virtual power tools you should start the development process by figuring out how the tools will work, how a user switches between different tools, and how they will apply to the environment and experience as a whole.

Test, prototype, and iterate on your core controls before going full steam ahead into production.

Test on Real People

Your team may be the best at what they do, but no one will be able to break your experience in the same way a novice user can. What tends to happen during testing is that you focus on particular areas and follow particular paths through the experience based on our own expectations of our users. New users will try things that you may not expect them to, which can often lead to finding issues that may even have been hidden in plain sight.

Another advantage to having other people test (other people not involved in production) is in seeing how their instincts align with yours. The way in which your interaction systems work will be pushed by users new to the experience and you will soon be made aware of problem areas by unpredictable usage.

If you know other VR developers, they may be able to bring another technical perspective to your project but for a true picture, test with both experienced and inexperienced users.

Look for Combination and Flow

Switching modes, game states, or virtual equipment should be a part of a larger flow through the entire experience. The way everything works in the virtual world should have a level of cohesion to it, relying on a consistency of ideas across multiple systems. Users bring along their own conventions and expectations based on other experiences—and regardless of whether those experiences come from real-world activities or simulations or videogames, we can leverage them to make for a smoother transition to the virtual. Many of the conventions we see from game controllers, such as which buttons do what in racing games, have come about through a shared opinion that those are the best ways of doing things. Not just because of opinions, but that the way we can switch modes or change the game state flows so well when these conventions are applied.

Make sure that it is easy to switch from one item to another, if you expect users to do the same. Ensure that when you switch from one system to another that there is consistency. This consistency makes it easier for users to transition between them. For example, changing from a laser blaster to a light saber might have the same method to switch on or off the power.

Realism Is Not Always the Most Realistic

Just because something is realistic in terms of math or physics does not mean it will feel good in the virtual world. The virtual is different to the real world and it is a place.

The best example I have of this is something I encountered whilst writing this book. It started as I was programming some code to pick up and throw objects for the HTC Vive controllers. When I picked up a ball and threw it, it did not feel natural. I sometimes felt as though I did not have enough power to throw objects in a way that felt right. I added a simple multiplier to the code that copied its speed and rotation from the controller and everything suddenly felt good. In this case, it was not at all realistic—I had given the user superhuman power of strength—but it helped the virtual world to work better.

RECAP

In this chapter, we took a journey into the past to find out how VR made its way from military and scientific simulation to the consumer market we experienced in 2016. We looked at devices from the 1990s and scrutinized some of their main flaws or shortcomings. Before we all proclaim that VR has learned from its earlier mistakes and is now ready to take over the world, we looked at some of the main problems that are either unsolvable or still in the process of being solved. The full Holodeck experience is not quite there yet, but it is very much on the road to getting there.

In this chapter, although we looked at many input options, I will be focusing on using only HMD and either remote or a game controller. The Rift ships with an Xbox One game controller, but you will be able to use an Xbox360 controller (wired or wireless) with the same methods shown later in this book.

CHAPTER 2

Setting Up Your Hardware for the First Time

I WAS VERY EXCITED WHEN a VR headset first arrived at my house. The idea of taking a journey into worlds I had been dreaming about since I was a kid, being able to create my own worlds and then visit them virtually, was something I never thought I would have an opportunity to do. My virtual dreams started long before the technology was powerful enough. I can remember riding in the back of a car at night when I was 9 or 10 years old and I was looking out of the window, watching the street lights as we passed them by. I watched the perspective of each one as it grew closer, then drifted away into the night. As they passed by, I imagined a future where we could draw computer graphics in three dimensions and make those street lights in pixels. I had no idea we would have 3D graphics as realistic as the ones we have now, let alone the idea of actually being able to go inside of those 3D computer worlds and explore them!

The arrival of VR to my own home was so exciting that I just wanted to plug it in and get going fast. Sadly, there was a little more to it.

WHAT HARDWARE AND SOFTWARE ARE YOU GOING TO NEED?

It did not take very long for me to realize that my poor old graphics card, a Gigabyte Radeon R9 280, was not quite up to the task of delivering crisp high-resolution VR at a steady enough rate. The 280 is a great card but the recommended specifications stated a 290. I had assumed that I would just drop down the detail levels in some higher-end VR but this was not the case and I found that all VR had visual jitter, as if the picture could not quite keep up with the action. My graphics card would run most modern games on full detail at 60 or more frames per second, but it was not good enough for VR. I also found that I needed extra USB ports, but there was a fairly cost-effective solution to that which I will get to a little later.

The recommended specifications for VR were a surprise to many, with a lot of people stating VR was already costly enough without having to buy a new PC to experience it with. It is not so much that VR cannot function on a lower spec system, but instead that the kinds of VR experiences you might get at a lower spec are something that we may not want take a risk with. Lower frame rates, stuttering or delays in the input systems can ruin the experience entirely. Access to VR experiences are considerably more expensive, but the experience will be much better for it.

HTC VIVE Recommended Specifications (Figure 2.1)

- GPU (graphics card): NVIDIA GeForce® GTX 970, AMD Radeon™ R9 290 equivalent or better

- Video Output: HDMI 1.4, DisplayPort 1.2 or newer

- CPU (Processor): Intel® i5-4590, AMD FX 8350 equivalent or better

- RAM (Memory): 4 GB or more

- USB: 1× USB 2.0 or better port

FIGURE 2.1   The HTC Vive headset. (Courtesy of HTC.)

- Operating System (OS): Windows 7 64-bit, Service Pack 1 or a newer Windows OS is required

OSVR HDK Recommended Specifications (Figure 2.2)

The HDK headsets aim to be compatible with as many different systems as possible, making the entry barriers low. The exact required specification will vary depending on the experience you are hoping to achieve. In the words of Razer, on the OSVR website it says you will need a mid-tier gaming PC or better (GTX660 or AMD equivalent or Intel i5 3.0 GHz or AMD equivalent). As with everything like this, the more powerful the better and the sky is the limit for how far you might want to take it. For mid-tier VR experiences, I would recommend something like the Intel i5 3 GHz or AMD A8 6500 3.5 GHz combined with a good graphics card like the GeForce GTX970 or similar. That said, if you want to be able to run high-end experiences such as Ubisoft's Project Cars or Frontier Developments Elite Dangerous, you are probably going to need a system closer to the level of the Vive's specifications.

Rift Recommended Specifications (Figure 2.3)

- GPU (graphics card): NVIDIA GTX 970 or AMD R9 290 equivalents or greater

- Video Output: HDMI 1.3 video output (directly on your graphics card)

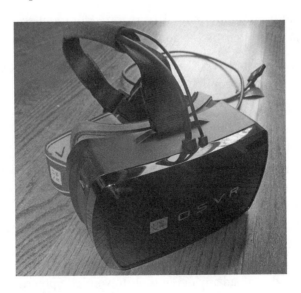

FIGURE 2.2   The HDK headset.

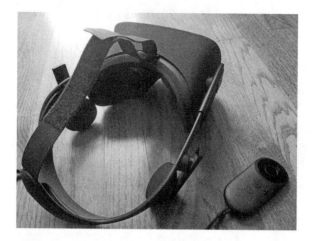

FIGURE 2.3   Oculus Rift headset.

- CPU (processor): Intel i5-4590 equivalent or greater

- RAM (memory): 8 GB + RAM

- USB:

  - Three available USB ports are required (2 USB 3.0 ports)

  - Additional USB 3.0 ports will be required for Touch controllers

  - Additional USB ports will be required for room-scale (1 per camera, which means 2–4 additional USB ports for room-scale)

- Operating System (OS): Windows 7 64-bit, Service Pack 1 or a newer Windows OS is required

- HD (disk space): 4 GB + free space

Compatibility Tools

If you did not purchase a VR ready PC already built, the best thing you can do is run the compatibility tests provided by the manufacturer of your HMD. It is not worth waiting until your headset turns up to find out whether or not you can actually use it. It makes for a very disappointing first day! The manufacturer's compatibility tool will tell you if you already have the right hardware or what components, if any, you need to replace.

Before you download any of the tools to your computer, the first thing you must do is to update your graphics drivers. This is important.

When you have the latest drivers installed, you can go ahead and download the tools for your head-mounted display.

The SteamVR Performance Test Tool

Open the Steam client and search for SteamVR Performance Test, or you can use the URL http://store.steampowered.com/app/323910/ in a web browser and have it open the Steam client from there (Figure 2.4). The download is over 1 GB so it may be time to put the kettle on for a cup of tea as you wait!

Click the green button marked Free to start the download. Once the test has fully downloaded, you can launch it from inside the Steam client and see exactly what you have.

The Rift Compatibility Tool

Download the Oculus Compatibility Tool from https://ocul.us/compat-tool and run it. The tool will check the specs of your computer and advise (Figure 2.5) on the aspects that may not be up to scratch. The download is nice and small, weighing in around 7 MB.

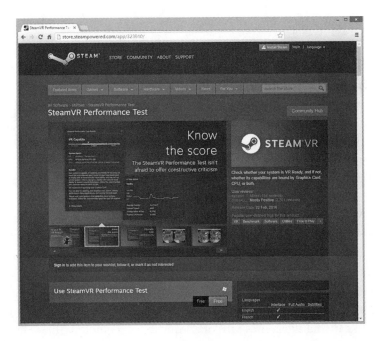

FIGURE 2.4 The SteamVR performance test lets you know if your computer system is ready for VR experiences.

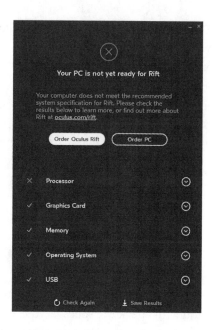

FIGURE 2.5 The Rift Compatibility Tool will report whether or not your system is ready for the Rift experience.

OSVR Compatibility

There is no compatibility tool you can use for OSVR, but if you are looking to develop VR at a quality level similar to those on the Rift or Vive then you can use the SteamVR performance test, instead. This will be a good guide as to whether or not your system can perform well enough. The minimum spec for OSVR is listed later in this chapter—it is less than the other two headsets here and you should be able to get into VR on a mid-tier gaming PC or better (NVIDIA GTX660 or AMD equivalent or Intel i5 3.0 GHz or AMD equivalent)—but it really will depend on the kinds of experiences you are hoping to run and/or develop.

Dealing with Compatibility Tool Results

If you are unsure as to how to go about performing upgrades to your system, modifying your computers components is something best left to the experts. Most computer shops will either be able to carry out the upgrades for you on-site or they should be able to recommend someone who can. Tasks like fitting a graphics card or adding extra memory will not take too long for the professionals to carry out, but do try to remember that you are likely to be one of many people waiting and that they may have several systems to take care of before they get to yours. Always be patient and kind to your computer people!

Graphics Cards

If the graphics card is flagged by the compatibility tool, you probably need to look at sourcing a new card so that you can enjoy a wider range of VR experiences without compromise. If the card is just outside of the recommended spec, it may be possible to overclock the graphics processing unit (GPU) to a faster speed that might allow you to experience at least some of what VR has to offer. But if you can afford it, upgrading is the best option. Newer VR-ready graphics cards have features specific to enhance VR rendering that older units do not have.

USB Ports

The Rift requires at least three USB ports to work. Two of them need to be USB 3.0, which on two- or three-year-old systems may be an issue. Before you modify anything, take a look at what is already plugged into the computer to see if there is anything you could unplug to make room for the new hardware. If you have a peripheral plugged in that you will not be using when you are in VR, such as a webcam or perhaps a standalone microphone or anything like that, you could always unplug them to make room for the head-mounted display as and when you need to.

If you do not have enough USB ports, it may not be time to throw out your computer just yet. Providing that your motherboard has a spare Peripheral Component Interconnect (PCI) slot, you may be able to purchase a PCI card to provide a number of new USB ports. Fitting is relatively straightforward, a case of finding an empty slot on the motherboard and plugging it in, but if you are at all unsure about installing it yourself, take your computer into a specialist repair shop to have it fitted by a professional. It is not worth risking your computer!

PCI cards currently run for around $30. If a lack of USB ports being flagged as the only problem with your system, a PCI USB card can prove to be a cheap and easy solution. Much cheaper than replacing the system.

INSTALLING SteamVR

Once your hardware is ready, you need to download Steam and SteamVR applications. You will need these for the HTC Vive, as well as for all of the examples in this book. All of the examples are targeted for SteamVR and the SteamVR libraries for Unity. It is entirely possible, however, to develop VR applications without the Unity SteamVR libraries, for example by using hardware-specific libraries or Unity's native VR support. But the biggest advantage of using the SteamVR libraries is the cross-platform compatibility between headsets. There are some other gems in the SteamVR libraries, too, such as the Chaperone system to help users know where the boundaries are during room-scale VR. We will not be going into too much detail over Chaperone, as there is not really all that much to cover. All you need to know is that whenever the user steps too close to the play area boundaries, Chaperone takes care of showing a grid to show where those boundaries are. This acts as both a guide and a warning to users, telling them not to go any further toward the closest boundary. It is possible to disable Chaperone by changing the tracking space, but outside of that the process is automatic and handled by the SteamVR system.

Install the Steam Client

To get SteamVR you first need the Steam client software. Traditionally used for purchasing and installing games, Steam has grown to feature all kinds of software and now VR libraries and apps. It is necessary to download the Steam client first, to be able to install SteamVR and all of the games and software SteamVR requires.

Download Steam from your web browser at this address: http://store.steampowered.com/.

Look for the Install Steam button somewhere along the top of the main page. The installation process is simple, with a standard Windows installer. Follow the on-screen instructions to get Steam.

Set Up a Steam Account

Everything you need is free but you do need a Steam account.

Start Steam and follow the instructions for setting up a new account or logging in with your existing account.

Install SteamVR

Once you have an account set up and the Steam client software running, you need to download and install SteamVR. Find this in the Library > Tools section. Right click on SteamVR and click Install Game. Yes, it says Install Game but it is not a game. We can ignore this—it says game because Steam has always been a platform for downloading games and having tools on there is still a relatively new thing for them!

GENERAL INSTALLATION HINTS AND TIPS (FOR ALL DEVICES)

Early VR development kits took a rather involved process to install, but consumer versions have a much more straightforward and user-friendly installation process. The process should be a simple one that is mostly automated, but there are a few things you can do in preparation for a better experience.

Make Room for Your Motion Tracker(s)

Non Room-Scale VR with a Single Station/Motion Tracking Camera

If, like mine, your space is small then you need to try to clear enough room for sensors first of all. The radius of the sensor's base is around the size of a large food can. When you place the sensor on your desk, it needs to be in a place where there is clear visibility between everywhere your head-mounted display is going to be and where the sensor is. As an example of how not to arrange your desk, I have a steering wheel attached to its front edge. Whenever I duck down or lean too far forward in a sitting position, the steering wheel blocks the visibility between the sensor and the headset so that my system loses positional tracking. I should really remove the steering wheel!

Room-Scale VR/Multiple Positional Tracking Cameras

If you have multiple positional trackers, such as those required for room-scale VR, take a look around the space you intend to use and think about how you can get the sensors up around head-height in four corners of the room. You will need to think about methods to power them (extension cords?) and provide safe, sturdy surfaces for the sensors to live on as well as making sure that each sensor has clear visibility for the entire space. If the line of sight between a sensor and the headset is blocked, you may find that positional tracking will stop working until it is clear. Try to avoid sharing the shelf with anything that might get in the way and, if possible, avoid sharing the shelf space with plants that may be watered regularly—sensor electrics really do not like being watered and a small spill could end up costing a huge amount for a replacement!

Organize Your Environment to Clear Some Space!

Having a place to put your head-mounted display when it is not in use between simulations is a good idea, too. As a developer, it's very likely that you will be putting the headset on and taking it off quite a lot and resting it on your lap is not an ideal solution. Your beautiful piece of technology will not take kindly to being dropped on the floor multiple times, so it is best to try to give it a good, solid, and easily accessible surface to rest on.

When you are in VR, you will not be able to see much and it is a good idea to know where your game controller or remote control are so that you can easily find them without taking of the headset. When you are organizing your space, think about how you can place the controller and remote so that they are easy to find.

Walls: Try to Avoid Them

If you have a massive empty space for VR, or you can keep your desk well away from walls, you probably do not have much in the way of worry about space. For those of us who do not have the luxury of space, try to allow for maximum distance between your normal seating position and the walls. If having obstacles is unavoidable, one trick I do in the virtual world is to reach out with my hand before I move my head. Feel ahead into the space you intend to move your head into so that you do not injure yourself hitting the headset against the wall. Sure, it sounds silly now but once you spend a decent amount of time in the virtual world you will understand that hitting your face is a real danger. VR can be utterly immersive and you can easily lose track of the real world. Always feel ahead with your hand! As well as seemingly silly advice to "feel ahead" I would also like to offer you the suggestion to consider the cable that connects your head-mounted display to the computer. It is very easy to accidentally sweep items like cups or controllers from the desk when you put them in the path of the cable and forget or assume that you will be able to avoid them.

What Is Interpupillary Distance and Why Should I Care?

You may have seen the term Interpupillary Distance (IPD) used in VR. When hardware manufacturers use this term, it refers to the relationships between the distance between the lenses on the headset and the distance between the viewer's eyes. Both the Rift and HTC Vive include an adjuster for this and it is important that you set this correctly for the most comfortable experience. The short of it is that if the IPD is not set right, this may cause eyestrain and act as a contributor to VR sickness.

There are two types of IPD you need to know about; real IPD and virtual IPD.

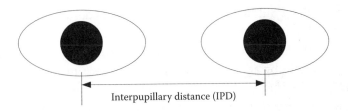

Interpupillary distance (IPD)

FIGURE 2.6   Real IPD.

Real IPD

The real IPD is the distance between the viewer's eyes in the real world (Figure 2.6). This is the measurement you need to know for setting the IPD on your headset. On the Rift, alignment software features a visual section that guides you through the process of correct IPD alignment.

On the HTC Vive, you will need to measure this yourself and adjust the headset to a number. It is not too difficult to find out what your IPD is and the benefits outweigh the inconvenience, so I highly recommend you take the time to do this properly.

How to Measure Your IPD   To measure your IPD you will need either a ruler or some sort of measuring tape. You may also find that you can do this with a home improvement tape measure or even digital caliper, but for these instructions we will stay low-tech. You also need a mirror to stand in front of.

1. Stand in front of the mirror. Hold the zero part of the measure below your left eye and extend it out past your right eye. Keep the measure straight, rather than following the contours of your face.

2. Close your right eye. Make sure that the zero end of the measure is directly below your pupil, in the middle of your eye. Keep still.

3. Close your left eye and look at the measure under your right eye. The mark directly underneath the center of your right pupil is your IPD.

It may be a good idea to write this down for future reference. If other people use your headset, they will need to adjust the IPD correctly too, so keeping a written record of everyone's IPDs may be a good idea.

Virtual IPD

The virtual IPD is the distance between the two cameras used to represent the viewer's eyes in the virtual world. With the SteamVR library, the virtual IPD is automatically taken care of. Its default settings will be matched to the real IPD. So you may be wondering what this has to do with scale? Well, it turns out that we can change the perceived scale of the virtual world by adjusting the virtual IPD to something other than the real IPD. By changing the scale of the virtual eyes (the cameras used by Unity in the VR scene) we can make the viewer feel as though they are anything from looking up at large architecture on an epic scale all the way down to looking at a tiny toy village. With SteamVR, scaling the virtual IPD is as simple as scaling the main camera in the Scene. Note that is not recommended to do as your simulation or game is running. Once it is set in the scene, it is best to just leave the camera scale alone during runtime. The visual effect of changing the IPD is very uncomfortable, particularly for viewers who may be sensitive to VR sickness.

INSTALLING YOUR VR HARDWARE

HTC Vive Installation Instructions

The HTC Vive demands a minimum of a 4 × 3 meter play area to get started in. Once you have decided where you are going to set up, it will be time to open up the box and start unpacking. It can be quite intimidating, to be honest. As you unpack all of the numerous cables, boxes, and power adapters you may well begin to wonder just what you are supposed to do with them all. Do not panic! You do not need to have everything set up and plugged in before downloading. Go to the website http://www.htcvive.com/setup and follow the instructions from there. There is no need to worry about all the stuff you have unpacked so far. It will all become clear soon enough, as the set-up procedure is very well handled. Just in case you do have any issues, there is a great tutorial video provided by the Vive team over on YouTube at https://www.youtube.com/watch?v=rv6nVPPDmEI.

Important Note: *These instructions are provided here for informational purposes and you should always be cautious to follow the manufacturers recommended procedures. In essence, you will be solely responsible for any damage caused by plugging the wrong things into the wrong things!*

1. Start the download.

   The first step is to go to the website http://www.vive.com/ca/setup/ and hit the button marked "Download Vive Setup." This includes a full setup tutorial and an installer for the Vive desktop app.

On the Vive setup website, there are some great tutorial videos for getting up and running.

2. Clear your space.

With most Vive experiences, you are going to be moving around quite a bit so it is vital to clear the space properly so that there are no tripping hazards or obstacles you could walk into. Keep expensive electrical equipment like televisions away from the edges of your play area in case you reach out a little too far over the boundaries.

If you have small animals, keep them away from your VR play area. You will not know where they are or, if you are wearing headphones, you may not be able to hear them. Keeping animals away from your VR area will hopefully keep you, your pets, and your VR headset safe from harm.

The VR zone is no place for small children. Talk to your kids about how they need to stay well back when you are in VR, as it may be very easy for them to forget that you cannot see them. Young children should be supervised, so if you are going to be using VR please try to make sure that there is someone else around to look out for the kids!

3. Mount your base stations.

For room-scale VR, you will need to consider the mounting and placement of your base stations. HTC recommend that you place them in opposite corners of your play space, no further than 16.4 feet (5 meters) apart. HTC also recommends that your base stations are mounted 2 meters (6 feet 5 inches) from the ground, and angled down by around 30°. None of my desks were high enough to mount my base stations on, so in one corner I used a standard low-cost camera tripod. The guys at HTC have made it so that the mount on the bottom of the base stations will fit a standard camera tripod so you do not need to buy any sort of expensive custom stand. My cheap camera tripod was enough for my base station to get the height up over 6 feet, on top of a desk. In the other corner, I attached the base station to the top of a high book shelf. Do not forget to remove the clear plastic film from the front of the base stations.

Plug the base stations in to the mains. You may notice that they vibrate. This is normal. It freaked me out when I first plugged in mine, so I asked some other Vive owners and they assured me that this is okay.

When the base stations are powered on, you should see the status light in green and you should also see a letter. On one base station, the letter should be a b and on the other, a letter c. These are known as the channel indicators. If b and c are not showing, press the channel button on the back of the base station to change the channel.

If one base station is not in view of the other, that status light will be purple rather than green. If this is the case and the light stays purple (give it 30 seconds just to make sure it does not change) you may have to use the included sync cable to connect the two base stations.

4. Set up the linkbox.

Grab the linkbox and the power adapter. Plug in the power adapter and connect it into the DCIN port on the linkbox. Grab a USB cable. Connect one end of the USB cable in to the computer side of the linkbox (i.e., the same side you plugged the power cable into) and the other end of the USB cable into your PC. Next, connect one end of a HDMI cable from the linkbox computer side (the same side you plugged the USB cable into) and the other into the HDMI port of your computer's graphics card.

5. Set up the headset.

Remove the protective film from the lenses inside the headset. Carefully unwind the cable. You will see that the three plugs on the end of the cable are yellow. These yellow connectors correspond with the yellow ports on the linkbox. Connect the yellow HDMI cable to the yellow HDMI port on the linkbox, the yellow USB plug into the yellow USB port on the linkbox and then, finally, the yellow power plug into the yellow DCIN port of the linkbox. At this point, your computer may detect the new devices.

6. Switch on the controllers.

The power button is the button below the touchpad on the controller. Press this once to turn on the controller and the power light should show in green. The Vive ships with charged controllers, but if they do not show in green you may have to charge them using the included controller power adapters. HTC includes two adapters, one for each controller, and the connectors plug into the base of the controller.

7. Install the software.

Hopefully, by the time you have got to this step, the Vive software download from step 1 should have finished. Run the installer, then start the software. Follow the on-screen instructions. I am omitting instructions for this here, as the software may change in the future and there really is no point in parroting its content in this book when you can just read it from the screen!

8. Run SteamVR setup.

You will need to run a room-scale VR set up in SteamVR setup once the Vive software has been installed. The set up procedure is guided, which means you can follow the on-screen instructions to get up and running. The only things to note are that, by this stage, you should have a clear play area and you may need a tape measure or similar measuring device to hand. For full instructions on running the SteamVR setup, see the "Setting up SteamVR" section later in this chapter.

Potential Issues/Fixes
Check Everything is Powered Up before Launching SteamVR Before starting SteamVR, make sure that your base stations are switched on and that the headset is plugged into the computer and powered.

Performing a Headset Reboot Sometimes Fixes Things! If you have tried everything else, checked that everything is plugged in and you have tried turning it on and off again, you may benefit from rebooting the headset. To do this, find the SteamVR status window (the one that appears as a standalone window when you first launch into VR from the Steam client). In the Steam status window, click the SteamVR dropdown menu and choose Settings. Choose the Developer section on the left and scroll down the right side to find a button labelled Reboot Vive headset. If successful, SteamVR will close, the Vive headset will reboot and then SteamVR will reconnect to it and restart the SteamVR system.

OSVR HDK Installation Instructions

Open Source Virtual Reality (OSVR) is an ecosystem intended for many different brands and companies. The great thing about using SteamVR is that you can instantly support all of the major brand headsets in one sweep, as well as OSVR compatible hardware. More bang for your buck!

I am very excited about OSVR and I think that it has a great future democratizing VR so that the end users get the benefit of choosing the features they want at a price they want to pay rather than being locked into a particular headset for a particular range of software or DRM-locked store. At the time of writing, the Hacker Development Kit (HDK) VR headsets offer great value for solid hardware, but they are intended for users with a little more experience in getting things going (the clue is in the name Hacker Development Kit!) so you may need to get a little more involved in the installation and setup procedures than you might with the more expensive mainstream headsets. The HDK team is working to make the process as easy as possible. There is a straightforward installer that will have you ready for VR in four or five steps. It automatically installs all of the relevant drivers and companion software as well as a nifty little task-bar-based app you can use to start and stop the OSVR server and access tool apps.

1. Start the download.

    Grab the required files via your web browser. Go to http://developer.osvr.org/ and click on the OSVR Installer by Razer.

2. Set up the hardware.

    First, you should connect up the beltbox. On the bottom of the belt-box are three plugs. One of the included cables is a single cable with two plugs on each end. The end to connect to your PC has a USB plug and a HDMI plug. Connect the USB to a USB port on your PC, then the HDMI plug to the computer's HDMI port for your graphics card. Connect the two plugs on the other end to the bottom of the beltbox.

    The power adapter alone is a single plug, but included in the box is a splitter cable. Find the splitter cable. On the end of the cable that splits into two is a power cable. Plug that end into the bottom of the beltbox. The plug on the end of your power adapter does not plug directly into the beltbox. Instead, the lead from the power adapter goes into the plug that splits off from the cable (Figure 2.7).

FIGURE 2.7   The beltbox for the HDK1.

Mount your IR camera on top of your monitor, where it will be able to track your headset in VR. Plug in the included USB cable into the side of the IR camera and the other end into a spare USB port on your PC.

On the other end of the split cable you plugged into the beltbox, is a small jack plug. Plug the jack into the side of the IR camera for tracking synchronization.

The headset has a large proprietary connector. Plug this into the top of the beltbox. The beltbox has a clip on it that is designed to keep the beltbox clipped to the top of your trousers and within range of the cable.

3. Software installation.

Run the downloaded drivers and software. The installation process should go through and install everything you need. Although the installer does not mention it, I suggest a restart of the system after install. Keep the hardware plugged in as you restart.

4. Start the OSVR server.

To use OSVR, you need to have the OSVR server running in the background. We will start up the server, next. In the Windows toolbar you should now find a little OSVR icon. This taskbar application helps you get to the parts of OSVR you need quickly. Right click the icon and choose Start. The OSVR server application should start. Hold up your headset in-front of the camera for 20 seconds, or wear it of course, so that the server can get tracking info.

5. Run the test application.

To make sure that everything is working correctly, we will run a little test application. Right click the icon and choose OSVR Test Apps > Launch VR Sample.

The demonstration app shows a simple environment that you can look around. It should show a creepy forest with a campfire. Use this to test that your headset is working and that your movement tracking is working correctly. If you encounter any issues at this stage, you may have to restart the system again, but it may be worth taking a look at the Display Settings in Windows to make sure that the headset has been detected correctly.

6. Set up SteamVR to use OSVR.

OSVR SteamVR support is not built-in to the SteamVR system and you need a little set up to get it working. If you have SteamVR already open, you should close it before you start this process:

a. Open a File Browser and go to the folder Program Files (×86)\ OSVR.

b. Find the OSVR-SteamVR folder and click to browse inside it.

c. Click on the OSVR folder, inside OSVR-SteamVR, to highlight it. Press CTRL + C on the keyboard to copy it.

d. Open up Steam. Click Library at the top of the window, then choose Tools from the dropdown. Find SteamVR in the list.

e. Right click SteamVR and choose Properties.

f. Click the Local Files tab. Choose Browse Local Files.. to open a new file browser window that shows the folder containing SteamVR.

g. Double click the drivers folder in that SteamVR folder.

h. Press CTRL + V to paste the folder you grabbed from OSVR in stage C.

i. With the drivers installed, you just need to tell SteamVR to look for them. To do this, you need to modify the drivers.cfg file in that SteamVR/drivers folder. Open up Notepad (Notepad is a Windows app you can find by typing Notepad into the search window on Windows10).

j. With the Notepad window open, drag the drivers.cfg file out of the file browser and drop it into the Notepad window. You should see something like:

[vortex]

The items in square brackets are the drivers that SteamVR will look for when it starts. Add a new one. Click at the top of the window and add [osvr] so that your file now looks something like:

[osvr]

[vortex]

Press CTRL + S to save the file in Notepad.

The next time you launch SteamVR it should pick up the OSVR headset, but you may find that you need to restart the system for this to take effect.

Potential Issues/Fixes

Power Cycling   Many problems may be solved by rebooting the device. Close SteamVR. Close down the OSVR server (right click the OSVR taskbar app and choose Stop from the dropdown). Unplug the power cable from the beltbox first, then the USB cable. Count 10 seconds and re-connect the power cable first, followed by plugging in the USB cable. The system should detect two devices. Re-start the OSVR server, then restart SteamVR.

Nothing Showing in the Headset   If you find that the headset screen just shows black, make sure that the OSVR headset display is enabled. To do this, right click on the OSVR tray app and choose Configure > Launch CPI. Under the OSVR HDK tab, click the Enable HDK Display button.

Firmware Updates   The HDK firmware needs to be kept up-to-date for your devices to work correctly, but at the time of writing there is no built-in application to do that. Firmware updating is something you have to do manually with the HDKs. I will not be covering firmware updates, because it can be tricky. All of the software to do that may be found at http://osvr.github.io/using/.

Desktop Shown in Headset But No Test App   Open up Display Properties/Screen Resolution on the Windows desktop. Make sure that the HDK headset has been detected and that it is to the right of the main desktop in the display window. On Windows 8+ you can drag and drop the window previews around, if you need to. Make sure that the resolution of the display is set to 1920 × 1080 and that Multiple displays is set to Extend these displays. The HDK should not be your main display. That should always remain to be your regular desktop.

Rift Installation

Gone are the days when you could expect to throw a CD into the computer CD drive to install drivers! There are no CDs, drivers, or software included with the hardware. The first step to setting up is downloading:

1. Start the download.

   The first step is to go to https://www.oculus.com/setup/ to download drivers and software. The initial download client is around 3–4 MB but there will be a significantly larger download to follow via the client. As the download is taking place, you could perhaps spend a little time re-organizing the space around your computer if you did not already do so.

2. Run the installer.

   You can get started by plugging the Rift's HDMI cable, plug in the USB from the headset and the sensor into your USB 3.0 port. Finally, connect the Xbox One controller USB wireless adapter into any USB port. When you run the Oculus installation software, it will guide you through the process and even tell you if any of your devices are not connected into the correct ports or if they are not functional.

   Once everything is setup you will be treated to a short collection of VR experiences.

FIGURE 2.8 The SteamVR icon should be in the top right of the Steam client window.

SETTING UP STEAMVR

When SteamVR is fully installed, you should find that a new little VR icon appears in the top right of the Steam client near to the window option icons (Figure 2.8).

Click the VR icon.

Something I really like about SteamVR is the setup procedure. It is friendly and fun to do, oozing with personality. I wish all software set up was as much fun!

When you first launch SteamVR, you will be asked to run Room Setup. This is how you tell the computer about the real world space around you and how you plan to use it. You can also access Room Setup at any time by clicking on the SteamVR dropdown menu in the top left of the SteamVR status window and then choosing Run Room Setup from the menu.

Click Room Setup and you will be given two options, Room-Scale or Standing Only (Figure 2.9).

FIGURE 2.9 SteamVR allows you to set up room-scale VR or standing only.

If you choose Room-Scale, you will be prompted to "make some space"—that is, to clear your play area. Do so, if you have not already done that.

From here on in, the SteamVR set up has full step-by-step instructions on screen. To repeat them here would be a waste of paper, so just follow the on-screen prompts and come back here when you are done.

Party! SteamVR Is Set Up!

Well, maybe not party but at this stage you could do a happy dance. SteamVR is now set up and configured. Time to either play some games, or do some work. If you are in the mood to play some games, there are a few free VR apps and games on the Steam store you can download and try out. If you are on HTC Vive, I do recommend that you download and try Google Earth VR free from the Steam store. It really is a breathtaking experience and a good introduction. *Poly Runner* VR by Lucid Sight Inc. is a really fun free infinite runner/flyer game you can play with a game controller (such as Xbox 360 or Xbox One controller) and your headset. I also enjoy BigScreen by BigScreen Inc., which enables you to view your screen in VR as though it were on a virtual computer as well as share and chat in multiplayer. You can use BigScreen to watch videos on a giant virtual screen (perhaps your very own YouTube cinema!), hang out with other VR users on Steam and chat or maybe even watch other people play games.

FINDING YOUR VR LEGS

The saying "finding your VR legs" gets bounded around a lot by VR users and it is usually referring to the idea of getting used to VR simulations before diving in fully. There is no solid evidence to support the claim, but research points toward some sufferers of VR sickness finding their negative symptoms easing over time. As VR is a new experience for most of us, it makes sense to start out gently and build up some experience before spending long periods of time in the virtual world. Diving in to hour-long sessions may not be a good idea and there is more than just VR sickness to consider when you first visit the virtual world.

During your time inside the headset, you need to maintain awareness of your body in the real world just as much as you are aware of the virtual. It is too easy to lose track of yourself and wind up crashing into walls, reaching out and hitting objects with your hands or tripping over the cables running into the headset. It can be a bit of a clumsy experience to start with, but over time you will get more and more used to it all.

If you are using motion controllers like those with the Vive, beware of the floor. The floor level inside the virtual world may not accurately tie up with the floor level in the real world. Reaching down quickly to pick something up can easily end up with crashing the controller into the floor. Use your ankle as a guide. Keep the controller above ankle level, or move very slowly below that.

SOME COMFORTABLE VR EXPERIENCE RECOMMENDATIONS

There are some great experiences out there for you to dip your toes into the virtual river. In this section, I will highlight a few good experiences for you to get started with, which will provide a good grounding for your future VR adventures.

HTC Vive

For awesome Vive experiences, you are spoilt for choice! The Steam store and Viveport are your destinations to awesome.

The Lab: Start here. *The Lab* offers mini-games and fun little things to do to get you started in VR. Best of all, *The Lab* is provided free of charge on the Steam store. My favorite part of *The Lab* is Long Bow, where you get to stand on a castle and do some archery with the Vive controllers. It is a fantastic little game, hard as nails (the little dudes will always overrun your castle no matter what!) and a surprisingly good arm workout! Everything here is room-scale VR, so there is almost zero opportunity for VR sickness.

Space Pirate Trainer: One of my favorite VR games, *Space Pirate Trainer* by I-Illusions is an adrenaline fueled bot-blasting festival of room-scale combat. It is an awesome workout (although you may have to clean the lenses occasionally because it can get fogged when you sweat!) and with the music cranked up, possibly the most visceral VR experience you can have. It looks just like target practice, but it is so much more than that—it is target practice gone mad!

Job Simulator: My kids absolutely love this game! For a hilarious, crazy experience you can look no further than *Job Simulator.* It is silly fun for all the family. There are no time limits, which means you can take your time and play around with all of the numerous props and things to do.

Thread Studio: If you are wondering where the future of clothes customization might go, Thread Studio is a great place to look. You can flip through color swatches, lay out designs, import your own logo or graphic and then see them modelled on fully posable mannequins. There are also props littered around the environment to play with, throw around or have your mannequin pose with. It is a lot of fun and a great look into the possible future of VR clothes and merchandise design.

OSVR

You can find a host of OSVR-ready experiences via the OSVR website (http://www.osvr.org/featured.html).

Showdown: Showdown is an awesome tech demo made with the Unreal engine. There is no gameplay, it is literally just a walkthrough of an environment but oh boy is it ever a cool environment! The scene looks like something out of a movie in slow motion and it is a short experience designed purely to wow you into the virtual world. If you are looking to show off your awesome hardware, this is a great way to do that.

Elite Dangerous: The space trading sim is back and this time, it is available with full VR support. What better way to enjoy your HDK than in space? I will warn you, however, that although it is a mind-blowingly beautiful experience it does involve rotational movement that can trigger nausea. Try to move slowly and turn slowly until you get used to it all. In space, no-one can hear you barf!

Rift

The Rift has some great experiences included with it, as well as some available through the Oculus Store. Before you buy, be sure to double check that you have the correct hardware (Touch controllers, room-scale cameras, and so on) as there are multiple hardware configurations that games are targeting.

Lucky's Tale: is one of my favorite games of all-time. I genuinely believe that this game is a sign of things to come—being inside the platform game makes you feel connected with them on many levels. Lean in toward the Luckey, the main character, and he will react to you in a fun way. The level of polish and fun it delivers is second-to-none. Also worth noticing is that the other creatures will sometimes make eye-contact with you, which gives you a true sense of connection with Luckey's world and its inhabitants. For VR sickness, I only found moving vertically to be a minor issue.

Every now and then when the camera moves up or down, I had to close my eyes for a second, but for the most part I was surprised by just how comfortable the experience is.

Henry: is a cute, fun story experience narrated by Elijah Wood. I was truly amazed by the level of immersion I had watching this for the first time. Being inside its cartoon world is fun and emotional. You remain in a fixed location, which means that it is extremely easy to watch with almost no chance of VR sickness. Highly recommend watching this if you have a Rift.

BlazeRush: This is a great racing game where the vehicles appear around the same sizes of toy cars. It is like watching some sort of advanced toy car track racing. I have found myself getting a little nauseous from it, but I can normally play around 20 minutes without getting sick so I would recommend this as a good "finding your legs" experience all the same. *BlazeRush's* fun, short blasts of gameplay mean that you do not have to spend too much time in VR if it starts to get uncomfortable.

STAYING AWARE FOR A HEALTHY VR EXPERIENCE

Before we jump into the virtual world, this section of this book is intended to draw your attention to some important things to watch out for on your journey and to prepare you for healthy VR experiences throughout this book.

Knowing When to Stop (the Telltale Signs of Oncoming VR Sickness)

Extensive studies by the military, the medical profession and even NASA have still not led to a cure for VR sickness. We do not yet know exactly how to tackle it and VR sickness is a real thing that affects a great number of people in many different ways. Some of the most common types of sickness-inducing experiences are; first-person shooters, driving or flying simulators, cut-scenes with a forced movement camera, or any sorts of experiences where the camera twists or rotates a lot.

Remember that VR sickness is not something you can just "power through." Persistence will not make it go away. You will not be able to push through sickness and come out feeling good. It gets worse the longer you keep doing whatever is causing it, which means that the only way to stop it is to walk away and come back to VR once the ill feelings are gone.

Later in this book, we will look at some of the known techniques for reducing and avoiding sickness triggers. VR sickness affects different people in different ways and it is triggered by different factors in different people, too, which makes providing a definitive list of symptoms almost impossible. What we can do is look out for some telltale signs that may be your body's way of telling you to take a break.

Important Note: *This is not medical advice. If you need medical advice, please consult a medical professional. I'm a Unity developer, Jim, not a doctor!*

Dry Eyes

If you feel as though your eyes are drying out, that could be the beginning of eye-strain. First, take off the headset. If you have not already set up your IPD correctly, refer back to section "General Installation Hints and Tips" and follow the steps to do so.

Eye drops may be a good way to make the experience more comfortable. I keep eye-drops handy and use them every now and then before I put on the headset. A qualified optometrist/optician may be a good option if you find your eyes giving you trouble in VR.

If you have dry eyes, take a break.

Sweating

Sweating is not just central to your cooling system, it is also a way of the body trying to rid itself of poisons or sickness when the brain thinks that the body is under attack. Sweating is a very common symptom of VR sickness and the only way to stop it is to take a break. Preferably a break in a cooler space.

Try to keep the room to a comfortable temperature if you can, as wearing a headset can get hot quickly and exacerbate symptoms. Even more so if the VR experience is physical. Try to keep the temperature a little cooler than usual to allow for the extra heat generated by movement.

If you are sweating any more at all than usual, take a break.

Aching

What can I tell you about this? If you are experiencing aching, you need to rest. Rest well until it goes away completely. Eat well, fruits and veg. Look after yourself. VR can be surprisingly tiring. When you are new to it, build up slowly to get used to it all.

If you are aching, you probably know what is coming here; take a break.

Nausea

Getting dizzy or feeling sick is never a good thing but for many of us it is a regular part of the VR experience. If you start to feel sick at all, you should stop immediately and remove the headset. Take a break and see if it subsides before going back in. Sickness symptoms can last for more than a full day after you have been in VR. If you feel extreme nausea, the best way to combat it is to lie down and sleep. Always consult a medical professional if the problem gets worse or if you have any question as to its cause.

Take a break.

Headache

There are so many different reasons you could experience a headache that it may or may not be related to the VR experience. If you are getting headaches regularly from the headset, it may be eye-strain or related to your vision. Consult an optician or medical professional, as you may need corrective lenses.

Regardless of the cause, take a break if you get a headache.

Take Breaks

Take a 10 minute break every 30 minutes and a 30 minute break if you are playing for over an hour. At this stage, VR is still in its infancy. We should try to be cautious.

If in doubt, restrict your VR sessions to 10 minutes per day until you start to get a feel for your personal limits.

For children under 12, VR is not recommended by hardware manufacturers. Younger children's eyes are still developing and who knows how a headset could effect that?

My kids like to try out VR and, from time to time, I do let them but I restrict VR sessions to a very short time (10–15 minutes) to be safe.

Eat, Drink, and Be Virtually Merry!

Keep a bottle of water nearby during all of your time developing or playing in VR—it does not have to be anything fancy, just as long as the water is clean. I got my water bottle from the drugstore and I fill it from the tap before I sit down. Drink plenty, regularly.

Eating right before going into VR is generally not a great idea if you suffer from VR sickness, as doing so may exacerbate nausea. If you find yourself prone to sickness and you get hungry, try to eat good, healthy food an hour or so before you use VR and avoid rich or sugary snacks that might make you feel sicker.

Most importantly, always remember to look after yourself physically as your mind goes off on its virtual vacations.

Do Not Break Your Back Making VR Things! Test Carefully

In the next chapter, you are going to be diving into Unity and creating a VR experience. As you progress, you will need to test numerous things along the way such as object interactions, space limitations, scale, and so forth. Before we go ahead with that, I want to talk a little about safety. As I write this, a good friend of mine has injured his back during VR testing and I would hate for you to do the same. Developing for VR, especially room-scale, can be a risk. I am not trying to scare, but it is well worth considering how you test, how you move around, and how you can be a little extra cautious during testing. Check the space regularly to keep it clear of obstacles, watch out for cables trailing across places where they might pull things off desks (like cups, etc.) when you move around and prepare yourself for physical activity.

When you want to test something quick, it is easy to grab the headset or controller and make bad movements because you are half watching the screen and half the hardware. Not paying full attention to the hardware can mean hitting controllers against walls, dropping the headset or knocking things off the desk. Before you test with the hardware, stop and count to 5 as you consider the space around you.

Also, I know it takes a few seconds extra to put on the wrist straps, don the headset and so on, but if your movements are going to be physical you should take the extra time. If not just to help protect your hardware investment.

Wherever possible, try to make your experience compatible with mouse and keyboard so that you can test small features without having to don the headset and anything else you might be using (controllers, VR gloves, haptic suits, etc.). The novelty of the experience will wear off relatively quickly once you have tested it over and over, day after day. When it does; it is too easy to shortcut to testing without consideration for your environment.

In room-scale VR, pay strict attention to the Chaperone/boundaries. A developer friend of mine recently destroyed a monitor with a Vive controller as he was so immersed in a game battle (stupid skeletons!).

Be aware of the fact that you are holding expensive equipment that will sometimes negatively affect your sense of balance and space around you. A second of unforeseen dizziness caused by a technical issue, such as camera lag, can also be enough to knock you off-balance.

If you are making a room-scale experience that is particularly physical or taxing on the body, you may even want to do some warm-up or stretching before you start developing for the day. Room-scale experiences need your body to work, making the risk of a back injury or muscle injury a real prospect. This is serious stuff—you are dealing with body movement and you can sprain muscles, hit things, drop things, or even fall over. VR can be more physically demanding than you think. As you are testing your experiences, you will be exercising. Like all exercise, take care. Please do not break your back making VR things!

RECAP

It has been a busy chapter! With your hardware all hooked up, you should now be ready to develop a VR experience. In this chapter, we began by looking at installation as well as organizing and being aware of the space you are going to be using for VR. We then looked at installing the Steam and the SteamVR system, then setting it up for either a room-scale or standing only space. Setting up the space is essential for SteamVR, so if you skipped any of that you might want to go back and make sure you got all of the important parts!

We went on to look at some of the awesome VR experiences already available for you to try out. Following on from that, we looked for any telltale signs of VR sickness that may be creeping in as you play so that you will be aware of it once we start developing and testing. Being aware of the hardware and world space when you are testing is essential. Hopefully, this chapter's information will help keep you safe and more comfortable as you enter the virtual world. In the next chapter, we start exploring how Unity and SteamVR work together.

CHAPTER 3

Setting Up a Unity Project for SteamVR

IN THIS CHAPTER, WE get to get our hands dirty and delve into Unity to look at the setup procedure for building a project and importing the SteamVR libraries. Unity is free to download and one of the easiest game engines on the market. The Unity editor (Figure 3.1) is where you create, configure, and bring to life all of your graphics, sounds, music, and other elements that go to make up the virtual world in your projects.

In this book, we are focussed primarily on building with SteamVR as the main SDK. That means we will not be using built-in Unity VR outside of whatever bits the SteamVR libraries need to use under the hood.

SteamVR is free, with the added advantages of being easy-to-use and supporting Rift and Vive as well as just about anything compatible with Open Source Virtual Reality (OSVR) such as the OSVR HDK1 or HDK2.

To use SteamVR as a developer, you need the Steam client software and SteamVR running as a part of Steam, along with the SteamVR library to use with your projects. At this stage, you should have your VR hardware prepared, switched on, and ready to go.

DOWNLOAD UNITY AND MAKE A NEW PROJECT

If you have not already downloaded Unity, you can grab it from the Unity website at https://unity3d.com/get-unity/download.

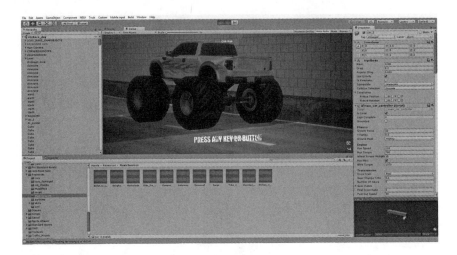

FIGURE 3.1 The Unity editor. Monster Truck model made by Ozgur Saral and available on the Unity Asset Store.

UNITY EDITOR CRASH COURSE

If you have never experienced Unity before, there are a few things you will need to know to get along with this book. If you have used Unity, it may be worth reading through this section just to make sure that we are using the same terminology.

This is not an extensive view of the Unity editor and I am aiming for accessibility rather than in-depth analysis. If you require more information on the editor, Unity provides some really good documentation on the subject on their website (https://unity3d.com/learn/tutorials/topics/interface-essentials).

Editor Views and Panels

The Unity editor is the result of a lot of hard work to make it as intuitive and easy to use as possible. As everyone likes to work differently, the layout is customizable. There are a number of different presets available to help you find the best configuration for how you like to work. The presets are a great way to start to make Unity your own, but for this book I will be using the 2 by 3 layout instead of the default one that Unity starts with.

Choose the 2 by 3 Layout preset from the dropdown menu in the top right of the editor window (Figure 3.2). The view will switch to reflect the change.

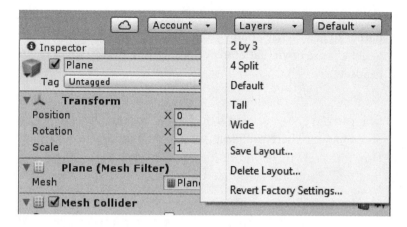

FIGURE 3.2 The Layouts preset button allows you to quickly switch around the layout of the editor.

The Unity editor is split into different views and panels. In Figure 3.3, I have highlighted the following sections:

Game View: In regular game development, this is where most of the action happens. It shows a preview of whatever the cameras in your Scene can see, so that you can see how your game will look before it runs. In VR development, you find that you actually refer to the Game view less and less, as it becomes so much more important to

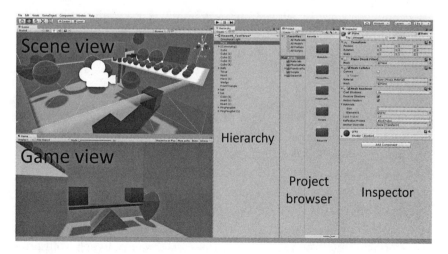

FIGURE 3.3 The Unity editor, broken up into sections.

see how everything looks in VR. In a preview window, it is much harder to get a sense of how your work is going to feel. The only way to get a sense of virtual presence is to be surrounded by it inside the headset.

Scene View: In VR development, this is possibly the most visual interface you have to your simulation other than the headset itself. The Scene view is where you place, move, and manipulate objects visibly. How you view the world in the Scene view is quite different to the headset, so you still need to test regularly.

Hierarchy: Your Scene is made up of many different GameObjects, which are Unity's placeholder entities that go to form the meshes, sounds, and other elements that build the virtual world. GameObjects and the relationships between them affect how the world works, with some GameObjects linked to others, moving together or individually. The structure of your Scene is shown in a text format in the form of the Hierarchy—a text-based visual map of the world. Note that there is also a search function at the top of the Hierarchy that will come in handy for finding GameObjects whenever a Scene starts to get complex.

Inspector: GameObjects have position information, scale, and rotation as well as different Components applied to them to make them do things when the engine runs. Some Components are made from your scripts and code, other Components are built-in to Unity. Any configurable values, properties and so on, will be displayed in the Inspector. The Inspector panel allows you to inspect the currently selected GameObject's Components and alter any available properties.

Project Browser Window: Essentially, a Unity project is a huge bunch of files. You need to be able to do all sorts of things to the files, like move them around, edit them, and organize them, and so forth. The Project panel (I call it the Project browser) is where you can do that. It has a preview system so that you can see a file without having to open it—something that is essential for dealing with larger projects. All the images, sounds, and scripts you need for a major project can soon mount up and the Project browser is designed to help your project stay organized. Note the search bar at the top, too, which makes finding files easier.

Terminology and Common Use Things
There are a few general use parts of the editor that fall outside of the views and panels.

Main Toolbar   The toolbar is made up of seven different tools, which are useful for different parts of the editor (Figure 3.4).
   From left to right, the toolbar is made up of:

   Transform Tools: Every GameObject has something attached to it called a Transform Component. The Transform gives us information about position, rotation, and scale of the GameObject. The Transform tools allow you to move, rotate, and manipulate the GameObjects visually in the Scene view; changing a GameObject's Transform in the Scene. You may also want to know that any modifications with Transform Tools have to take place when the editor is not in play mode, as changes are not saved if they are made when the simulation is running (Figure 3.5).

   The hand icon (1) is used for moving the camera. The little crossed arrows icon (2) is for moving objects. The two arrows in a circle icon (3) is for rotation. The small box with four arrows coming out of it (4) is for scaling objects. Finally, the icon that looks like a circle with a cube around it (5) is the Rect Tool. The Rect Tool is a multi-purpose tool primarily aimed for manipulating 2D graphics, such as user interface or 2D game sprites, but it can be handy sometimes for 3D objects too.

   Transform Gizmo Toggles: On the left is the Pivot toggle. On the right, the Pivot Rotation toggle. The state of these toggle buttons affects how objects will react when you move or rotate them. The Pivot toggle decides the point that the object rotates around. The Pivot

FIGURE 3.4   The toolbar.

FIGURE 3.5   The Transform Tools.

Rotation toggle switches from Local to Global world space (either tool handles work in global rotation or the active object's rotation).

Play/Pause/Step Buttons: Play/Pause/Step buttons control the simulation preview.

Cloud Button: The little cloud icon accesses Unity Services (things such as cloud-based storage and so on).

Account Menu: You need an account to use Unity (free or otherwise) and you can access account settings via this icon.

Layers Menu: Layers are used by the Unity engine to decide how collisions affect each other. The Layers menu lets you create and edit layers.

Layout Menu: We already saw the Layout dropdown earlier, to switch between the Default Unity editor layout to a 2 by 3 layout.

Unity Terminology

Scenes: Unity splits its worlds into Scenes. Scenes work as you might imagine they would, acting as holders for all of the entities that make up a scene of a game. You can switch between Scenes at runtime to move between different environments, for example.

Components: Components are made either from your scripts, or built-in to Unity. They provide behavior to GameObjects such as collisions or sounds, and Components are added to GameObjects.

GameObjects: Think of GameObjects as empty entities that make up the entities in a game or simulation inside Unity. By assigning Components to GameObjects, such as Components to render objects or resolve collisions, GameObjects become the players, enemies, and worlds in a Scene.

Transform: The Transform is a Component that Unity automatically applies to all GameObjects. It contains information about position, rotation, and scale. We communicate with the Transform Component whenever we need to move, turn, or change sizes of objects.

Prefabs: You will often find that you need to create pre-configured GameObjects or groups of GameObjects at runtime, for example projectiles or particle effects. Prefabs are files which can contain one or more GameObjects with Components attached and Components configured, that you can add to your Scenes at any time.

Tags: Unity provides Tags to help you organize and identify GameObjects. In the Unity editor, you set up Tags with names (such as Player, Enemies, Terrain, and so on). In code you can use Tags to find or identify GameObjects.

Layers: The collision system is the main intended use for Layers. In the editor, Layers are given names but in code we often refer to them by index number. Unity also allows you to choose the Layers that will be allowed to collide with each other via the Physics Manager's Layer Collision Matrix (Figure 3.6), which is accessible through the menus Edit > Project Settings > Physics.

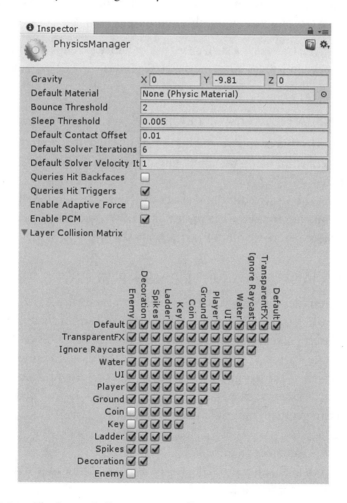

FIGURE 3.6 The Layer Collision Matrix allows you to choose which Layers are allowed to collide.

Triggers: Unity allows its collision system to register, but not actually attempt to resolve collisions between GameObjects. By checking the IsTrigger checkbox on a collision Component, such as a Box Collider Component or a Sphere Collide, the game engine will register when the collision happens but not do anything physically to resolve it. You can add functions to your own scripts that will be called automatically by the game engine whenever these events occur, so that you know when a collision happens and you can react to it in your own way. As an example of usage, Triggers are often used to tell when a player crosses a checkpoint—the checkpoint exists in the Scene as a GameObject and a player is free to move through it without having its physics affected by the checkpoint.

Canvas: The Canvas is a surface we use in Unity to render user interface onto, when using Unity's newest User Interface (UI) system.

CREATING A NEW UNITY PROJECT

The project in this chapter is aimed at making first steps into VR. If you are experienced in using the Unity engine, you will probably zoom right through it.

Open up the Unity editor and select the New icon. Unity will open up to show your new project. The project is ready to go, but we need to do a little bit more before we jump into the virtual world.

DOWNLOADING SteamVR LIBRARIES FOR UNITY

The required files for SteamVR are available on the Unity Asset Store. The Asset Store is a shop where you can purchase and instantly download all kinds of useful assets and scripts for your projects. Products on the Asset Store include scripts, 3D models, full projects, textures, and graphics, and more. As well as the paid products, the Asset Store provides a convenient home for free assets such as the SteamVR libraries. It is provided by Unity and you can get to it from right inside the Unity editor.

Open up the Asset Store inside Unity by accessing the menu Window > Asset Store (Figure 3.7).

The search field runs across the top of the Asset Store page that appears in the main editor window.

For SteamVR VR features to work, you need to download the libraries. The easiest way to find them is with the search function.

FIGURE 3.7   The Unity Asset Store opens in the main editor window.

Type SteamVR into the search window and press enter on the keyboard. After a short time, the search results should appear. Look for the SteamVR Plugin asset (Figure 3.8) and click on either the graphic or the name to view more details. If you have any trouble finding it, the SteamVR libraries are categorized under the Scripting section. Using the name of the category as an extra keyword may help to narrow down your search.

At the top left of the product description you will find the Download button (Figure 3.9). Click on Download and then let Unity download it.

FIGURE 3.8   The Asset Store search results, showing the SteamVR Plugin.

FIGURE 3.9   The SteamVR Plugin asset store product description.

When the download has finished, the button will change to Import (sometimes, a bug in the Asset Store browser causes this button to be unresponsive. If you find that the button doesn't do anything when you click on it, click the Back arrow and then click the forward arrow again to reload the page. After a reload the button should be active again). Unity will start importing SteamVR libraries after you click the Import button.

Before the files are actually copied over into your project, a small window will appear prompting you to look at the files contained in the package (Figure 3.10). On an empty project, it may seem pointless to have to

FIGURE 3.10   Unity checks with you that the files it will import are correct before it imports assets.

go through this extra step, but later on when you are updating libraries to new versions or importing assets that you may have modified during your own development, you may not want the entirety of the asset package overwriting the files in your project and this little check will help you not to overwrite any changes or newer files.

As we do not have anything else in this particular project just yet, you do not need to worry about overwriting files and you can just go ahead.

Click the Import button to have Unity complete the import process and copy in the SteamVR libraries and code.

Some of Unity's default settings will not be suitable for SteamVR. Rather than having to go through and find each setting to change manually, Valve developers have done an excellent job in automating the process with a single button press. If the project settings are not quite right, a pop up will appear to tell you all about it. The SteamVR settings window (Figure 3.11) shows the settings that need changing and what they need changing to.

Hit the Accept All button to have the SteamVR system automatically change the project settings. When the process is complete, a message appears saying something along the lines of "You've made the right choice!" The SteamVR developers take a lighthearted approach to it all but don't let that fool you. Those guys know what they are doing!

Two new folders will appear in the Project panel (Figure 3.12): Plugins and SteamVR. Any APIs suitable for working with the hardware go into

FIGURE 3.11 The SteamVR settings window helps you to make sure that your project is ready for VR.

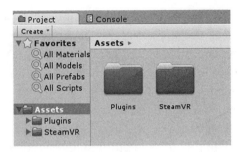

FIGURE 3.12   SteamVR adds two new folders to your project.

the Plugins folder and all of the Unity code, examples and so forth, go into
the SteamVR folder.

Expand out the SteamVR folder by clicking on the little expand arrow
in the Project folder list. Look in there for the Scenes folder and click on
it. Inside, you should find the example scene named example (Figure 3.13).

You can go ahead and close the Asset Store window now, if you like. We
are done with that for now.

Press the Play button in the center of the editor window to try out the
Scene. It is possible that the computer will stall a little as it launches all of
the extra background libraries and applications for VR. Once it has finished preparing, you should see a world full of cubes and what looks like a
browser window giving you a little bit of information about what exactly
SteamVR is (Figure 3.14). Feel free to have a little look around the scene.

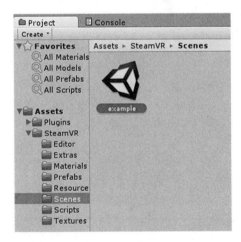

FIGURE 3.13   Use the small arrows to expand folders in the Project browser. In
the Scenes folder, you will find the SteamVR example scene.

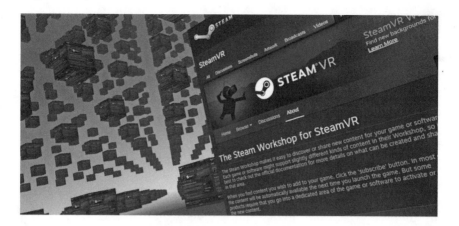

FIGURE 3.14   The SteamVR example scene.

Did you hit some sort of error? If you did, don't panic!

At this stage, you might want to take a quick look at the SteamVR status window that should have appeared after you pressed Play in the editor. If SteamVR wasn't ready to talk to your headset, you will see a status window similar to the one shown in Figure 3.11. If everything is OK and your headset detected, you should see a status window more like the one in Figure 3.12.

Why would you get an error? If the base station(s) do not have a line of sight to the headset, SteamVR may assume that the headset is not connected and will sometimes report a status of "Not Ready." It is an easy fix—either put the headset on your head, or just hold it out somewhere that the base can track it. Stop and press Play again, in Unity, keeping the headset within view of the base station to have it work correctly. As long as your SteamVR status window looks like the one in Figure 3.12, Unity should play nice with it.

Welcome to VR in Unity!

If you are using a HTC Vive, you should try out the example Scene Interactions_Example in the SteamVR/InteractionSystem/Samples/Scenes folder. For Vive owners, this Scene is amazing. It features a whole host of examples for using the Vive controllers for UI, teleportation, and interfaces. It also features a longbow ready to use, complete with loading in arrows manually and firing them at a target. We will not be using the SteamVR InteractionSystem in this book, but it could be a good direction to look in, for Vive-specific systems more advanced than those I will be writing about.

A ROOM WITH A (VR) VIEW

In this section, we are going to make a new scene and bring in a 3D garden environment for you to hang out in. There is nothing particularly complex—it will literally be a garden environment and you can stand in it. To create the garden environment, I used the amazing free voxel-based 3D modeling software MagicaVoxel (https://ephtracy.github.io/). I doubt I have the skills to model such a nice garden in a regular 3D package, so I have to thank the awesome @ephtracy and the ease of use of MagicaVoxel for making this possible!

What I hope to achieve through this is to demonstrate how easy it is to get SteamVR up and running inside the Unity engine.

Make a New Scene in Unity

Keep the project open from the previous section, or reopen it and navigate the menus File > New Scene. If Unity asks whether or not to save changes to the current scene, just click no and continue to the new blank scene.

All of the 3D models and project files for this book are included in the example files you can download free of charge from this book's page on the CRC Press website. If you want to skip following along through this chapter, you can open up the example project from the next chapter (Chapter 4) and open the Scene named chapter 3 scene. The chapter 3 scene contains a finished version of the project we are building here.

Copy in the Models from the Example Files

If you have not already extracted the example files into a folder on your hard drive, extract them somewhere where you can easily access them.

Open a File Explorer by holding down the Windows key and pressing E on the keyboard. When the Run box appears, type explorer and hit enter. When the File Explorer window appears, browse to find your example files folder. In the example files, find the 3DAssets folder and drag the folder into the editor window, dropping it into the Assets folder, so that the whole folder gets imported into the Unity project.

If the import is successful, a 3DAssets folder will appear inside the Project browser (Figure 3.15).

Add a New GameObject

Just below the Hierarchy tab, find the Create button. Click this to show the create menu and select Create Empty to make a new GameObject (Figure 3.16).

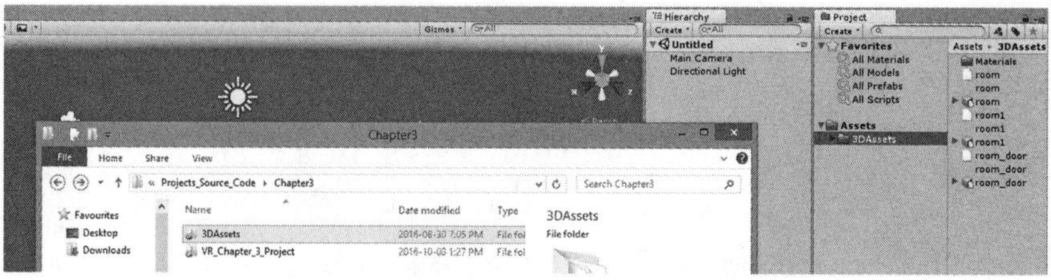

FIGURE 3.15 The 3DAssets folder imported into a new Unity project.

FIGURE 3.16 The Create dropdown menu to add a new GameObject to the Scene Hierarchy.

The new GameObject will start out selected already. Notice that a GameObject has no form, mesh, or shape etc.—it is just an empty placeholder.

Right click on the GameObject in the Hierarchy and click Rename from the dropdown.

Rename the new GameObject to SCENE. This GameObject will act as a parent object to the models used to make the environment.

Empty GameObjects are a great way to keep your Scene organized. We will add models or elements related to the scene, as child objects of this new GameObject. By organizing it like this, we keep everything associated with the scene separate from any other GameObjects and easy to find whenever we want to delve into it. As your project grows, it will get easier and easier to become disorganized, so always try to keep it in order to avoid pain later on!

Add the Garden Model to the Scene

Click 3DAssets in the Project browser.

In the Project window preview, click the garden model. A preview image of the garden should appear at the bottom of the Inspector (Figure 3.17).

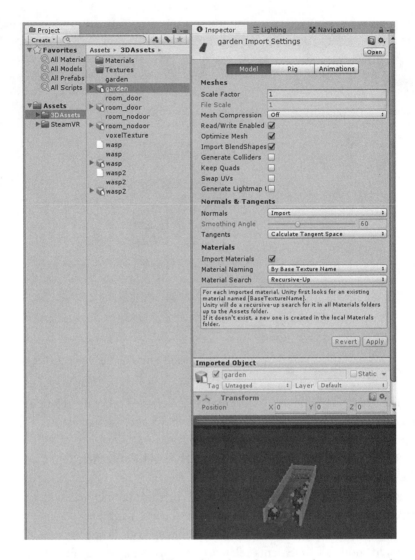

FIGURE 3.17   The garden model is selected in the Project browser, revealing a preview in the Inspector.

Drag the file named garden (the one with the cube icon next to it) out of the Project panel, and drop it right on top of the SCENE GameObject you added to the Hierarchy earlier. When you release the mouse, you should see that Unity has now added the garden to the scene (Figure 3.18) as a child object of SCENE.

The garden is nice, but there is a bit missing: a nice little house.

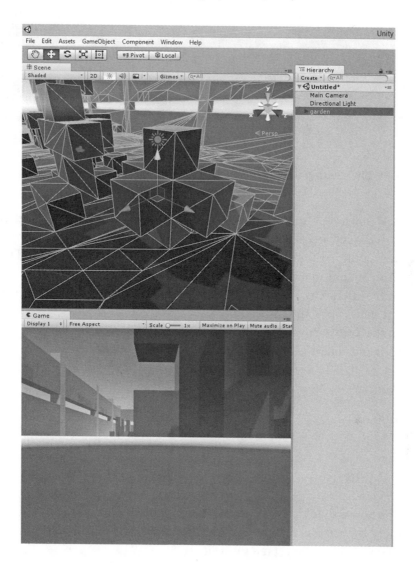

FIGURE 3.18   The garden model, added to the Scene.

Add the House Model

Look to the Projects browser, inside the 3DAssets folder, and find the room_nodoor file. Drag the room_nodoor model over to the Hierarchy and drop it on top of the SCENE GameObject the same way you did for the garden in the last section.

Move the mouse pointer so that it is over the Scene View and then zoom out to get a better view. You can zoom out by either using the mousewheel,

FIGURE 3.19   Setting the room_nodoor Transform position in the Inspector.

or hold down ALT and hold the right mouse button. Once you get a better view of the entire scene, you can see that the house has been dropped right in the middle of the garden. Having a house in the garden may be good for goblins, but not so much for humans. We need to fix this up.

In the Hierarchy, find and click on the room_nodoor GameObject so that it shows up in the Inspector.

In the Transform section of the Inspector (Figure 3.19), click each box in turn and enter the following values:

Position:

X: −1

Y: 0

Z: −46

The house should now be where it is supposed to be, at the top of the garden. The scene is set which means the next step is to add a VR camera so that you can go and stand inside it.

Setting Up the VR Camera Rig

Click the Main Camera in the Hierarchy. Hit the Delete key on the keyboard (alternatively, you can right click the GameObject and choose Delete from the dropdown). The Game view will change to show a message about there being no cameras in the Scene. This is just to let you know that if you were to hit Play now, there would be no camera to render anything and it would just show an empty screen. We will add the VR camera next.

The SteamVR package includes some prefabs to help get things moving. One of them is a camera rig all set up and ready to go. FYI: The term rig is used by developers to describe a setup. In this case, that setup is made of GameObjects with Components attached to them and configured.

In the Project browser, find SteamVR > Prefabs. Inside that folder is a prefab named [CameraRig]. Grab [CameraRig] and drag it over to an empty space in the Hierarchy. Drop it there to add the new camera set up to the Scene. That is all we need to do to get SteamVR working in the Scene. Before continuing, however, we should take a quick look at what the [CameraRig] contains and why.

Digging into the SteamVR Camera Rig
Hold down the ALT key on the keyboard, then in the Hierarchy, left click on the little arrow to the left of [CameraRig]. This will expand out [CameraRig] to show its child objects. It looks something like this:

[CameraRig]

    Controller (left)

        Model

    Controller (right)

        Model

    Camera (head)

        Camera (eye)

        Camera (ears)

Starting from the top, we have the [CameraRig] GameObject itself. It contains a Component to manage controllers, named SteamVR_Controller Manager. It also has a Component named SteamVR_Play Area. What this does is draw the blue frame around the area that we will be allowing users to move around. If you are using HTC Vive, the Chaperone system works regardless of this, independent from it, but the SteamVR_Play Area Component provides a good guide to the play area for working in the editor.

The next GameObject down, a child under [CameraRig], is Controller (left). The Controller (left) and Controller (right) GameObjects are essentially the same. If you have an HTC Vive, this set up will render models that in the virtual world to show where the controllers are—Controller (left) and Controller (right). There is a single Component attached to the

Controller (left) and (right) GameObjects, which is SteamVR_Tracked Object. This allows the virtual controller to follow the one in the real world.

Note that the rig is intelligent enough to know whether or not the controllers are connected and it will not raise any errors if they are unused. If you do not use the controllers, or you are developing for a platform that does not use them, the Controller GameObjects will not affect performance.

Below both the left and right Controller GameObjects is a GameObject named Model. This GameObject is interesting because although it is named model, it does not actually contain any 3D mesh or model. SteamVR will add the model when the simulation runs, which is all the information I will give you right now. You do not need to know how this works unless you plan to use Vive controllers. We will cover Vive controller support in detail in Chapter 9.

Moving down the Hierarchy to the next item, Camera (head) is the start of a set of GameObjects that make up the head system. Camera (head) contains three Components, a Camera, SteamVR_Game View, and the SteamVR_Tracked Object Component. The SteamVR_Game View Component is actually a leftover from previous versions of Unity. It was required to render the view to the Game window prior to Unity 5.4. 5.4+ makes this Component optional, but do not worry as it has compiler-time code that will exclude itself from the build if you are using the newer Unity that no longer requires it.

Also attached to Camera (head) is a SteamVR_Tracked Object Component. If you take a look at the SteamVR_Tracked Object Components attached to the controllers (left and right) you will see that the Index field is set to None. As there may be one, two or maybe more controllers, their Index ID numbers are never hardcoded and always set up at runtime by the SteamVR_ControllerManager script.

For this Camera (head) GameObject, the Index field of SteamVR_ Tracked Object is set to HMD, which stands for Head-Mounted Display. The Camera (head) GameObject will be moving along with the headset. This SteamVR_Tracked Object Component makes sure that the head part of the camera rig gets positioned where it needs to be—mimicking the position of the headset in the real world by referring to the device with the Index set up for the HMD.

Camera (eye) is where you can find the actual headset's view into the virtual world. It is positioned the same position as the Camera (head) object, but here we have the Camera Component used to render the main part of the view. As you will see later in this book, the Camera (eye) is where we will add Components that are reliant on the view, such as Components to find out what the viewer is looking at in the virtual world, or a reticle image to help targeting and so on. It contains a Component named SteamVR_Camera, which deals with taking the view and sending it over to SteamVR for rendering out to the headset. During runtime, SteamVR_Camera will also set up some extra objects needed to do this (when you look at the Hierarchy when the simulation is running, you will notice that its structure changes somewhat). If you are ever making your own camera rig for VR, you can start out by adding a standard camera to the Scene and this SteamVR_Camera Component can be added to use the camera in VR. In terms of the view and how it goes from the Scene to the headset, the SteamVR_Camera Component is central.

Finally, there is Camera (ears). This GameObject is where the Audio Listener sits, which is a Unity-provided Component that deals with "hearing" in a Scene and passing what it hears out to the sound system. SteamVR also includes a Component named SteamVR_Ears, which will align the audio listener correctly when you are using speakers. If you are wondering how it knows whether or not you are using speakers, it is a property of the OpenVR libraries. I assume that it will use some sort of property built into the device to detect when the audio is going through the headset, but in all honesty I found it impossible to get any information about how this value actually gets set by SteamVR if it is actually ever used.

Test the Scene

Press the Play button to preview the scene and put on your VR headset.

Feeling small? The scene may seem quite large. When you are standing in this world, you are about the size of an insect!

The best way to solve scaling problems is inside the 3D modeling package that it was made in—it is best to have the level built to the correct scale right from the beginning. If possible, resizing should be done before the models are imported into the engine, but that is not always an option especially if you are using stock assets. We are going to scale the scene to make you feel the size of a regular human. It is a quick fix that you can do right inside the editor.

VR Environment Scale

In Unity's 3D space, there are no meters, centimeters, or any other kind of measurement other than arbitrary units. Units can be anything you want them to be, but the scale of the world will dramatically affect how the simulation feels. In reality, arms and legs are a certain size and physics behaves in a particular way dependent on our world's scale. For example, gravity causes objects to fall at a certain speed and this reaction depends on the ratio between space and weight. Change one of the two for a different outcome.

Unity physics will behave most naturally (at least, as naturally as it can) when the scale means that 1 unit represents 1 meter. Using 1 unit to 1 meter means that the physics engine is set up to simulate physics reactions at a similar scale to the real world. SteamVR assumes the same, with regard to scale. If you are developing for room-scale VR, the real-world scale will only match the virtual world when the scale is 1:1. That is, the room size that you set up during SteamVR set up will only truly correlate with sizes in the virtual world when the scale is 1 unit to 1 meter.

As a side note, another option to adjusting scale might be to scale the camera. By scaling the camera, you adjust the way that the viewer perceives scale. This works in terms of adjusting the apparent size, but again, due to the scale not being at 1:1, the physics may or may not behave in a way you might expect. Scaling the camera works for visual effect, but it is not useful for changing virtual world objects' physical scale.

Scale the Garden Model

In Unity, select the room_nodoor GameObject in the Hierarchy. Over in the Inspector, you need to enter the following numbers in to the Transform fields:

Position:

    X: −0.2

    Y: −0.2

    Z: 33.66

Rotation:

    X: 0

    Y: 0

    Z: 0

Scale:

X: 0.2

Y: 0.2

Z: 0.2

Next, you need to move and reposition the house so that it matches up with the garden.

Click the garden GameObject in the Hierarchy. In the Inspector, enter the following:

Position:

X: −0.4

Y: −0.2

Z: 24.46

Rotation:

X: 0

Y: 0

Z: 0

Scale:

X: 0.2

Y: 0.2

Z: 0.2

The house should now align nicely with the garden (Figure 3.20).

Press Play again to preview the scene. This time, you should feel regular human size!

STEAMVR CAMERA POSITIONING AND REPOSITIONING

Developing for room-scale VR calls for the hardware to track the position of the headset in the room. When you position the [CameraRig] prefab in your Scene, you are in effect setting up the positional link between the real and virtual worlds. The blue rectangle you see in the Unity editor

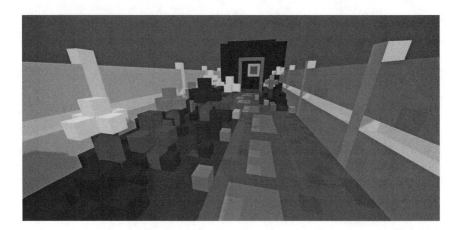

FIGURE 3.20   The garden Scene in Unity.

represents the default bounds of the play area, and you can use those to position the room where you want the simulation to start.

It is possible to move the virtual room area around at runtime. We will look at teleporting in detail in Chapter 6, where we see that it is the entire camera rig that gets repositioned. When a teleport occurs, the entire rig moves to the new area and it is possible to move around in the same physical space but it then correlates to a different space in the virtual environment.

If you intend to move the user, such as having them moving around inside a vehicle like a car or spaceship, you will need to change the tracking configuration. By default, tracking is set to allow the user to move around the space with the Chaperone system displaying boundaries when the player gets too close to the edges of the play area. With seated experiences (such as those inside vehicles) we need to turn off the boundaries and change the tracking configuration so that our camera no longer acts like a person in a room and more like a person in a static position. We will be looking at this in detail in Chapter 11.

Unless you are setting the vertical position of the player in your own code, when you place the camera rig the blue graphics showing the virtual room boundaries need to be positioned at the correct vertical height so that the bottom of the play area aligns with the ground level in your virtual environment. One common mistake is misaligned floor levels leading to objects positioned lower down than the physical space will allow. This becomes especially important when you are using motion controllers to pick up objects from the ground. If the virtual ground is positioned too high, the user may not be able to grab objects or, worse still, may end up hitting controllers against the floor in the real world. We always need to be extra careful about putting our users in situations that may lead to equipment damage, so keep an eye on your floor levels.

SAVE THE PROJECT AND KEEP BACKUPS!

I do not mean to preach, but this is one of the most important lessons you can only fully appreciate when everything goes wrong. If you do not already do it, saving is almost certainly something you need to get used to doing regularly. Very regularly. Working on something for hours at a time means it can take just a single crash to wipe out a whole lot of work. Crashes happen. Especially with new or cutting edge technologies like VR. The best way to avoid losing your work is to save regularly and make regular backups of your projects. Seriously, I know backing up can be a real chore but it is the best way you can spend 5 or 10 minutes of your day. Hard drives do not live forever and backups may be our only hope.

Save the project with File > Save Project.

But wait! That's not all! The current scene has not been saved yet. Saving the project does not save the scene at the same time and you need to do that separately.

Save the scene with File > Save Scene.

Unity will ask for a name. Call it "garden" and click OK.

RECAP

In this chapter, we took a crash course in the Unity editor by looking at its views and panels. We defined some common terms before diving in to setting up a Unity project and downloading the SteamVR library from the Unity Asset Store. The project was set up to be VR-ready and, if all went well, you should have taken the first steps into your own virtual world. It started out a little large, so we scaled it. By importing 3D models, you got to build up a simple garden scene that we used to learn about the camera, scaling, and the basics of a VR scene.

It is time to open the door to the next chapter or, rather, it's time to open a virtual door in the next chapter! In the next chapter, we will look at adding interactivity. We will be using a framework of code that Unity provides as part of its sample VR assets. The framework is free to download from the Asset Store and it is constructed in such a way as to provide an extensible base for building interfaces with.

Adding Interactior

B y now, you probably already know that Unity is a great engine
backed up by an awesome team. If you need any evidence, just take a
look at all of the documentation and free code they give you to get started
on your projects. It really is impressive how much they give; free assets,
free code, and online tutorials. One tutorial session offered by Unity is
the VR Samples series (https://unity3d.com/learn/tutorials/topics/virtual-
reality) which is all about building VR user interfaces. It not only includes
a video tutorial but you get also all of the code and assets to use in your
own projects. Most importantly, it includes a great framework for interaction that we can use to save a ton of time by having the basics in place.

The framework that Unity provides in their tutorials is top class code,
well written, and well thought out. Rather than repeating their work and
repeating what you can read on their website for free, we are going to use
the framework and build on it. This framework will form the basis of
interactive elements in this book, as it provides a solid event-based system
for dealing with the viewer's gaze, controller input, and interaction. You
will not need to study the framework for this book, but if you are interested in what is going on under the hood, you can find full tutorials on
the Unity site: http://unity3d.com/learn/tutorials/topics/virtual-reality/
interaction-vr.

For the examples, I have already extracted the interaction framework
scripts out of the original project provided on the Asset Store (https://
www.assetstore.unity3d.com/en/#!/content/51519) to help future-proofing
the book examples.

te: HTC Vive users may want to look at the SteamVR Interaction System as an alternative way to use standard Unity UI. SteamVR's UI system allows you to use standard Unity GUI elements in the virtual world and we look at this in detail in the section "Using the SteamVR Interaction System for User Interface" in Chapter 9.

ADD THE INTERACTION FRAMEWORK TO YOUR PROJECT

Open the example project for Chapter 4 and open the interactiveDoor Scene in the Unity editor.

With Unity open in the background, open up a File Explorer window and open this book's example files. Inside the example file folders, find the UnityVRUI folder. This contains all of the files that make up the interaction framework provided by Unity. Drag and drop the folder into the Assets folder inside your Unity garden project.

Inside the folder, you will find:

- A GUI folder containing images

- The Utils folder, containing some Utility scripts

- The VRStandardAssets folder containing a subfolder named Scripts, which contains the main framework scripts

ADDING A RETICLE FOR AIMING

One definition of reticle is "an aid in locating objects." In our simulation here, the reticle will take the form of a little dot in the center of the view. It is simply a visual aid to help the viewer aim accurately. Before we can display any sort of UI, however, we need to add a UI Canvas.

Adding a UI Canvas

You may recall adding the [CameraRig] prefab in the previous chapter. We will be adding the reticle to the camera that this rig uses as the viewpoint for VR.

In the Hierarchy, find [CameraRig] and unfold it out. One of the child GameObjects under it is named Camera (eye).

Right click on Camera (eye) and choose UI > Canvas to add a Canvas GameObject. The new Canvas will appear as a child of the Camera (eye) GameObject.

A Canvas is used to display user interface. Literally, you can think of the Canvas as a canvas in the traditional sense, where the interface will be rendered onto it.

Right click your new Canvas GameObject and select Rename from the menu. Rename the Canvas to VR_HUD.

Making a Canvas Suitable for VR

With a regular game, displayed on a regular desktop monitor, the approach to most interfaces is to overlay all of the user interface elements on top of the game display as if they were on a clear plastic sheet in front of the camera. In VR, overlaying the UI in the same way would position our images so close to the camera that it would be impossible for the viewer to actually focus on them. The UI would be a blurry mess. This overlay approach (called Screen Space-Overlay in the Unity UI system) is disabled in VR mode for this reason. We need to use World Space canvas render mode, instead.

The Canvas set to use World Space looks a bit like a flat screen TV in the 3D space. Your Canvas acts like a regular 3D object. You can move it around, rotate it, scale it, and do everything that you could with a regular GameObject and it has the UI rendered onto it. You can move a World Space rendering Canvas in front of the camera to make it viewable, or attach it to other objects in the 3D world such as the controllers or perhaps a screen in the 3D world. We will use World Space for all Canvas in this book.

Unity's UI system allows you to align objects in several different ways, such as automatically centered, left, or right aligned. The alignment system bases its calculations on the parent object of the object you are trying to align, for example if you had a Panel and you added a Button image as a child object of the Panel, telling the Button to align to the center will align it to the center of the Panel. If you were then to add a Text object as a child of that Button, and then set the Text to center, it would center the text to the center of the Button. That hierarchical relationship continues. With a World Space Canvas, the top alignment level would be the Canvas itself. As the Canvas remains at a fixed size, this makes it very easy to align UI elements because you can rely on the Canvas size for element positioning. That said; you need to choose a Canvas size and position that will be easily readable for the viewer and that does not make images too large or too small.

It is important for VR UI designers to keep in mind how the interface will work in the actual simulation, not only looking at the aesthetics but

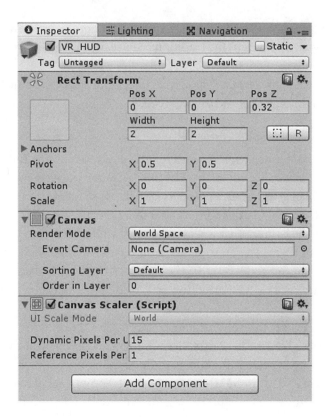

FIGURE 4.1 Properties for the Canvas for the reticle.

the effect as a whole. A huge, complex heads-up display (HUD) may look great in Photoshop but turn out to be unreadable in the virtual world. Iteration is the key. Start simple and build up.

Note that this Canvas will be parented to the main camera, which means that it will move and rotate with the camera at all times. This is good for certain types of interface (like the reticle) but not ideal for full menus as having some types of interface glued to the face of the viewer can make for a rather uncomfortable experience. We will deal with a menu later in this book, but it is good for you to know that parenting the interface to the camera is only a good idea in certain situations.

The Canvas for the reticle will be small and positioned close to the camera. The Canvas only needs to be large enough for a small circular image. Rather than you having to play around and experiment to get the best result, you can copy the parameters below (or see Figure 4.1):

Position:

X: 0

Y: 0

Z: 0.32

Width: 2

Height: 2

Also, make sure that the scale is set to X: 1, Y: 1, and Z: 1.

That is the Canvas all set up. Now you need to add an image to act as a reticle.

Right click on the (now renamed) VR_HUD canvas and choose UI > Image.

The new image is just a small white square. Now, let us switch out the image and change that to a nicer shape more conducive to targeting.

When you dragged in the folder UnityVRUI, it contained a folder named GUI, which was full of images. Whenever you import images into the game engine, it will default to bring them in as textures. These textures are stored in memory in a format that is suitable for 3D models but not suited to Unity's interface system. Unity defaults to importing images as textures that are ready for making 3D games with, but that is not what we want in this situation. The image import settings need to be changed so that those images become available for UI rather than 3D models.

To change the image import settings, in the Project browser, click on the little arrow to the left of the UnityVRUI folder. This should expand out the folder so that you can see its contents. Now, click on the GUI folder so that you can see all of the images it contains.

Click any one of the images to highlight it. On the keyboard, press CTRL + A to have Unity select all of the images in that folder rather than just the one. They should all be highlighted and, over in the Inspector, you should now be able to change the properties for all of the images at once.

Change the Texture Type from Texture to Sprite (Figure 4.2). Now, all of the images in the GUI folder can be rendered as UI on canvases. Next step is to change that square image to a nice circular one, instead.

Click Image in the Hierarchy (remember that it is a child of the VR_UI canvas). With Image selected, you should be able to see its properties in the Inspector.

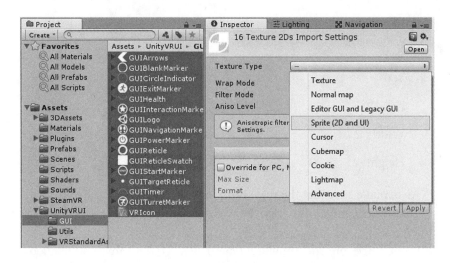

FIGURE 4.2   Image import settings are modified in the Inspector.

Find the Source Image field. To the right of that there is a little circle with a dot inside it, which represents a target. Click on that target icon to show a popup where you can choose from all of the images in your project. The popup appears on the left side of the editor.

In the image popup, find the GUITargetReticle image. It should be about half way down if you move the scroll bar at the side of the pop up. Select GUITargetReticle. The next step is to set up its Transform.

Use these values:

Position:

X: 0

Y: 0

Z: 0

Width: 1.28

Height: 1.28

Scale:

X: 0.02

Y: 0.02

Z: 0.02

The decision as to positioning is actually best made inside VR. That way, you can see exactly where it is and what sort of experience the viewer will have. The reticle needs to be far enough away so that there are no focus problems, but close enough so that it is still visible and at a reasonable size. The antialiasing process and also the resolution of the headset will have an impact on how far away you can reasonably position it.

The reticle image is ready and you should be able to see it now in the center of the Game preview. Before we can move on, there is a little set up work still to be done on the camera.

ADD VREyeRaycaster AND RETICLE COMPONENTS TO THE CAMERA

VREyeRaycaster and Reticle are a part of the interaction framework scripts you imported earlier in this chapter.

The way we find out what the user is looking at is to utilize a method known as raycasting. Raycasting is where we fire out an imaginary line and find out what it is the line intersects with. In this case, the VREyeRaycaster script casts out a ray from the camera's viewpoint, in the direction that the camera is facing, to find the first object in view. Unity's raycaster will grab collision information on any objects the ray hits, such as its Collider and the point that the ray hit.

The Reticle script makes sure that the reticle remains the correct size and controls its position when the viewer looks at an object. To help the viewer understand the depth of objects in front of the camera, the reticle will move to the ray intersection point where the viewer's gaze meets the object. This helps us to judge where the object is in the 3D world.

Back in the garden Scene, in the Hierarchy, find [CameraRig] and unfold it out if it is not already. Find Camera (eye). Click the Add Component button at the bottom of the Inspector, and find Scripts > VRStandardAssets. Utils > VR Eye Raycaster.

Next, with Camera (eye) still selected in the Hierarchy, click the Add Component button again and find Scripts > Reticle

These Components are connected in different ways and they need to be able to communicate with each other. For example, the VREyeRaycaster Component needs to be able to communicate with the Reticle script and it also needs to track input from the viewer. For VREyeRaycaster to do this, it will need to hold references to the other Components it needs to talk to, in the Inspector. We will set up those references now.

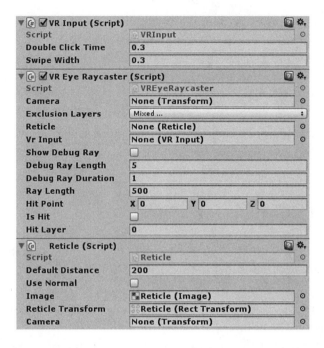

FIGURE 4.3   Script Components attached to the Camera (eye) GameObject, to handle aiming and interaction.

Setting Up Inspector References

In a script that makes a Component to be attached to a GameObject, public variables will be shown in the Inspector as text fields that you can either type into, or drag references in (wherever the variable type is an object). Components can be dragged into these fields in the Inspector, then wherever the variable appears in code it will be referring to the instance set up in that field. This is one way we can get Unity to communicate between scripts and Components.

If you do not already have Camera (eye) selected in the Hierarchy, select that now so that you can see its Components in the Inspector. Look for the VR_Input, VREyeRaycaster, and Reticle Components (Figure 4.3).

We will set up the fields one by one:

COMPONENT: VR EYE RAYCASTER (SCRIPT)

CAMERA

Left click and drag Camera (eye) into the Camera field.

Exclusion Layers

Click the drop down and select Everything, so that all of the Layers shown in the dropdown are highlighted.

Reticle

Grab the Reticle(script) Component from the Inspector and drop it into this field.

Vr Input

Grab the Camera (eye) GameObject and drag it into this field. Unity will automatically use the first instance of the Reticle Component that it finds attached to the GameObject. I am only demonstrating using the GameObject this time, rather than the Component previously, to show that you can either use the Component directly or have Unity automatically find the Component by dragging in a GameObject with one attached to it.

COMPONENT: RETICLE

Reticle Transform

The Reticle Transform field is the Image GameObject attached to the VR_HUD Canvas. VR_HUD is a child of Camera (eye) and you will need to unfold out Camera (eye) followed by VR_HUD to get to the Reticle GameObject with the Image Component attached to it. When Reticle is visible in the Hierarchy, re-select the Camera (eye) GameObject again to show its Components in the Inspector. Find the Reticle Component, then click and drag Reticle from the Hierarchy into the Reticle Transform field.

Camera

Grab Camera (eye) and drop it into this field. Unity will find the Camera Component attached to it, for this field.

Press Play to try out the scene. The reticle should be nicely positioned in the center of the view when you look around.

Stop the Reticle from Clipping

An issue you may come across with the current set up is that the reticle can end up clipping inside other 3D objects in the Scene and be drawn inside them. If the reticle is drawn inside other objects, it will be no use in helping targeting since it will no longer be visible. There is a quick fix for this, which involves using a shader. In the 3DASSETS folder from the example files for this book, there is a Shaders folder containing some of the shaders provided by Unity as a part of the VR Samples files. One of the shader files named UIOverlay will draw images above/in-front of everything else in view.

I have already set up a Material in the example files that will use this shader, but you will need to change the Reticle image to use it. In the Hierarchy, find Reticle again (under VR_UI) and select it. In the Inspector, find the Image (script) Component and click the little target icon to the right of Material. A pop up containing materials should appear. Choose UIMaterialWithUnityShader by clicking on it. With this shader in place, the reticle should no longer clip inside other objects.

With the reticle all setup and ready to go, we should go ahead and make something interactive to try it out with. In the next section of this chapter, you will add a door to the scene and some code to make it open and close.

ADD A DOOR TO THE SCENE

In the Project browser, click the 3DASSETS folder to show its contents in the browser. Find the room_door model (i.e., the one with the small cube icon next to it). Drag that file over to the Hierarchy and drop it there so that Unity adds the model to the scene.

The door starts out in the wrong place (Figure 4.4), which means the first job here is going to be to correct its position.

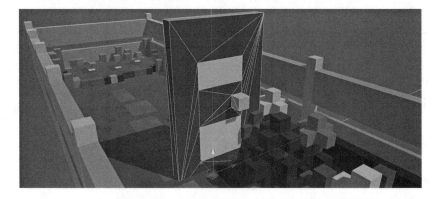

FIGURE 4.4 The door model will not be correctly positioned when it is first brought into the Scene.

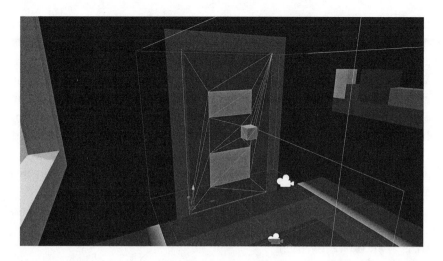

FIGURE 4.5   The door model needs to be correctly positioned against the house, inside the door frame.

Click on the new room_door GameObject in the Hierarchy and then set its Transform properties in the Inspector to the following:

Position:

X: −2.05

Y: 1.05

Z: 6.84

Rotation:

X: 0.77

Y: 0.77

Z: 0.77

The door should look like the one in Figure 4.5 when it is positioned correctly.

Next, we will add some new Components to make the door interactive.

MAKE THE DOOR INTERACTIVE

Adding interactivity to the door requires two Components. The main Component is VRInteractiveItem, provided as part of the interaction framework by Unity, which will catch events triggered by button presses or whenever the headset gaze affects it (such as the gaze hitting a Collider attached to the same GameObject, or the gaze moving away from it). VRInteractiveItem will raise its own events when it catches button or gaze events, and we can tap into VRInteractiveItem's events with our own scripts so that we know when things happen and can react to them. In effect, VRInteractiveItem acts as an interface between our scripts and the Unity interaction framework.

Open up the main Scene from the previous section, if you do not already have it open.

Select the room_door GameObject in the Hierarchy. In the Inspector, click the Add Component button and find Scripts > VRStandardAssets. Utils > VR Interactive Item.

VRInteractiveItem is a standalone script that does not require any set up, but it will need a Collider added to the door that will act as the collision area for our door handle. This will be covered further in this chapter, in the "Add a Box Collider for the Door Handle" section.

The second Component we need for interactivity will be scripted by you and it will catch those events raised by VRInteractiveItem. Your script will be a door controller script to open or close the door whenever the door handle is being looked at and an OnClick event (button press) occurs.

Create a Door Controller Script

Now, click the Add Component button again. This time, right at the bottom of the Components list find New Script and name it DoorController. Ensure that C# is selected in the Language drop down and click Create and Add. The new DoorController script Component will appear in the Inspector.

Double click on the script name DoorController on this new Component, to open it in the script editor.

Here is the DoorController.cs script in full:

```
using UnityEngine;
using System.Collections;
using VRStandardAssets.Utils;
public class DoorController : MonoBehaviour {
    public bool isOpen;
    public Vector3 openRotation;
    public Vector3 closedRotation;
    public Transform ObjectToRotate;
```

```
    public VRInteractiveItem VR_InteractiveItem;

    void Start () {
        // update the current state of door
        UpdateDoorState();
    }

    void ToggleDoor()
    {
        // this will just use isOpen to toggle the
door open or closed
        if(isOpen)
        {
            CloseDoor();
        } else
        {
            OpenDoor();
        }
    }

    void OpenDoor()
    {
        // set isOpen and call to update the actual
door in the scene via the UpdateDoorState() function
        isOpen = true;
        UpdateDoorState();
    }

    void CloseDoor()
    {
        // set isOpen and call to update the actual
door in the scene via the UpdateDoorState() function
        isOpen = false;
        UpdateDoorState();
    }

    void UpdateDoorState()
    {
        // here we adjust the rotation of the door so
that it is physically open or closed
        if(isOpen)
        {
```

```
              ObjectToRotate.localEulerAngles =
openRotation;
        } else
        {
              ObjectToRotate.localEulerAngles =
closedRotation;
        }
    }

    private void OnEnable()
    {
        // subscribe to events from VR_InteractiveItem
        VR_InteractiveItem.OnClick += OnClick;
    }

    private void OnDisable()
    {
        // unsubscribe from events from
VR_InteractiveItem
        VR_InteractiveItem.OnClick -= OnClick;
    }

    void OnClick()
    {
        // call to toggle the door open or closed
        ToggleDoor();
    }
}
```

Script Breakdown

The only additional library needed for this script to work is the VRStandardAssets.Utils namespace. Without this reference, we would not have access to other Unity-made scripts like the VRInput or VRInteractiveItem code:

```
using UnityEngine;
using System.Collections;
using VRStandardAssets.Utils;
```

Next it is the class declaration, again this is just a standard MonoBehaviour derived script (so that we can tap into Unity's built-in automatically called functions like Start and Update and so on) followed by the variable declarations:

```
public class DoorController : MonoBehaviour {

    private bool isOpen;

    public Vector3 openRotation;
    public Vector3 closedRotation;
    public Transform ObjectToRotate;

    public VRInteractiveItem VR_InteractiveItem;
```

Rather than describing each of the variables in the code above, I will describe them as they are used in the code. I will draw attention to the fact that isOpen is a private variable whereas everything else is public. This is because everything except isOpen will be exposed in the Inspector so that you can enter values into them or set up references as required. isOpen is a variable used by the DoorController script to track door state and does not need to be accessible from any other class.

```
void Start () {
    // update the current state of door
    UpdateDoorState();
}
```

Above, the first function is Start(), which is one of the functions automatically called by Unity when playback first begins. The variable isOpen is a Boolean type variable (i.e., its value can only be either true or false) we will be using to track door state. We want to make sure that the door model in the Scene starts out in a state synchronized with the script, so when the script first starts we call the UpdateDoorState() function to take care of rotating the door open or closed as needed.

```
void ToggleDoor()
{
    // this will just use isOpen to toggle the
door open or closed
    if(isOpen)
    {
        CloseDoor();
```

```
        } else
        {
            OpenDoor();
        }
    }
```

In the ToggleDoor() function, we track the door state with isOpen. When ToggleDoor is called, if isOpen is true then we call the function close the door (which will rotate the door model). If isOpen is false, the door is opened, toggling the door either open or closed.

```
    void OpenDoor()
    {
        // set isOpen and call to update the actual
door in the scene via the UpdateDoorState() function
        isOpen = true;
        UpdateDoorState();
    }

    void CloseDoor()
    {
        // set isOpen and call to update the actual
door in the scene via the UpdateDoorState() function
        isOpen = false;
        UpdateDoorState();
    }
```

The function names in the code above are no coincidence. OpenDoor() sets the isOpen variable to true and the UpdateDoorState() function is called to handle the rotation of the model itself.

CloseDoor() does the opposite, of course. It sets isOpen to false, the closed door state, then calls UpdateDoorState() again to update the door model's rotation.

```
    void UpdateDoorState()
    {
        // here we adjust the rotation of the door so
that it is physically open or closed
        if(isOpen)
        {
            ObjectToRotate.localEulerAngles =
openRotation;
```

```
    } else
    {
         ObjectToRotate.localEulerAngles =
closedRotation;
    }
}
```

The UpdateDoorState() function takes care of rotating the model to an open or closed position in the Scene. There are no fancy animations or transitions here, though, it is just a straight jump between the open or closed states.

It works like this; If isOpen is true, ObjectToRotate has its localEulerAngles set to the Vector values in the variable openRotation. If isOpen is not true, the localEulerAngles of ObjectToRotate is set to the closedRotation. The vectors in openRotation and closedRotation are set by you in Unity's Inspector. We will cover this, in the next section.

That is all there is to the opening and closing of the door. I wanted to keep it nice and simple for this example. If you wanted to, you could play an animation here or use Vector3.Lerp to transition between rotations.

The next part of the script deals with subscribing to events from VRInteractiveItem:

```
private void OnEnable()
{
    // subscribe to events from vrInput
    VR_InteractiveItem.OnClick += OnClick;
}
```

OnEnable is automatically called by Unity when a Component (or the GameObject it is attached to) becomes active in the scene. VR_ InteractiveItem is a variable containing a reference to the VRInteractiveItem Component attached to the same GameObject this script is attached to. Here, we say to VR_InteractiveItem to add a listener to its OnClick event. If you were to open up the VRInteractiveItem C# script, you would see that it has a variable declaration for OnClick that looks like this:

```
public event Action OnClick;
```

To explain this, I will employ an analogy. Let us pretend that VRInteractiveItem is a HiFi sound system that you are setting up in your house. In the code, when you declare a variable as an Action, it is as though you are making a speaker for your sound system. The speaker starts out silent. Further on in the VRInteractiveItem code, we make a call to switch on the speaker—OnClick.Invoke()—and it makes a noise. At this stage, however, the music may be playing but nobody is listening to it. Now, imagine that another script (your DoorController) wants to listen to the music, so it subscribes to the OnClick event—essentially becoming a listener to the speaker. When VRInteractiveItem switches on its loudspeaker (triggering the event), the DoorController hears it and can react with its own code. Maybe it will do the funky chicken?

You could add any number of other scripts as listeners, by subscribing to the same event, and it would be as though all of the other scripts will stand around listening to the music. A script party! We only need the speaker to play when there are scripts around to hear it, so we also do a quick check to make sure that the event has at least one listener. OK so now, forget about the speakers.

The way this code works is that VRInteractiveItem will fire an OnClick event, but it will only do so when a button is pressed and it has listeners subscribed to it. Our DoorController subscribes to OnClick like this:

```
VR_InteractiveItem.OnClick += OnClick;
```

We pass in OnClick, which is the name of the function in the DoorController class that we want to call whenever VR_InteractiveItem fires its own OnClick event. OnClick in DoorController will now be called when the viewer presses a button or clicks the mouse. As long as they are looking at this GameObject, VRInteractiveItem will take care of triggering its own OnClick for you, which in turn triggers your function in DoorController.

Just as you may want to listen to an event, you will also need to stop listening when you no longer need to listen. In the next part of the code, we remove the subscription to OnClick—in effect, at the end of the scene, we stop listening to it:

```
private void OnDisable()
{
    // unsubscribe from events from vrInput
    VR_InteractiveItem.OnClick -= OnClick;
}
```

There are two operators you use to either subscribe or unsubscribe to/ from events:

To subscribe	+=
To unsubscribe	-=

Notice that these operators are the same ones you can use to add or subtract numbers. Think of it as adding or subtracting listeners to events.

The OnDisable() function is the opposite of OnEnable(), in that it is called when the Component (or the GameObject) becomes disabled or inactive. OnDisable() is a good place to put important code that needs to happen when an object is destroyed (such as when a new scene is loaded and you need to do some cleanup on the way out).

Now, the final code in this class:

```
void OnClick()
{
    // call to toggle the door open or closed
    ToggleDoor();
}
}
```

As you know, we subscribed to VRInteractiveItem's OnClick event back in the OnEnable function, telling Unity to call the function above whenever VRInteractiveItem's OnClick event happens.

Finally, the call to ToggleDoor() will flip the door open or closed.

Note: A click, by definition, is considered to be a button that has been pressed and depressed.

ADD A BOX COLLIDER FOR THE DOOR HANDLE

There is not much left to do to make this work, now. All of the scripting is done, so switch back to the scene to do a little more work on the GameObject in the Inspector.

If it is not still selected from earlier, click on the room_door GameObject in the Hierarchy. Over in the Inspector, click Add Component and find Physics > Box Collider

I will provide the numbers I used for my Collider, but you should feel free to position and scale the Box Collider any way you like, via the Inspector (Figure 4.6) or by using the Scene Tools. The collider will be the hotspot for the headset's gaze, so you need to position the Collider in a

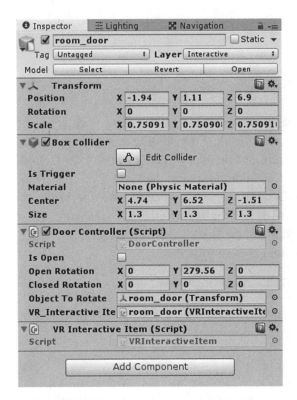

FIGURE 4.6   The Inspector shows all of the Components attached to the room_
door GameObject, including the Box Collider Component.

place that will make sense to the user as being the right place to look when
trying to open a door. The collider might cover the entire door, or just the
door handle. I chose to only cover the door handle, so here are the properties you will need to do that:

Center:

X: 4.74

Y: 6.52

Z: –1.51

Size:

X: 1.3

Y: 1.3

Z: 1.3

With the Box Collider in place, all that is left to do is set up some references on the DoorController Component.

SET UP REFERENCES ON THE DOORCONTROLLER COMPONENT

The DoorController Component has four fields visible in the Inspector. Those are

OPEN ROTATION

This is the rotation vector for the door in its open state. Enter the following values:

X: 0

Y: 279.5

Z: 0

CLOSE ROTATION

This is the rotation vector for the closed door. You can leave this at 0,0,0.

OBJECT TO ROTATE

This is the GameObject which is going to have the rotation applied to it when the call is made to open or close the door. In this case, we just need to rotate the room_door object.

Drag the room_door GameObject from the Hierarchy into this field.

I chose to expose this variable to the Inspector just in case you decide to re-use this script in the future and, for whatever reason, need to rotate a parent object or a different object to the one with the script attached.

VR_INTERACTIVE ITEM

You might remember this variable from the coding sections earlier in this chapter. It needs to reference the VRInteractiveItem Component attached to this GameObject.

Click on the VRInteractiveItem Component, still in the Inspector, and drag it into this field.

The final DoorController Component should look like Figure 4.7.

Hit Play to preview and to give the Scene a test. In VR, you should now be able to look at the door handle and press a button on your controller to open it. If you don't have a controller, you can use the mouse, but you need to be

▼ ⓒ ☑ Door Controller (Script)						🖻 ⚙,
Script	ⓒ DoorController					⊘
Is Open	☐					
Open Rotation	X 0	Y 279.56	Z 0			
Closed Rotation	X 0	Y 0	Z 0			
Object To Rotate	⊥ room_door (Transform)					⊘
VR_Interactive Ite	ⓒ room_door (VRInteractiveIte					⊘

FIGURE 4.7 The DoorController Component with all of its values and references set up.

sure to position the mouse somewhere inside the Game preview before you put on the headset, then use the left mouse button to interact. If the mouse is not hovering over the Game View in Unity when you click, it will not be registered by Unity as being a click into the game and it may lose focus.

SAVE YOUR WORK!

You have reached the end of this project. Stop playback if Unity is still in Play mode. Save your work.

Click on the menus File > Save Scene

RECAP

This chapter was our most in-depth so far! You have set up a reticle to help viewers to be able to aim at an object, set up the VREyeRaycaster to find out where the viewer is looking, added a door model to the scene, and then added Components to it. We programmed a new behavior to work with VRInteractiveItem to know when to open and close a door. You have seen how the VRInteractiveItem Component may be used to add interactivity easily by subscri4bing and unsubscribing to events, passing in functions to call when events are triggered. This is at the core of Unity's VR interactive framework. Add VRInteractiveItem to any object you want to make interactive, register to its events, and you can make scripts for viewers to interact with, in whatever way you like.

In the next chapter, we will take a look at the SteamVR teleportation system to allow the viewer to move around the garden. When you are done opening and closing the doors, beam yourself over to the next chapter!

CHAPTER 5

Building User Interface for Headset and Game Controller

MAKING A MAIN MENU SCENE

A main menu scene provides a menu for players to load the game or exit. Having a screen before the game is a great way to make sure that your user is set up correctly with the headset and ready to go before starting the game.

In this chapter, we start with putting together a reusable button script so that we can easily add buttons anywhere they may be needed and potentially use the same script again in future projects. From a simple user interface to interactive Awooga buttons, by the end of this chapter you will know how to implement interface-like interactivity. The Unity interaction framework we have already seen in the previous chapter will be employed to take care of the raycasting and core event setup. The button script will tap into the interaction framework, extending on the basic interaction model to demonstrate how you will be able to develop your own behaviors for interactive content and interface.

It will use the viewer's gaze (where the VR headset is looking) to establish which button is being looked at. When a button is being looked at, the button has a built-in progress bar that will increase over a set time. When the progress bar reaches the top, we assume that this is the button the viewer wants to select and go ahead to perform whatever action

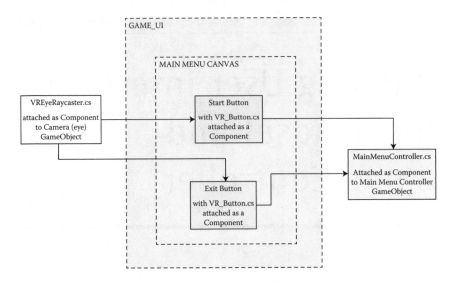

FIGURE 5.1   The UI system structure.

is attached to that button. This type of button is already commonly found in VR and the way that it works is nice and straightforward for a viewer to understand. The timed button may also be familiar to anyone who may already have experience in VR.

The structure of the UI system looks like Figure 5.1.

Open the Example Project

Open up this chapter's example project. We are going to use the reticle, from Chapter 4, for aiming the VR_Input Component to track game controller input and the VREyeCaster Component to find out what the headset is looking at.

In the Project window, click on Scenes to show what is inside. Find the mainMenu Scene and double click on it.

Create a Canvas for the User Interface to Be Drawn On

To stay organized, add an empty GameObject to the scene to act as a parent to the UI. Click the Create button at the top of the Hierarchy to bring up the Create dropdown menu. Select Create Empty and rename the new empty GameObject to GAME_UI

Right click on GAME_UI and select UI > Canvas.

Rename the Canvas to MainMenuCanvas.

In Chapter 3, we looked at creating a Canvas for the reticle and it was noted that the standard setting for a Canvas is not intended for VR. We need to change some parameters of the Canvas Component attached to MainMenucanvas to have it visible inside the headset, such as its Render Mode setting.

In the Inspector's Canvas section, set the Render Mode to World Space.

Drag the Camera GameObject from the Hierarchy and drop it into the Camera field.

Sorting layer should be set to Default.

Order in Layer set to 0.

In the Canvas Scaler Component, ensure that the following values are set:

UI Scale Mode should be grayed out. This is because we are using the World Space render mode in the Canvas.

Dynamic Pixels Per Unit should be set to 1.

Reference Pixels Per Unit should be set to 100.

With the Canvas set up, at this point we are almost ready to go. For the interface to work well in the virtual space, we will use the UIMovement Component.

Add a UI Movement Component to the Canvas

The reticle, in Chapter 3, was a child object of the main Camera so it would be attached to the viewer's head and move around with it, to aid aiming. When we are making a menu system, this type of camera locking behavior does not work. We need to be able to look at different areas of the screen in order to have more than a single item on the menu, so we need the menu to be fixed at least to some degree but still allow movement. One approach to tackling this is to lock the interface on two axes, having it follow the viewer's head movement side-to-side. It may move in perfect sync horizontally with the headset, or lag behind a little for a different feel. The vertical axis of the menu may be locked in the 3D space so that the headset can move up or down to select different items easily yet have the horizontal lock keeping the menu positioned in front of the view. In this section, we will add a script to the Canvas that will move with the headset in a nice way. Personally, I prefer completely static menus as a part of the environment around me, but I understand that this is not always an option and some designers will want to do something more similar to what we see here. Not all UI designs are suitable to be included as a part of an environment. This

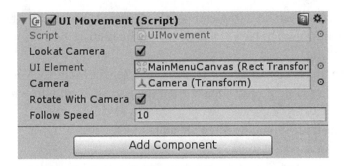

FIGURE 5.2 The UI Movement Component in the Inspector, attached to the MainMenuCanvas.

approach allows us to support a more abstract design that will be easy for the viewer to find and interact with.

With MainMenuCanvas selected in the Hierarchy, click the Add Component button in the Inspector. Select Scripts > VRStandardAssets. Utils > UI Movement.

You should see the new Component appear in Inspector (Figure 5.2). There are five fields in the UI Movement Component. Those are

1. Lookat Camera.

   Should this script make the Canvas always face the camera? The answer is yes, so go ahead and check this box by clicking in it once.

2. UI Element.

   Click and drag the MainMenuCanvas into this field. Do this just so that the script knows which UI element to move around.

3. Camera.

   This is the camera that the UI will be following and put in front of. Find the Camera in the Hierarchy and drag it into this field.

4. Rotate with Camera.

   Should this script make the canvas rotate with the camera, too? The answer is yes, again. Check this box.

5. Follow Speed.

   You can easily adjust how much smoothing this script will apply by changing this number. I find 10 is a nice, comfortable value. Enter 10 into this field.

The Canvas should now move around nicely with the camera, but you will not be able to see much until we actually add elements to be drawn.

Building a Button

First, we need to make an empty GameObject to use as a button.

Right click on the MainMenuCanvas object in the Hierarchy. Select Create Empty. Rename the new GameObject to StartButton.

Next, we need to add Components to the button to make it work. There are three Components that make our VR buttons function. They are

1. VR Interactive Item (script).

   The Unity interaction framework provides this Component. It is used by our buttons to monitor when the viewer's gaze is over this GameObject.

2. Box Collider.

   For any sort of collisions or raycast intersections to be tracked, objects we want to interact with must have a Collider Component. Without any sort of Collider, the raycast will not be able to "see" the object. For buttons, the Box Collider makes total sense as it is rectangular, like a button.

3. VR_Button (script).

   The VR_Button Component is a custom script Component that we will be coding in the next section. It hooks into the VR Interactive Item Component and acts when the viewer's gaze is on the button.

Click Add Component in the Inspector, to add a new Component to the StartButton.

Choose Scripts > VRStandardAssets.Utils > VR Interactive Item

The VR Interactive Item Component has no properties or anything to change in the Inspector, so we can just move on and add the next Component.

Click Add Component. Find Physics > Box Collider

Keep the center of the Box Collider at 0,0,0 but we will need to change the size. Enter the following into the Size fields:

X: 344

Y: 57

Z: 1

Before we go ahead and start programming the VR_Button Component, set up the graphical element for the button.

Add a UI Slider to Show Button Progress

A UI Slider is normally used as an interface element for people to be able to drag and drop to change a numerical value or to scroll around an area. An example of a Slider in action is a scrollbar.

The Slider has a method for showing a value (between 0 and 1) as a progress bar. We will remove the interactive parts of the Slider so that it is just a progress bar and then use it to show how long the player has been gazing at the button. When the progress reaches full, the button action will be triggered.

To add a UI Slider, right click on the StartButton GameObject in the Hierarchy and choose UI > Slider.

Expand out the Slider in the Hierarchy and click on the Handle Slide Area object (Figure 5.3). Press Delete on the keyboard to remove it from the Scene.

Select the Slider in the Hierarchy. You need to change some of its settings in the Inspector. Those are

1. Interactable.

   Set this to false (unchecked) as we do not want the viewer to be able to do anything with this object. Everything we need to do will be handled by code.

FIGURE 5.3 The Handle Slide Area object should be deleted to use a UI Slider as a progress bar.

2. Transition.

Select None from the dropdown. The default setting is Color Tint, but we do not want to do anything with the Slider except show progress.

3. Navigation.

The default setting of "Automatic" means that navigating between UI elements on the Canvas will be dealt with automatically. Since there will be no navigation via controllers or other input device, set the Navigation to None in the dropdown.

4. Fill Rect.

Here, you can pass in the image to use to fill the progress bar with. Fill Rect, by default, will be set to the Fill image you can find deeper in the Hierarchy as child objects of the Slider. This is fine. You do not need to change this setting.

5. Handle Rect.

The Handle Rect is an image to use as a handle. On a typical scroll bar, the handle would be the part you click and drag on to change the view. Here, we are not using a handle and its value will currently be Missing (Rect Transform). It is acceptable to leave it as Missing, but I prefer to keep things tidy. Click on the small target icon to the right of the field. Select None from the list.

6. Direction.

Left to Right is the correct value for this. Unless you decide that your progress bar makes more sense going in another direction, this is the correct way to show progress of the button selection.

7. Min Value.

We will be passing in numbers to this slider, to tell it where progress is at. Rather than assume that the progress bar should show nothing when the value is zero, the nice people at Unity have provided a Min Value field so that you can decide where "no progress" should be on the scale. For our purposes here, however, keep it to 0.

8. Max Value.

Just as we have a minimum value for a slider, we have a maximum value. The progress bar will be full when its value (that numerical value we will pass into it) is at Max Value. Leave this at 1.

9. Whole Numbers.

This box should be unchecked, as our script will be using decimal values between 0 and 1.

10. Value.

You can decide where a Slider starts without having to pass anything in through code. The Value slider is also a good way to visualize the Slider in the editor. Feel free to drag it up and down to see how the slider is working. When you are done, return this to 0.

11. On Value Changed Events.

This can be left empty. It is provided to trigger events when the user drags the handle to change slider value, but since we are not using the slider in that way we don't need anything to happen if a user happens to click here.

The Slider GameObject is ready to go, but you now need to change the sizes and colors of the graphics so that progress is more visible on the screen.

Change Slider Background Color
The background color defaults to a grayish sort of color, which is a little bright for what we need here. The button would work better in a darker color.

In the Hierarchy, click on the Background GameObject (you can find it right under the slider). In the Inspector, look to the Image Component and find the Color field. It should be a white rectangle. Click on the Color rectangle to show the color picker and choose black.

The fill color is also not as visible as I would like. We should change it.

Change Fill Color
Expand out Fill Area in the Hierarchy to show the Fill object. Click on the Color rectangle to show the color picker and choose a nice, bright red color. This will make the progress very easy for the viewer to see as it increases.

Resize the Slider
There are actually two components belonging to the slider that you will need to resize for the right effect.

First, click on the Slider GameObject. In the Inspector Rect Transform area, set the following fields:

Width: 334

Height: 37

To get to the numbers above for sizing, I just picked sizes that looked like they could accommodate a few different sizes of menu button text (we need these buttons, at the very least, to be able to fit Play Game and Exit text in them). You can easily resize them if you do choose different sized fonts at a later time.

The way this works is that the Slider size determines the whole area that will act almost like its own mini-canvas. When you change sizes of the child objects that make up the Slider, their sizes will fall within those set by the overall Slider. You will see first-hand how this works when we resize the Background GameObject in the next section.

Resize the Background Image

The Slider is the right size, but you may notice that the actual graphics have not changed size at all. You need to edit these individually. The first graphic to resize is the Background.

Find the Background GameObject. In the Inspector, find the Rect Transform Component and click the Anchor Presets button in the top left (Figure 5.4). The Anchor Presets helps you quickly choose how the GameObject will be affected and anchored to its parent GameObjects.

In the bottom right of the Anchor Presets is a button that will make this interface element stretch to fill the boundaries of its parent GameObject. It does this by setting anchors to be automatically positioned in each corner of the allowed display area. Whenever the parent object changes position, since the anchors are in the corners, this object will continue to stretch to fill. We need to click it three times, but each one a little differently:

1. Click the Stretch (Figure 5.5) button once. Clicking the button like this says "stretch the size to fill."

2. Hold ALT on the keyboard and click the Stretch button for a second time. Clicking with the ALT key held down effectively says "make sure that the objects pivot moves with the stretch, too."

3. Hold CTRL on the keyboard and click Stretch again. With CTRL pressed, this says "move the position of this element along with the stretch, too."

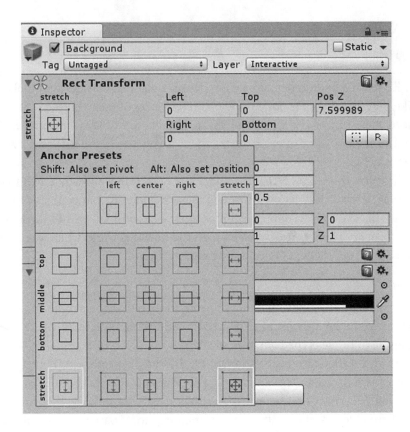

FIGURE 5.4   The Anchor Preset button in the top left of the Inspector will have Unity display the Anchor Presets menu for user interface elements.

FIGURE 5.5   The Stretch Anchor Preset is used to make UI elements stretch to fill the available Canvas area.

With the anchors set up to stretch to fill, the Background will now stretch to fit the area of the Slider.

Next, you need to resize the Fill GameObject.

The process is the same for the Fill object as it was for the Background. Select Fill and use the Anchor Presets menu to stretch it to fill the area.

PROGRAMMING A C# BUTTON SCRIPT

The interaction framework provided by Unity is a great way to track viewer's gaze and track controller buttons or mouse clicks. Although Unity
does provide sample files, I think it is more useful to look at how to expand
upon the framework to build your own Components. In this section,
we will see how a gaze-based button can work.

The VR_Button.cs script in full:

```csharp
using UnityEngine;
using System.Collections;

using UnityEngine.UI;
using VRStandardAssets.Utils;
using UnityEngine.Events;

public class VR_Button : MonoBehaviour {

    public VRInteractiveItem VR_InteractiveItem;
    public Slider slider;

    [Space(20)]
    public float activationTime =2; // in seconds

    private float gazeTimer;
    private bool gazeOver;

    public UnityEvent OnActivateEvent;

    void Update()
    {
        // if we are not looking at this button, reset
the gaze timer to zero
        if (!gazeOver)
        {
            // reset timers to zero
            gazeTimer = 0;
        } else
        {
            // as we are looking at the button, let's
go ahead and increase gaze timer to time how long the
gaze lasts
            gazeTimer += Time.deltaTime;
        }
```

```
        float theSliderNum = gazeTimer /
activationTime;
        slider.value = theSliderNum;

        // check to see if we are ready to activate
        if ( gazeTimer >= activationTime)
        {
            // tell the event attached to this button,
to go!
            OnActivateEvent.Invoke();
        }
    }

    private void OnEnable()
    {
        // subscribe to hover events from
VR_InteractiveItem
        VR_InteractiveItem.OnOver += OnGazeOver;
        VR_InteractiveItem.OnOut += OnGazeLeave;
    }

    private void OnDisable()
    {
        // subscribe to hover events from
VR_InteractiveItem
        VR_InteractiveItem.OnOver -= OnGazeOver;
        VR_InteractiveItem.OnOut -= OnGazeLeave;
    }

    void OnGazeOver()
    {
        gazeOver = true;
    }

    void OnGazeLeave()
    {
        gazeOver = false;
    }
}
```

Script Breakdown

There are quite a few libraries in action for this script:

```
using UnityEngine;
using System.Collections;
```

```
using UnityEngine.UI;
using VRStandardAssets.Utils;
using UnityEngine.Events;
```

If you are going to be writing code which accesses Unity's user interface elements, such as the Slider, you will need to use the UnityEngine.UI namespace.

The VRStandardAssets.Utils namespace contains the collection of scripts provided by Unity for the interaction framework. We will be referencing a VRInteractiveItem Component further down in the script, which is only accessible with this library referenced at the start of the script.

Finally, we see UnityEngine.Events, which is a library that needs more explanation. If you have not already come across the UnityEvent before, it is a really convenient way to add customizable behavior to Components. We will take a look at this system in detail, a little further down in the script.

The class declaration follows, derived from MonoBehaviour, so that we can tap into the automatically called functions like Update(). Following that, we have variable declarations:

```
public class VR_Button : MonoBehaviour {

    public VRInteractiveItem VR_InteractiveItem;
    public Slider slider;

    [Space(20)]
    public float activationTime =2; // in seconds
    private float gazeTimer;
    private bool gazeOver;
    public UnityEvent OnActivateEvent;
```

Most of the variables in the code above, we can explain as they come up but there are a couple of things to note.

The first thing is the line that reads [Space(20)]. This is not a variable, but instead something known as an Attribute. Unity has several different attributes that can provide a degree of customization to the way the Inspector displays your variables. The Space attribute will make a space between variables in the Inspector. In this case, a 20 pixels high space will appear between the variable above the attribute and the variable below it.

The final variable declared above is OnActivateEvent and it is the type UnityEvent. As mentioned earlier, Unity Events are a great way to add customizable behavior to Components. In the Inspector, the way that a

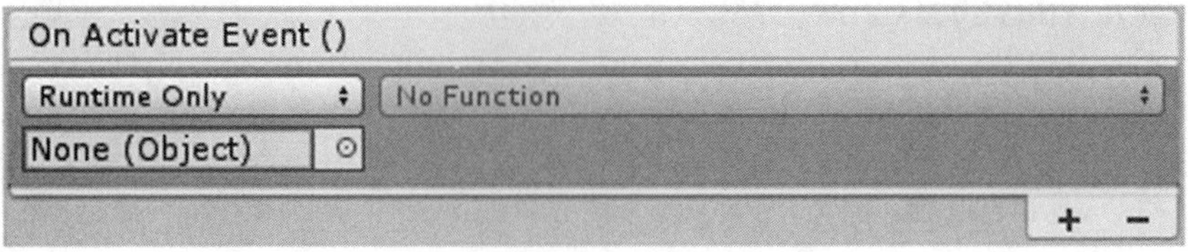

On Activate Event ()		
Runtime Only ⬍	No Function	⬍
None (Object) ⊙		
		+ −

FIGURE 5.6 The UnityEvent type adds an interface to the Inspector.

UnityEvent field is displayed is different to other variables and it includes an interface for setting up behaviors (Figure 5.6).

The way we use it is to set up a behavior for the button in the Inspector. Essentially, we drag in the script we want to call and then select a function from the script via a dropdown menu. All part of the UnityEvent interface in the Inspector.

When we need to trigger the button's behavior, we can call a function on the OnActivateEvent variable that will carry out the function call to the script set in the Inspector.

The next part of the script deals with making the progress bar rise whenever the viewer's gaze is on this button:

```
void Update()
{
    // if we are not looking at this button, reset
the gaze timer to zero
    if (!gazeOver)
    {
        gazeTimer = 0;
    } else
    {
        // as we are looking at the button, let's
go ahead and increase gaze timer to time how long the
gaze lasts
        gazeTimer += Time.deltaTime;
    }
```

It is only when the viewer looks at the button that we want the progress bar to raise and when the viewer looks away from it, the progress bar needs to reset back to zero. In the code above, we look to see if gazeOver is false, which will only happen when the viewer is not looking at this button, and then reset progress held in the variable gazeTimer to reset the progress bar.

The else statement catches whenever gazeOver is not false and adds Time.deltaTime to gazeTimer. Time.deltatime is the amount of time that has passed between this frame update and the last update. That is, the time since Update() was last called. If the viewer is looking at the button, we know that they have been looking for this amount of time between frame updates so we can add it to gazeTimer and this will keep a track of gaze time.

This means, in gazeTimer, we always have a clear count of how much time the viewer has been looking at this button. The next job is to convert that into a percentage value between 0 and 1 so that we can set the Slider value to display it graphically:

```
float theSliderNum = gazeTimer / activationTime;
```

theSliderNum is declared first in the code block above. gazeTimer is how much time has gone by with the viewer looking at the button and activationTime is the amount of time (in seconds) we want them to look at the button before we activate it. theSliderNum is set to the gazeTimer divided by activationTime, which gives us a number between 0 and 1 to use as a value to set the Slider with.

The Slider UI element has a property named value, which we set next to the value of theSliderNum:

```
slider.value = theSliderNum;
```

All that is left to do in the Update() function is to keep a tabs on where we are with the gazeTimer:

```
        if ( gazeTimer >= activationTime )
        {
            // tell the event attached to this button,
to go!
            OnActivateEvent.Invoke();
        }
    }
```

Above, the condition asks if gazeTimer is greater or equal to activationTime. That is, questioning whether the viewer has been looking at this button long enough to activate it. If this condition is met, the Invoke() function is called on OnActivateEvent. Remember earlier I mentioned this UnityEvent type variable, OnActivateEvent? Whatever behavior is set up in the Inspector will be called here by this single Invoke() call.

Next, we need to tell the VR_InteractiveItem Component that we would like to receive events:

```
private void OnEnable()
{
```

The OnEnable() function is another function that gets automatically called when a script deriving from MonoBehaviour is first activated or enabled in the Scene.

As it occurs before any sort of main loop update takes place, it is the right place to subscribe to events. We do it here as a safety measure; so that by the time that the first main loop updates happen, this script is set up and ready to go right away.

In Chapter 4 we looked at the VRInteractiveItem Component and used it to register for clicks on the door, to open it. As well as OnClick, VRInteractiveItem provides a few more events useful to user interaction. Above, we subscribe to its OnOver and OnOut events. They speak for themselves, really; OnOver will be triggered when the viewer first looks at the GameObject that has the VRInteractiveItem Component attached to it, and OnOut is triggered when the viewer looks somewhere else.

As with the OnClick() event we put together in Chapter 4, we pass in the name of the function that we want to trigger whenever the applicable event in VRInteractiveItem triggers:

```
// subscribe to hover events from VR_InteractiveItem
    VR_InteractiveItem.OnOver += OnGazeOver;
    VR_InteractiveItem.OnOut += OnGazeLeave;
}
```

Just a reminder: the += operator is used to add to variables. In the code above, we are effectively adding OnGazeOver to VR_InteractiveItem. OnOver. You can add multiple functions, using that same operator (+=) and multiple functions will be automatically called by the event. This also applies to multiple scripts. Any script that is subscribed to an event will get triggered. For example, if you wanted to make another script that will play a sound whenever OnOver occurs, you could subscribe to VR_ InteractiveItem in the exact same way from another script and it would not affect the behavior of this button.

Following on from the code above, the OnDisable() function contains the code to unsubscribe from VRInteractiveItem gaze events:

```
private void OnDisable()
{
    // subscribe to hover events from
VR_InteractiveItem
    VR_InteractiveItem.OnOver -= OnGazeOver;
    VR_InteractiveItem.OnOut -= OnGazeLeave;
}
```

The operator −= is used to subtract. Above, we subtract those functions from the events we previously subscribed to in the OnEnable function so that they will no longer be triggered by the events.

Finally, we have the OnGazeOver() and OnGazeLeave() functions themselves (which are the functions that are called by our subscriptions to VR_InteractiveItem events):

```
void OnGazeOver()
{
    gazeOver = true;
}
void OnGazeLeave()
{
    gazeOver = false;
}
}
```

gazeOver is a Boolean type variable used to track whether or not the viewer is looking at the button. Back in the Update() function, we checked the state of gazeOver to decide whether or not to reset the gazeTimer used for the progress bar, or to add more time to it.

The final parentheses above closes the class and we are done with the VR_Button script! Save the script (CTRL + S on the keyboard) and switch back over to the Unity editor.

ADD A REFERENCE FOR THE VR_BUTTON COMPONENT TO USE

In the last section, we saw how the VR_Button class registers for events from VR_InteractiveItem. In order for this to work, we need to populate the VR_InteractiveItem variable with a reference to the VR Interactive Item Component in the Inspector.

In Unity, select StartButton in the Hierarchy. In the Inspector, click and drag the VR_InteractiveItem Component into the VR_Interactive Item field on the VR_Button Component.

The VR_Button class also needs to set the value of the progress bar. To do that, it needs to talk to the Slider. In the Hierarchy, expand out StartButton so that Slider is visible. Reselect StartButton again to show the VR_Button Component in the Inspector, then click and drag the Slider GameObject from the Hierarchy and drop it into the Slider field on the VR_Button Component, in the Inspector.

The On Activate Event() section, at the bottom of the VR_Button Component, will point to the script that will have one of its functions triggered when the button is selected/pressed. We do not need to set that up right away and we will set up the On Activate Event subscription later in this chapter, once we have programmed behaviors for the buttons.

ADD A TEXT LABEL TO THE BUTTON TO SHOW WHAT IT DOES

A nice progress bar for a button is awesome but we still need to tell the viewer what this button is supposed to do. We will do this by adding a text label.

Right click on the Slider GameObject and choose UI > Text

Default size and color of text means that it can be a little difficult to see. It will be fairly small and dark gray. In the Hierarchy, find this new Text GameObject and right click. Choose Rename and change its name to Label

In the Inspector, find the Text Component (Figure 5.7) and change its fields to:

Text: PLAY GAME.

Font Style: Normal

Font Size: 39

Line Spacing: 1

Rich Text: Checked.

Paragraph:

Alignment: Centered Horizontally and Vertically

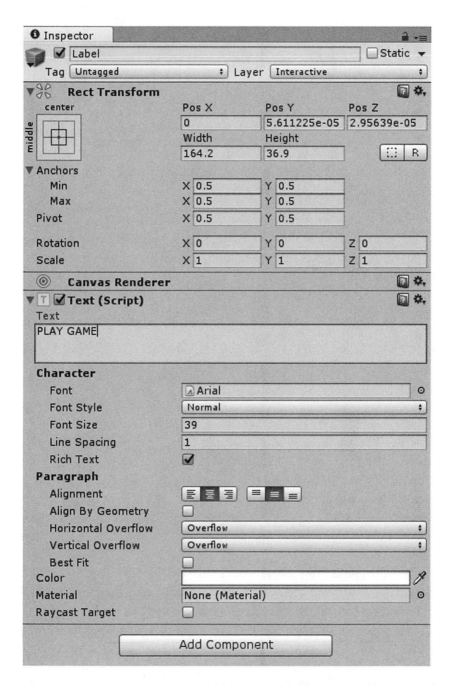

FIGURE 5.7   The Text Component used for the start game button.

Align by Geometry: Unchecked

Horizontal Overflow: Overflow

Vertical Overflow: Overflow

Best fit: Unchecked

Color: Choose a nice bright, color (white?) so that it is easy to see!

Material: Leave this one—it is okay for it to say None (Material)

Raycast Target: Unchecked

The last thing to do with the button here is to move it to a good position. From the default center point on the Canvas, it needs moving up a little.

In the Transform Component in the Inspector, change the position fields to:

X: 0

Y: −38

Z: 0

If you are wondering why it is that the Y position is −38, that is because the position value is relative to the GameObject's pivot point location. Earlier, we anchored the pivot and position to the center of the GameObject, which means that the position should be −38 units from the center of the Canvas.

A couple of quick notes about the settings for the Text Component above:

The overflow settings are how text will be affected when it reaches or goes over draw boundaries. I tend to use the setting of Overflow by habit, as it means I can get the text size close to the boundary without the text jumping onto another line or not being drawn at all. Experiment with the overflow settings on a per-use basis to attempt to get the effect you like.

The position of the GameObject within the Hierarchy affects how it is drawn to the Canvas. Higher up in the Hierarchy will be drawn first, and hence be further behind. In this case, the Label is at the bottom of the chain, beneath the other child objects under Slider, so that it is drawn on top of the others.

TEST THE BUTTON

Now, your button should be set up correctly. The text should be drawn on top of the progress bar. To test the bar out, before we move on, click Slider in the Hierarchy to select it. In the Inspector, look to the Slider Component and find the Value slider bar. Move it left and right between 0 and 1 and see the progress bar go from empty to full. If this is the case, we can move on and copy it to use as a template for the Exit button.

ADD A SECOND BUTTON TO THE MENU SCENE

The great thing about the button rig we are building in this chapter is that it is easy to re-use. We have put it together in such as a way as to be flexible in that it just takes a single change to the text to make a new one.

Duplicate the Button

Click StartButton in the Hierarchy. Right click and choose Duplicate (or press CTRL + D on the keyboard) to duplicate the GameObject. This will create a duplicate of StartButton and every child object it contains. Rename this new GameObject to ExitButton

Change the Text Label

Expand out the new ExitButton GameObject to show its child object, Slider. Expand out Slider, too, so that you can see the Label.

Click on Label and, in the Inspector, find the Text field and change the text to read EXIT.

It is up to you how you deal with the next part; you need to move the button down the Canvas so that it is no longer being drawn in the same location as the StartButton. Either do this via the Scene window or just enter −95 into its Y Position field in the Transform Component (in the Inspector).

ADD BEHAVIORS TO THE BUTTONS

With the buttons in place, you now need to make them do something when the progress bars reach 100%. To do that, we will add an Empty GameObject and put a script on it. The buttons will be told of their functions to call.

Add a Main Menu Controller GameObject to the Scene

At the top of the Hierarchy, click the Create button and choose Empty.
Rename the GameObject to MainMenuController.

Making a Main Menu Script

The new MainMenuController GameObject needs a C# script Component adding to it. In the Inspector, click the Add Component button. Select Add Component > New Script. Make sure that the Type is set to C# and name the script MainMenuController

The buttons will take care of themselves, acting as independent systems that do not have any behavior code directly attached to them. The buttons call out to MainMenuController when they are fully activated and the progress bar reaches 100%.

Here is the mainMenuController.cs script in full:

```
using UnityEngine;
using System.Collections;
using UnityEngine.SceneManagement;
public class MainMenuController : MonoBehaviour {
      public void LoadGame()
    {
        SceneManager.LoadScene("interactiveDoor",
LoadSceneMode.Single);
    }
    public void ExitGame()
    {
        Application.Quit();
    }
}
```

Script Breakdown

The script starts by referencing the namespaces it will need to talk to:

```
using UnityEngine;
using System.Collections;

using UnityEngine.SceneManagement;
```

The only addition namespace here is UnityEngine.SceneManagement, which is a part of the Unity engine used for managing the loading and manipulation of scenes. Our menu will load the main game scene using something called SceneManager, which is a part of UnityEngine. SceneManagement.

The next part of the script is the class declaration and button functions:

```
public class MainMenuController : MonoBehaviour {

    public void LoadGame()
    {
        SceneManager.LoadScene("main", LoadSceneMode.
Single);
    }
```

LoadGame() is a function that will be called by the Play Game button to start the game. It uses SceneManager.LoadScene to load the main scene. LoadScene takes two parameters, the name of the scene followed by a parameter to tell Unity how to load the Scene.

When you use the LoadScene function, you can tell Unity how to load the Scene using either LoadSceneMode.Single or LoadSceneMode.Additive as the second parameter. Unity can load a Scene in two ways, either one at a time or by loading multiple Scenes into memory and combining them. Here in the code above, we are loading one Scene at a time with LoadSceneMode.Single.

```
    public void ExitGame()
    {
        Application.Quit();
    }
}
```

ExitGame() just calls Application.Quit(), a function provided by Unity to close the game. If the game is running as a standalone executable file it will close the file and return to Windows. In the editor, on the other hand, Application.Quit() will do nothing.

With the script complete, the final part of the puzzle is to tell the buttons about these new functions.

Add Event Functions to the Menu Buttons

To make a button work, we have a really cool interface for telling it what to do courtesy of the UnityEvents system (Figure 5.8). At the bottom right of the VR_Button Component, in the Inspector, you should see plus and minus icons. These buttons will add or remove event watchers to this event, but we only need a single event for this button. Beneath the On Activate Event() text is a small dropdown for Runtime Only. The dropdown containing Runtime Only refers to when this button should work. You can have it work inside the editor, as well as only when the game is running, which may be useful for testing when used with a regular button.

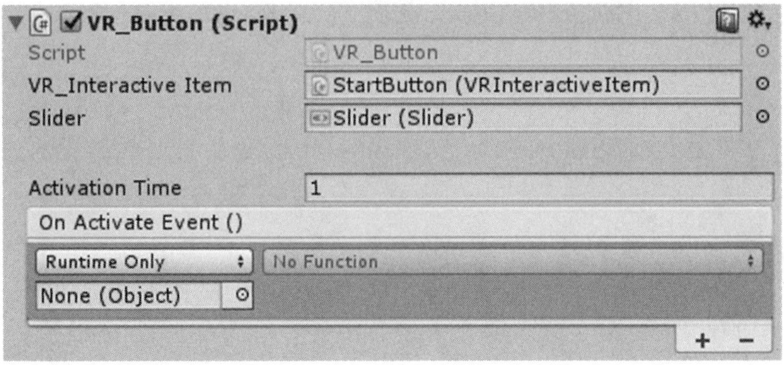

FIGURE 5.8   The UnityEvents interface in the Inspector.

Our VR buttons will not work unless we are running the game due to its reliance on the headset (which is only enabled at runtime).

Just under that dropdown is a field reading None (Object). In here, we can provide the script containing whatever function needs to be called when the button is activated.

Click the MainMenuController in the Hierarchy and drag it into this field inside the VR_Button Component area. Notice that another dropdown button to the right of the Component is no longer grayed out. It says No Function in it.

The newly available dropdown lets you choose which function to call from the script object you provided previously. Click the dropdown to see the available options (Figure 5.9).

From the function dropdown, choose MainMenuController > LoadGame

This tells the button script to run the LoadGame function you coded in the previous section to make MainMenuController.cs.

That is all there is to do to make StartButton work.

In the same way as you just did for StartButton, click on the Exit button in the Hierarchy and set up the MainMenuController to use for its behavior. In the dropdown for Exit button, this time choose MainMenuController > ExitGame.

ADD SCENES TO BUILD SETTINGS

The menu uses the SceneManager to load a different scene when the Play Game button is selected. Unity's build system does not include all scenes by default and you need to tell Unity which scenes it should include.

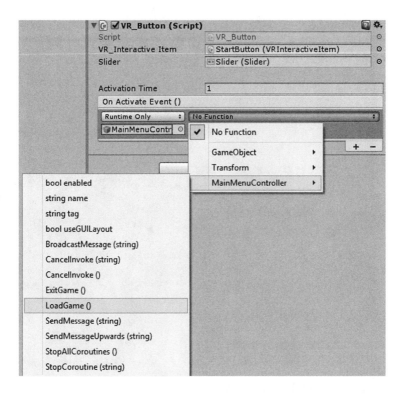

FIGURE 5.9 The LoadGame() function will be called when this UnityEvent is invoked by the script.

Open the File menu in the top left of the Unity editor and choose File > Build Settings.

The Build Settings window (Figure 5.10) allows you to add scenes to the build in its Scenes In Build section.

In the Project window, find the Scenes folder and click it so that you can see the two scenes it contains (Figure 5.11). Drag and drop the main-Menu scene out of the Project browser and drop it into the Scenes In Build section of the Build Settings window. Then, do the same for the interactiveDoor scene.

Both scenes should now be in the Scenes In Build area in Build Settings so that Unity knows to include them at runtime.

TEST THE MENU

Grab your headset and press Play to try out the scene. Your menu should appear in front of the headset and move with it if you rotate side to side.

FIGURE 5.10   The Build Settings window.

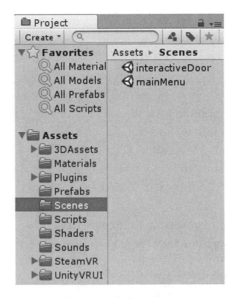

FIGURE 5.11   There are two scenes in this project and they must be added to Build Settings for the build to work.

Look at the Play Game button and wait for the progress bar to fill. It should take one second to fill and the garden level should appear.

SAVE YOUR WORK!

You have reached the end of this project. Save your work. CTRL + S is the shortcut to save the project in Unity, but you should also make sure that the Scene is saved. Click on the menus File > Save Scene

In the file explorer window, click the Scenes folder and name the scene interactiveDoor.

VR User Interface Design Tips

Keep it simple. Text should be very easy to read, or the user should be able to get as close as they need to, to read it. VR headsets come in a number of resolutions and quality, some of which may make it harder to read smaller text than others. Small text may look great, but as well as different quality of tech, you will also need to cater to a range of people with a range of different vision capabilities. Make sure that all text is clear and that the text colors you use are sensible. If in doubt, make it huge and bold. Better ugly than unusable (I can also feel designers out there cringing at that but experience is king!).

Professional designers will use a specific range of colors that will reinforce the themes of the interface. The colors that a designer chooses affect the atmosphere, theme, and usability. If you are not a professional designer, aim to use contrasting colors and attempt to make sure there are significant visual differences between backgrounds and foregrounds. You may also want to consider looking at the color laboratory website (http://colorlab.wickline.org/colorblind/colorlab/) to select colors and see how they appear next to one another in various foreground/background combinations. The color lab website also allows you to see those colors as they might appear to colorblind users, which is something to consider if your simulation is going to be public.

Finally, a menu screen inside VR helps to make sure users are ready to play before you launch them into the full experience. If you do not include a menu, you should at the very least provide some sort of "press a button to start" stage inside VR before starting any sort of simulation or play. There are some experiences out there that have their menu systems outside of VR, using mouse-based interfaces, then expect the users to quickly switch over to VR as the main experience loads. I strongly recommend you do not take this approach. Not only is this really messy in terms of consistency and flow, but it can also lead to incorrect alignment as the user may struggle to get the headset on before the VR scene loads and does its initialization and alignment routines. Give the viewer a chance to get ready and prepare for the experience to start.

Using a Word Space Canvas means that you can easily attach the canvas to 3D objects in your virtual world. This means that you can make your menu a part of the environment, perhaps showing on a virtual screen or projected onto a wall. If you are using motion controllers such as the Vive controllers, you can use a Word Space Canvas to add instructions around or on top of the controller. When the viewer looks down at the controller, the instructions will be there. Another use for World Space canvases is for menus. Menus work well when they are parented to a controller. As an example, you might attach a menu to a right-hand controller and have users use the left-hand controller to pick items with. This not only looks good, but it can help solve readability issues with users themselves getting to choose how far to hold the menu from their eyes.

RECAP

In this chapter, we made a Canvas suitable for user interface and made it follow the viewer's headset rotation using the UI Movement Component from the VR Samples. We constructed buttons suitable for VR by re-purposing the UI system's Slider and adding a custom VR_Button script Component to it. By making the VR_Button script, we saw how to build on the Unity interaction framework using VRInteractiveItem for handling gaze. With what you have used for VR_Button, you should be able to go on to create your own behaviors and VR-ready user interface elements.

We looked at UnityEvents and how they can be used to create a flexible script that can be re-used to provide more than one single button in the menu scene. By duplicating the main button GameObject and changing its Label and behavior, you can now easily make a fully-fledged game menu system.

Finally, we added the correct scenes to the Build Settings so that the SceneManager class could be used to switch between Scenes.

In the next chapter, you will see the framework in action again as we use VREyeCaster to figure out where the viewer is looking and teleport around the virtual world and explore it properly in VR.

CHAPTER 6

Moving around the Virtual World with the SteamVR Teleportation System

STEAMVR INCLUDES CODE FOR virtual teleportation. The script allows a viewer to point the controller to the location they want to teleport to, hit a button, and be teleported there. The SteamVR_Teleporter.cs script is designed to be used in conjunction with HTC Vive controllers, but we can modify it to work without. In this chapter, we are going to use the teleporter code in a way it was never intended to be used. With a few modifications, the teleporter code will work with the viewer's gaze combined with a mouse or a standard game controller button press.

The SteamVR_Teleporter script uses Unity's raycasting system to cast a ray out from the Transform of the GameObject it is attached to and it uses an intersection between the ray and a Collider as a potential position to move to. For example, if the script were attached to a motion controller (such as a HTC Vive controller) it would cast a ray out along the controller's forward direction vector. Wherever the controller pointed to would be the target teleportation point.

If we attach SteamVR_Teleporter to the headset camera as a Component, it will use the camera's forward vector instead. The only

129

thing we need to do is to make a little bridge code to tell it when to teleport. Note that if you are using any other type of motion controller, you could also use this code to tell SteamVR_Teleporter when a button on your controller is pressed.

If you are using HTC Vive controllers, you may want to use the teleportation method outlined in Chapter 9 rather than the one we build in this chapter. In Chapter 9, we set up the teleportation system to use the controllers for aiming whereas here we use the viewer's gaze to target with.

SETTING UP THE SCENE FOR TELEPORTATION

Open Unity and open the example project for this chapter. In the Scenes folder, find and double click the Scene named teleporting to open it.

Create Colliders for Teleport Ground Position Detection

When the teleporter script tries to establish where to teleport to, it casts out an invisible ray. When the ray intersects (hits) with a Collider, it reports back with some information about the intersection, such as the point of contact and what it hit and so on. The Colliders the raycasting system looks for are Collider Components attached to the objects we want to interact with, such as the door from Chapter 5 or, in this case, the ground areas where we want to allow the viewer to teleport to.

One thing you will quickly learn about me is that I insist on staying organized in the Hierarchy. To stay organized, we start out by making an empty GameObject to act as a parent for Colliders. I like to use GameObjects to keep things neat (Figure 6.1).

Right click in an empty space in the Hierarchy panel and choose Create Empty, to add an empty GameObject. Rename GameObject to Collisions.

Right click on the Collisions GameObject you just added and choose Create Empty to add a second empty GameObject as a child object of Collisions. Rename this newest GameObject to GroundTeleportColliders. This is where the ground colliders will go. This hierarchical approach to organizing the Hierarchy makes it easier to find what we need quickly, as well as to configure groups of objects quickly. A good example of this might be times when we need to disable a group of objects for whatever reason: We can just disable the main parent GameObject and all of its children will be disabled at the same time.

As a Collider is a Component, it needs to belong to a GameObject. We could add a new GameObject and add a new Collider Component to

FIGURE 6.1   Colliders for teleport-safe areas.

that, or perhaps take the quicker option of adding a Cube that already has a Collider attached to it. Using a cube will also mean that we have a very obvious visual representation of where the ground collisions will be. Normally, you do see a wireframe representation of the Collider in the editor, but it can be difficult to see and if we use a cube we can see it as a solid object that will make placement easier.

Right click on GroundTeleportColliders in the Hierarchy and choose 3D Object > Cube. Rename the new Cube to GroundCube.

We need three Colliders, but instead of having to trawl the menus over and over, you can highlight the one you added last (GroundCube) and press CTRL + D on the keyboard to duplicate it. A new GroundCube will appear in the Hierarchy with a number after it.

Hit CTRL + D to duplicate GroundCube for a second time. Then once more. Now you have four cubes set up with Colliders and ready to be placed, all neat and tidy as child objects of the GroundTeleportColliders GameObject you made earlier.

If you have already spent a lot of time in the Unity editor, you may already know about the Scene Gizmo. The Scene Gizmo is located in the upper-right of the Scene View, allowing you to switch viewing angle and toggle projection modes. Here, you will use the Scene Gizmo (Figure 6.2) to change view.

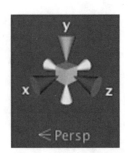

FIGURE 6.2   The Scene Gizmo is in the upper-right of the Scene View. It allows you to choose preset views and toggle between perspective or orthographic views.

The orthographic projection mode provides a view that has no perspective, making it a good choice for exact object alignment. An overhead orthographic view of the garden will be easier for placement of the ground cubes. Switching between perspective and orthographic views is done by clicking on the gray cube in the center of the Scene Gizmo. Move to an overhead view by clicking on the green arrow marked with a y to represent the y axis.

How you deal with the next part is up to you. You can easily select each GroundCube GameObject and enter the following coordinates into the Transform section in the Inspector, or you can use the Scene View to drag and drop them into place so that the objects are placed like those in Figure 6.3. Your choice!

If you want to use my coordinates, select each GameObject in turn and enter the following into the Inspector:

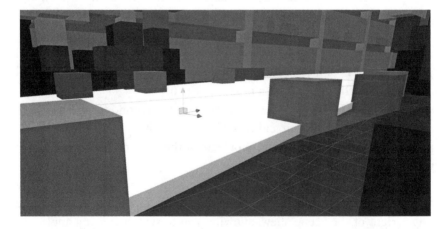

FIGURE 6.3   The Colliders for teleportation cover the ground where teleportation is allowed.

GroundCube:

Position:

    X: 3

    Y: 10.2

    Z: 37.5

Rotation:

(leave at 0,0,0)

Scale:

    X: 19

    Y: 1.4

    Z: 13

GroundCube (1):

Position:

    X: −1.8

    Y: 10.2

    Z: 17.5

Rotation:

(leave at 0,0,0)

Scale:

    X: 8.85

    Y: 1

    Z: 38

GroundCube (2)

Position:

    X: 2.7

    Y: 10.2

    Z: −10.7

Rotation

    X: 0

    Y: −10.5

    Z: 0

Scale:

    X: 9

    Y: 1

    Z: 30

GroundCube (3)

Position:

    X: 2.6

    Y: 10.2

    Z: −28.6

Rotation:

(leave at 0,0,0)

Scale:

    X: 19

    Y: 1.4

    Z: 14

It is important to make sure that the tops of the collider cubes are near to, or just above, ground level in the environment (Figure 6.4). If they are too far above ground, the raycast, to detect where the viewer is teleporting to, will either start out inside the cube or end up intersecting in unexpected parts of the cubes. If you used my coordinates, they should already be in the correct place, but if you chose to drag and drop the boxes around then just make sure that your GroundCube objects look something like those in Figure 6.4.

Layers are a good way to organize objects and how they collide with each other in your projects. You can decide which layers collide with

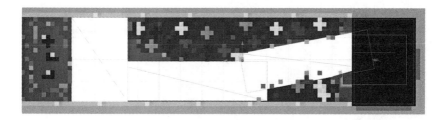

FIGURE 6.4 The tops of the Colliders for teleportation need to match up with the ground level in the garden scene.

which, customizing the collision system to suit your needs. For the teleport areas, we will use a layer named TeleportSafe.

Setting Up Layers

Click on the GroundTeleportColliders GameObject so you can see its properties in the Inspector. In the top right of the Inspector is a dropdown button next to Layers. Click the Layers button to show the layers dropdown menu.

From this menu, you can select which layer to use for this GameObject, but we have not added a layer for teleport collisions yet so click the Add Layer... option from the bottom of the menu.

Whenever you are using SteamVR, you should not use layer number 8. It turns out that SteamVR uses layer number 8 for its own messages—to avoid any future confusion, we should give it a text description so we know not to use it Figure 6.5.

Click next to layer 8 and type in SteamMessages.

Next, add a layer we can use for the teleport areas—click layer 9 and name it TeleportSafe

That is everything we need in terms of setting up the Colliders for the scene.

Set Up the Camera Rig and Add Components

Download, if necessary, and import the SteamVR unitypackage from the Unity Asset Store, exactly as shown in the section "Downloading SteamVR Libraries for Unity" in Chapter 3.

In the Project browser, find SteamVR > Prefabs. Drag the [CameraRig] prefab out of that folder and in to the Hierarchy so that it is added to the Scene.

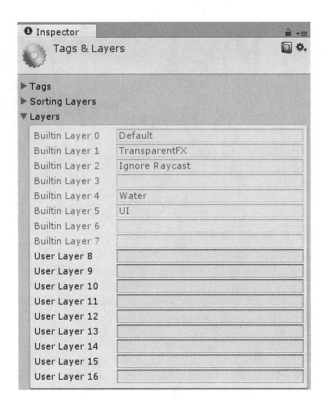

FIGURE 6.5   The Tags and Layers interface.

The Camera SteamVR uses for the headset is a couple of levels down under the main [CameraRig] GameObject. You can expand out the [CameraRig] in the Hierarchy until you find Camera (eye), or type Camera (eye) into the search box at the top of the Hierarchy.

Once you find Camera (eye) in the Hierarchy, click Camera (eye) to highlight it and show its properties in the Inspector. In the Inspector, click Add Component and choose Scripts > Steam VR Teleporter.

Next, we need to provide a VR_Input Component that our script can tap into to find out when the user provides input.

In the Inspector, click Add Component > Scripts > VRStandardAssets. Utils > VR Input. Its default settings are fine for what we need and there is no further setup needed for the VR Input Component.

Next, click Add Component and choose New Script. Type in the name box ControllerTeleporterInputProvider and make sure that the Language dropdown reads C Sharp. When the new script is added as a Component, double click on the script name to open up the script editor.

WRITING A C# SCRIPT TO PROVIDE INPUT TO THE TELEPORTER

In the Hierarchy, click on the Main Camera GameObject to show its properties in the Inspector. Click the Add Component button and select the New Script item from the very bottom of the menu. You may have to scroll down to display it.

After selecting New Script, Unity will ask for some details on the script you want to make. Those are

Name—Enter the name for the script ControllerTeleporterInput Provider.

Language—Select C# from the drop down menu.

Click Create and Add to make the new script.

Once the new script Component appears in the Inspector, now attached to the GameObject, double click on the script name to open it in the script editor.

Here is the completed ControllerTeleporterInputProvider.cs script in full:

```
using UnityEngine;
using System.Collections;
using VRStandardAssets.Utils;

// here we fake the Vive controller output when its button is
clicked. That way, we can
// tap into the SteamVR teleport code without too much modification.
This should help with
// keeping the code backward compatible when, in the future, the
SteamVR libraries are updated

public class ControllerTeleporterInputProvider : MonoBehaviour {

    public VRInput VR_Input;
    public SteamVR_Teleporter theTeleporterComponent;

    private ClickedEventArgs theArgs;

    private bool isTeleporting;
    public float totalTeleportTime = 1;

    void Start () {
        // grab a reference to the SteamVR teleporter Component
        if (theTeleporterComponent==null)
        {
            if(GetComponent<SteamVR_Teleporter>())
```

```
                {
                    theTeleporterComponent = GetComponent
<SteamVR_Teleporter>();
                }
            }
        }

    void OnClick()
    {
        // make sure that we are not already teleporting
        if (isTeleporting)
            return;

        // call the function to handle the actual fade
        OnTriggerClicked();
    }

    // this function will call the teleporter and pretend to be a
controller click
    public virtual void OnTriggerClicked()
    {
        // start a nice fullscreen / full headset fade out effect
        SteamVR_Fade.Start(Color.black, totalTeleportTime /2);

        // we set isTeleporting so that the teleporter is locked
during the fade out
        isTeleporting = true;

        // the actual teleport will happen in 0.5 seconds, at the same
time the fade out reaches full darkness
        Invoke("DoTeleport", totalTeleportTime /2);
    }

    void DoTeleport()
    {
        // start a nice fade in effect
        SteamVR_Fade.Start(Color.clear, totalTeleportTime /2);
        // done with the teleport, so we can allow the user to
teleport again now if they want
        isTeleporting = false;

        // tell SteamVR to take care of the actual teleport move
now
        theTeleporterComponent.DoClick(this, theArgs);
    }

    private void OnEnable()
    {
        // when this script is first enabled in the scene,
        // subscribe to events from vrInput
        VR_Input.OnClick += OnClick;
    }
```

```
    private void OnDisable()
    {
        // unsubscribe from events from vrInput
        VR_Input.OnClick -= OnClick;
    }
}
```

Script Breakdown

The ControllerTeleporterInputProvider.cs script starts out with the usual namespaces (the default ones added by Unity to all C# scripts). Here, as the VR_Input class is a part of the VRStandardAssets code, I've also added VRStandardAssets.Utils so that we can use VR_Input as an object type in variable declarations. If we did not reference the namespace here, then trying to use VR_Input as a variable type would raise an error because it would be unavailable:

```
using UnityEngine;
using System.Collections;
using VRStandardAssets.Utils;
```

After the class packages, we move on to the main declaration, where there are five variables the script requires:

```
public class ControllerTeleporterInputProvider : MonoBehaviour {

    public VRInput VR_Input;
    public SteamVR_Teleporter theTeleporterComponent;
    public event ClickedEventHandler TriggerClicked;
    private ClickedEventArgs theArgs;
    private bool isTeleporting;
    public float totalTeleportTime = 1f;
```

VR_Input will hold a reference to the VRInput script that will track when buttons get pressed on the viewer's controller. theTeleporterComponent holds a reference to that SteamVR_Teleporter script, which is a part of the SteamVR libraries that will deal with the actual teleportation. TriggerClicked will crop up again in the next section of this chapter, when we modify the SteamVR_Teleporter.cs script. TriggerClicked is an event that the SteamVR_Teleporter will subscribe to. When this script detects input coming from the VRInput script, the event will be triggered and SteamVR_Teleporter should pick it up and act on it (once we have modified SteamVR_Teleporter to subscribe to it, which we will do in the next section).

Of course, this script is going to need a reference to that VREyeRaycaster script you saw in the previous section. The VREyeRaycaster will tell us about the viewer's gaze and that info will then be passed on to the teleporter.

theArgs is used as a temporary store for information about the click when input is detected. When the teleporter is used with Vive controllers, ClickedEventArgs is used to pass around information about the state of the controller, but here we fake the state and pass it over to the teleporter as though it came from a controller.

When we start a teleport the variable isTeleporting will be used to track when a teleport is in progress. The last variable above is totalTeleportTime. This variable is used to time the whole teleport process from start to finish.

Next, the Start function runs when the game engine does its first frame update. It is the ideal place for the initialization code:

```
void Start () {
    // grab a reference to the SteamVR teleporter Component
    if (theTeleporterComponent==null)
    {
```

The code above starts by looking to see if a reference is already set in the theTeleporterComponent variable. This is purely convenient so that you can set the reference via the Inspector. If the teleporter script (SteamVR_Teleporter) was attached to a separate object, you can set the reference via the Inspector, but if the teleporter script is attached to the same GameObject as this one, the script will find it automatically here:

```
        if(GetComponent<SteamVR_Teleporter>())
        {
            theTeleporterComponent = GetComponent<SteamVR_Teleporter>();
        }
    }
}
```

GetComponent<SteamVR_Teleporter> looks for the Component on the same GameObject this script is attached to. If it finds something, the return value from GetComponent will not be null and therefore the condition met. Inside the condition, theTeleporterComponent is set to the SteamVR_Teleporter Component.

The next function is OnClick:

```
void OnClick()
{
    // make sure that we are not already teleporting
```

```
    if (isTeleporting)
        return;

    OnTriggerClicked();
}
```

The OnClick() function above will be triggered by an input event in the VRInput Component. Above, we start with a quick check to see if isTeleporting is true. Note that we do not need to explicitly ask if isTeleporting is true—a quicker way is just to put the variable inside brackets. Unity will assume that the condition is only met whenever the condition inside is true.

If isTeleporting is true, we know that a teleport is already happening. The teleport takes place over a full second of time, allowing for a nice fade effect to make the transition smoother between locations. So, isTeleporting will be true during a teleport. As we only want a single teleport to happen at any one time, when the isTeleporting condition is met, we call on a return statement to drop out of the function without running any more of its code.

Assuming that we are not already teleporting, we call the OnTriggerClicked function, which also happens to be the next code block:

```
public virtual void OnTriggerClicked()
    {
        // start a nice fullscreen / full headset fade out effect
        SteamVR_Fade.Start(Color.black, totalTeleportTime /2);

        // we set isTeleporting so that the teleporter is locked
during the fade out
        isTeleporting = true;

        // the actual teleport will happen in 0.5 seconds, at the
same time the fade out reaches full darkness
        Invoke("DoTeleport", totalTeleportTime /2);
    }
```

OnTriggerClicked will start the teleport, first with a call out to SteamVR_Fade to begin a nice effect to fade the view out to black. SteamVR_Fade.Start() takes two parameters; a Color object to fade to and the duration in seconds. The Color class is provided as part of the Unity engine and provides lots of different colors such as Color.white, Color.red, Color.blue, and so on. In this script, I used a float variable named totalTeleportTime to make it easy to change the time of the teleport in your own projects. As it is the total time, the fade out should take half of it so we divide it by two—the fade back in again, after the teleport, will take the other half.

Now that the fade is started, the next statement sets isTeleporting to true to lock out new attempts to teleport until this one is done.

At the end of the above code, the Invoke command is used to schedule a call to make the actual teleport happen. The time is passed in as the second parameter, in seconds, timed using that totalTeleportTime variable again, divided by two. At this stage, all that will be happening is a nice fade out effect. What we want to do here is have the fade out effect take half of the time allowed for teleporting, then we teleport, and then the fade in, in the new location, takes the second half of the allowed teleport time. With the fade out started here, the scheduled call to DoTeleport() will kick in right when the screen gets fully black. The teleport jump and position change is handled by Steam_VR code, but the DoTeleport() function will take care of the second half of our teleport process by starting the fade in and telling SteamVR to teleport.

DoTeleport() is next in the class:

```
void DoTeleport()
{
    // start a nice fade in effect
    SteamVR_Fade.Start(Color.clear, totalTeleportTime /2);

    // done with the teleport, so we can allow the user to
teleport again now if they want
    isTeleporting = false;

    // tell SteamVR to take care of the actual teleport move now
    theTeleporterComponent.DoClick(this, theArgs);
}
```

Above, the call to SteamVR_Fade class starts a fade in effect. The Color object we pass in, this time, is Color.clear, used to completely remove the fade from the view. Timing comes from totalTeleportTime divided by two again, meaning that the fade in effect will go for the remaining second half of the total allowed time for the teleport.

As we fade in, it is now safe to go ahead and reset isTeleporting to false, which we do in the next line, so that another teleport is allowed, from here on, if the user wants to.

Our code pretends that the input for the teleporter system is coming from a SteamVR-ready controller such as the HTC Vive controllers. To do that, we have to pass in some arguments that would normally come from the controller. When you use the Vive, each controller has a unique

ID number assigned to it and the Steam_VR teleporter code expects this information to be passed to it whenever it is called upon to teleport. The arguments the teleporter requires are passed in as a ClickedEventArgs object, which is a class from the Steam_VR libraries of code.

We do not actually put anything into the theArgs variable and it is not essential do so. We are, in effect, just passing in a ClickedEventArgs object with all of its variables set to their default values—this is enough to get the teleporter to work.

OnTriggerClicked takes theArgs and passes it in to the SteamVR_Teleport script via a call to a DoClick() function. You may see this line highlighted or receive an error if you try to compile it, but that is okay. After we are done making this script, we need to modify the SteamVR_Teleporter code to make this function public. Right now, SteamVR_Teleporter's DoClick() function is not accessible from this script. We will fix that in the next section.

The last two functions in this ControllerTeleporterInputProvider class deal with subscribing to the required events:

```
private void OnEnable()
{
    // when this script is first enabled in the scene,
    // subscribe to events from vrInput
    VR_Input.OnClick += OnClick;
}

private void OnDisable()
{
    // unsubscribe from events from vrInput
    VR_Input.OnClick -= OnClick;
}
}
```

You may recall from the last chapter how we go about subscribing to events. In Chapter 6 we looked at subscribing to OnOver and OnOut events on the VRInteractiveItem class. Here, we need to bypass everything and go straight to the input system to find out when a button is being pressed. For that, we reference the VR_Input Component in the VR_Input variable. To track a click, the event to subscribe to is OnClick. This works for any of the input devices that VR_Input tracks, which is linked into Unity's input system so that you can customize it via the Input Settings of the Unity editor if you need to.

When OnEnable() is called, we subscribe to OnClick and in OnDisable() we unsubscribe from it again.

Save the script you are working on, if you did not already do that, and return to the editor.

MODIFY THE SteamVR TELEPORTER CODE

There are two modifications we need to make to the SteamVR teleporter class. The first change is to expose one of its functions as public so that we can access it via the script you made in the previous section. The second change is to make the raycasting work with specified collision layers, rather than its current method of counting every raycast as a teleport location. You may recall that, when we set up the Colliders for teleport-safe areas, we used the layer "TeleportSafe" for our collision objects.

Find and open the SteamVR file in the Project under SteamVR > Extras > SteamVR_Teleporter. Double click SteamVR_Teleporter to open it in the script editor.

Change DoClick() into a Public Function

In the script editor, scroll down through the code to find:

```
void DoClick(object sender, ClickedEventArgs e)
```

And add public in front of it so that it now reads:

```
public void DoClick(object sender, ClickedEventArgs e)
```

Modify SteamVR Teleporter to Use a LayerMask

A LayerMask is a list of one or more layers which you can use to limit raycasting with. In the Inspector, a LayerMask is displayed as a popup menu of layers. Layers in the LayerMask will be shown in a dropdown menu and may be toggled on and off, meaning that you can easily select one, multiple, or all layers from it.

In this case, we are going to restrict the layers that register during the SteamVR_Teleporter script's raycasting routines.

Find the Start() function at the top of the SteamVR_Teleporter script. Add this line just above it:

```
public LayerMask teleportSafeLayer;
```

Next, we need to modify the raycasting statements to include this new LayerMask.

In the DoClick() function, find the line:

```
hasGroundTarget = Physics.Raycast(ray, out hitInfo);
```

And change it to read:

```
hasGroundTarget = Physics.Raycast(ray, out hitInfo,
teleportSafeLayer);
```

Save the script with CTRL + S and return to the Unity editor.

SET UP THE COMPONENTS ON THE CAMERA GAMEOBJECT

In Unity, click the Camera (eye) GameObject in the Hierarchy and, over in the Inspector, find the SteamVR_Teleporter Component. You should see the new Teleport Safe Layer dropdown menu you added in the previous section.

On the SteamVRTeleporter Component, check the Teleport On Click box.

In the Teleport Type dropdown (Figure 6.6), choose Teleport Type Use Zero Y. This needs a little explanation before we go on.

When you teleport, the teleporter code uses Vector coordinates: the world X, Y, and Z points of the position to teleport to. There are three options in the Teleport Type dropdown, each one causing the teleporter to act in a different way with regard to how it deals with the Y (vertical) position of the viewer during teleportation. Those options:

1. Teleport Type Use Terrain.

   This setting will cause the SteamVR_Teleporter script to use the Unity terrain currently active in the Scene and find the height of the terrain at those X and Z coordinates found during its raycasting.

2. Teleport Type Use Collider.

   This setting uses all three X, Y, and Z coordinates discovered by the SteamVR_Teleporter script's raycast; wherever the ray intersects with a Collider in the Scene will form the position to teleport to.

3. Teleport Type Use Zero Y.

   With Teleport Type set to Use Zero Y, it is assumed that the ground level set by SteamVR is the default ground level established during setup. That is, the height of the raycast intersection will be ignored. The point to use as a teleportation location will be the X and Z points of the raycast hit, along a flat plane at zero height.

Note: In this example, we want to use the Teleport Type Use Zero Y setting but, for whatever reason, if you try to use Teleport Type Use

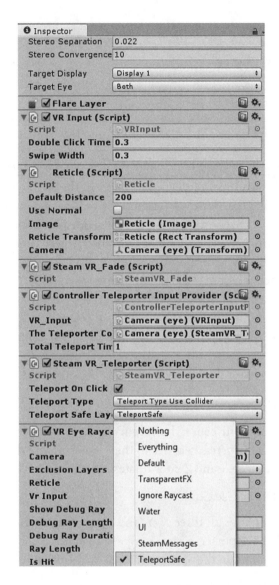

FIGURE 6.6 The SteamVR Teleporter Component in the Inspector.

Collider on this Component and it fails to do anything, check that the raycasting call actually sets the hasGroundTarget variable. I found a bug in the version I was using which was missing a small part of the raycast statement for this setting and caused it not to work. If you hit the same problem, open up the SteamVR_Teleport script and look for the condition:

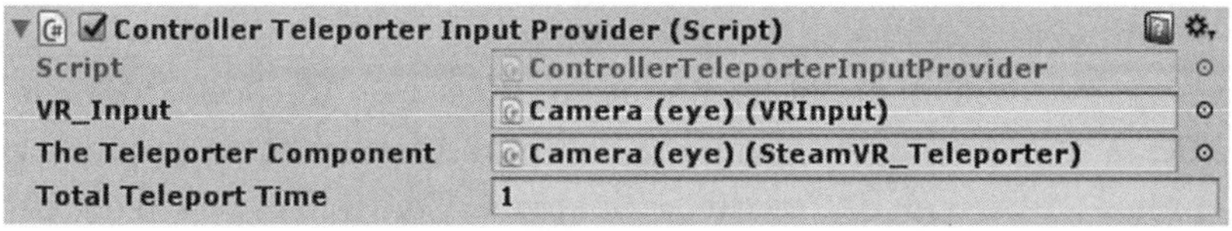

▼ ⓒ ☑ **Controller Teleporter Input Provider (Script)**		🔲 ⚙,
Script	ⓒ ControllerTeleporterInputProvider	○
VR_Input	ⓒ Camera (eye) (VRInput)	○
The Teleporter Component	ⓒ Camera (eye) (SteamVR_Teleporter)	○
Total Teleport Time	1	

FIGURE 6.7 The ControllerTeleporterInputProvider Component with its references set up to the other Components it needs to communicate with.

```
else if (teleportType == TeleportType.TeleportTypeUseCollider)
```

Inside the parenthesis (curly brackets!) for the above statement, look for:

```
Physics.Raycast(ray, out hitInfo, teleportSafeLayer);
```

And change it/make sure that it reads:

```
hasGroundTarget = Physics.Raycast(ray, out hitInfo, teleportSafeLayer);
```

Set Up ControllerTeleportInputProvider

You need to set up the references on the ControllerTeleporterInputProvider Component next. The two references we need to set up are VR_Input, the-TeleporterComponent. They can all be found on the camera already, so add drag and drop the Components down into the fields so that it looks like Figure 6.7.

That is it! The teleporter should be ready for action!

Save the file (File > Save Project), grab your VR headset, and hit Play to try out the Scene.

You should be able to look at a point on the garden pathway and click the mouse to teleport over to it. As you teleport, the view should fade out to black, move you to the new location, and then fade back into the scene again. Try clicking on different parts of the Scene, such as the walls of the house. You should not be able to teleport anywhere other than on the path, on those "TeleportSafe" collision areas.

OPTIONAL EXTRAS

The teleporter works great, but you can improve it a little more by adding the Reticule and Eyecaster from the previous chapter. The Reticule adds a dot to the center of the view so that it is easier to target where it is you will teleport to. Eyecaster will cast out a ray and move the reticule so that it sits close to wherever the teleport point will be, again making it a little bit easier to tell where the target point is.

RECAP

This chapter was all about teleportation. We set up the Scene to contain colliders suitable for raycasting against to find teleport target points. We modified the SteamVR teleporter script to use Collision Layers in deciding safe places to go to, and made a brand new script to figure out when input is happening and to connect the code for teleportation—faking input from a SteamVR controller. As a bonus, we also added a rather nice little fade effect. If you like, you could use this fading technique anywhere else in your projects for fading in or out as you need to. To fade out at any time, just add this line of code to yours:

```
SteamVR_Fade.Start(Color.black, 1f);
```

And to fade in, you can do:

```
SteamVR_Fade.Start(Color.clear, 1f);
```

The next chapter is going to be fun! We will be looking at how we can use the gaze to launch projectiles in a simple mini-game where you have to fend off evil flying insects from your garden. When you are ready, buzz over to the next chapter!

CHAPTER 7

Using the Headset for Aiming in a Game

A T THIS STAGE OF this book, I think that it is time to play a game. It will take place in the garden scene you have seen throughout this book so far (Figure 7.1). Invading flying insects fly at the player and the aim is to spray them with green bug spray. The bug spray will make them fly away rather than sting the player.

Elements such as score counting, game management, or insect behavior code are already set up and ready to go inside the example, but in this chapter we will go through adding the VR support, the headset, and some related game items such as the spray can and making it fire projectiles. The technique could also be used for other types of projectile firing devices (paintball, anyone?!) so it should be a nice little thing to have in the toolbox.

Before we get into it, take a look at Figure 7.2 to see how the scripts from this chapter will fit together in the Scene and Hierarchy.

ATTACHING A PROJECTILE FIRING SYSTEM TO THE CAMERA

We will be using the camera as an aiming device. To make it work, the projectile firing device will be attached to the camera, as a child object. Wherever the camera looks, the projectile firing device (the bug spray can) will look, too. We will hook up the spray can up to the VR_Input class so that it knows when the player presses button on the controller.

FIGURE 7.1   The garden environment is reused for a game in the example for this chapter.

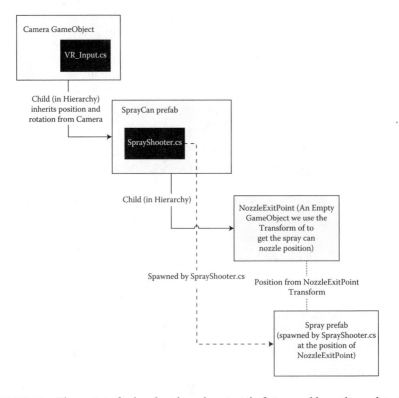

FIGURE 7.2   The scripts for headset-based projectile firing and how they relate to each other, and the scene, in this chapter.

Open the Unity project for this chapter. Open the Scene named game from the Scenes folder in the Project browser.

Find [CameraRig] in the Hierarchy. Hold ALT on the keyboard and click the little arrow to the left of [CameraRig] to expand its hierarchy out and show all of the objects parented to it.

You should see:

[CameraRig]

    Controller (left)

    Controller (right)

    Camera (head)

        Camera (eye)

            VR_HUD

                Reticle

        StringEnterTrigger

        WaspSpawnCenterPoint

        WaspTarget

        Camera (ears)

Go to the Project browser and find the Prefabs folder. Click Prefabs to show its contents and then find the SprayCan prefab inside it. Drag this over to the Camera (eye) in the Hierarchy and drop it there, so that it becomes a child of the Camera (eye).

The next step is to add a script to find out when a button is being pressed.

ADD A SCRIPT TO THE CAMERA TO GRAB PLAYER INPUT

Click on the Camera (eye) GameObject in the Hierarchy. With Camera (eye) selected, click the Add Component button in the Inspector (you may have to scroll the Inspector down to find Add Component). Choose New Script, right down at the bottom of the script popup menu.

Name the script SprayInputProvider and make sure C Sharp is selected in the Language dropdown before you click Create and Add.

Right click on the new SprayInputProvider Component in the Inspector and choose Edit Script.

Programming a SprayInputProvider.cs script

Here is the completed SprayInputProvider script:

```
using UnityEngine;
using System.Collections;
using VRStandardAssets.Utils;

public class SprayInputProvider : MonoBehaviour
{

    public VRInput VR_Input;
    public SprayShooter sprayCan;
    public event ClickedEventHandler TriggerClicked;
    public VREyeRaycaster eyecaster;

    private ClickedEventArgs theArgs;

    private void OnEnable()
    {
        // when this script is first enabled in the scene,
        // subscribe to events from vrInput
        VR_Input.OnClick += OnClick;
    }

    private void OnDisable()
    {
        // unsubscribe from events from vrInput
        VR_Input.OnClick -= OnClick;
    }

    void OnClick()
    {
        sprayCan.Fire();
    }
}
```

Script Breakdown

The script begins with the using statements to tell Unity which packages it will be using. The only one of note is VRStandardAssets.Utils and you may remember it from previous chapters. The VRStandardAssets.Utils code contains VR_Input, which is a script to grab controller input.

```
using UnityEngine;
using System.Collections;
using VRStandardAssets.Utils;
```

The class derives from MonoBehaviour so that we can tap into the Unity-called functions such as OnEnable() and OnDisable() etc.:

```
public class SprayInputProvider : MonoBehaviour
{
    public VRInput VR_Input;
    public SprayShooter sprayCan;
    public event ClickedEventHandler TriggerClicked;
    public VREyeRaycaster eyecaster;

    private ClickedEventArgs theArgs;

    private void OnEnable()
    {
        // when this script is first enabled in the scene,
        // subscribe to events from vrInput
        VR_Input.OnClick += OnClick;
    }

    private void OnDisable()
    {
        // unsubscribe from events from vrInput
        VR_Input.OnClick -= OnClick;
    }
```

To track input, this script subscribes to the OnClick event in VR_Input. When the OnClick is fired, the OnClick() function will be called:

```
    void OnClick()
    {
        sprayCan.Fire();
    }
}
```

In the code above, all the OnClick() function does is call a Fire() function on sprayCan, which is a reference to an instance of SprayShooter.cs. The SprayShooter script is attached to the spray can model to handle the actual spraying.

In the next section, we put together the SprayShooter.cs script.

ADD A SCRIPT TO THE SPRAY CAN TO MAKE IT FIRE

Keeping the logic separate between the spray can and the interface and separate between the input and the spray can, it makes it easier to be able to swap out input systems easily if we need to do this in the future. For example, I use the same SprayShooter.cs script with the HTC Vive controllers and call it from a different script in Chapter 9. Designing your project in such a way as to be reusable is not only a good way to think about your projects intelligently but it is a great way to future-proof the code. A modular approach to scripting may even save you time in the future, when you can re-use code instead of re-writing it.

Programming the SprayShooter.cs Script

Click on the SprayCan GameObject in the Hierarchy (it is under Camera (eye)). With SprayCan selected, click Add Component button in the Inspector. Choose New Script.

Name the script SprayShooter and make sure C Sharp is selected in the Language dropdown. Click Create and Add.

Right click on the new SprayCan Component in the Inspector and choose Edit Script, to open it up in the script editor.

The complete script looks like this:

```
using UnityEngine;
using System.Collections;

public class SprayShooter : MonoBehaviour {

    public Transform nozzleExitPoint;
    public Transform projectilePrefab;

    void Start () {

    }

    public void Fire () {
        // we only want to fire when the game is in
its 'ingame' state
        if (SceneController.currentState ==
SceneController.GameState.InGame)
        {
            Instantiate(projectilePrefab,
nozzleExitPoint.position, nozzleExitPoint.rotation);
        }
    }
}
```

Script Breakdown

First, we tell Unity that we are using the usual packages UnityEngine and System.Collections:

```
using UnityEngine;
using System.Collections;

public class SprayShooter : MonoBehaviour {

    public Transform nozzleExitPoint;
    public Transform projectilePrefab;
```

First, in the code above, we tell Unity that we are using the usual packages UnityEngine and System.Collections. The script derives from MonoBehaviour.

There are two variables, which are both references that need to be set up in the Inspector. nozzleExitPoint is a Transform positioned at the point at which we want the spray to appear. It is positioned at the front of the nozzle on the spray can.

projectilePrefab is the prefab that will be spawned at the nozzle exit point.

```
    public void Fire () {
        // we only want to fire when the game is in
its 'ingame' state
        if (SceneController.currentState ==
SceneController.GameState.InGame)
        {
```

The Fire() function above is the one called by the SprayInputProvider script we made in the previous section.

Inside the Fire() function, we see SceneController for the first time. This is a script used to track the game state and take care of things such as starting the game, showing messages, ending the game, and so on. In SceneController, the currentState variable is declared as a public static, like this:

```
public static GameState currentState;
```

Declaring a variable as public static means that it is visible (and usable) in all other scripts in the Scene just as long as an instance of the script it contains exists.

currentState is declared as type GameState, which is an enumerator declared in the SceneController to hold information about where the game is at. Over in SceneController.cs, the declaration for the enumerator looks like this:

```
public enum GameState { Loaded, GetReady, InGame,
Paused, GameOver };
```

So, the currentState variable we see in SprayShooter.cs can be in a state of either GameState.Loaded, GameState.GetReady, GameState.InGame, GameState.Paused, or GameState.GameOver.

To make sure that the player is not able to spray bug spray all the way through the "get ready" message, or any other inappropriate time such as when the game has finished, we do a quick check to make sure that the currentState is SceneController.GameState.InGame. This means the spray gun will only work when the game is ready, the get ready message is done, and it is not paused.

The last part of the SprayShooter.cs script:

```
Instantiate(projectilePrefab, nozzleExitPoint.
position, nozzleExitPoint.rotation);
    }
  }
}
```

In the code above we instantiate a projectile at the position of the noz-zleExitPoint Transform. This is all the code we need to do to fire out projectiles from the spray can, but you will need to switch back to the Unity editor to set up the prefab references in the Inspector.

SET UP COMPONENTS IN THE INSPECTOR

Click on the Camera (eye) GameObject in the Hierarchy. In the Inspector, find the Spray Input Provider Component. The field Spray Can will read None (Spray Shooter) but we need this to point to the Spray Shooter Component attached to the Spray Can.

With Camera (eye) still selected and the Spray Can field still visible in the Inspector, find Spray Can in the Hierarchy and drag it over to drop into the Spray Can field. With this reference set up, the Spray Input Provider can now tell the Spray Shooter when to launch its spray projectiles, but we now have to tell the Spray Shooter what it is going to be firing and where it should fire them from.

Find the Spray Can and expand it out with the little arrows in the Hierarchy. Look for the GameObject named NozzleExitPoint. It is located under Spray Can down under:

SprayCan

 CanBody

  CanLid

 CanNozzle

  NozzleExitPoint

Click the Spray Can GameObject and drag the NozzleExitPoint GameObject into the Inspector, in the field Nozzle Exit Point on the Spray Shooter Script Component.

In the Project browser, click the Prefabs folder. In there, drag and Spray prefab out and into the Projectile Prefab field in the Inspector.

TRY OUT THE GAME

Grab your VR headset, make sure you have SteamVR running (and the OSVR server if you are using OSVR) then hit the Play button to preview the game.

The spray can moves with the headset. Aim by looking at the invading insects and press a button on your game controller, or click the mouse (make sure that the mouse is over the Game view) to spray the insects. Keep them away for as long as possible!

RECAP

This chapter has been relatively straightforward, with the biggest portion of the work being in setting up the scripts and references to allow the spray can to fire spray projectiles. We begin by programming some code to take input from the VR_Input class and pass it over to our projectile firing script. The projectile firing was programmed next, in SprayShooter.cs, and then we set up the correct references so that the Components could "talk" to each other.

There is really nothing very complicated about this system. Essentially, we make an object to parent to the Camera. A script attached to that object instantiates GameObjects when we need them. Although this game is fun for a while, it is lacking in immersion. One big step further toward a good experience is going to be adding audio. In the next chapter, the goal is to bring the garden scene to life and to add sound effects to the insects to bring them to life, too.

CHAPTER 8

Making the Most of Virtual Reality with Audio

THE VIRTUAL REALITY SPACE AND BEYOND

Sound engineering and design is a deep and wide ranging subject that could easily merit its own book. What I could squeeze into a chapter is not going to qualify you to be a sound engineer. Rather, this chapter is more of a crash course in designing audio for VR, looking at ways to influence the focus and mood of the viewer in a scene without going into great depth about the more technical aspects of sound design.

A headset can only go so far in replacing the viewer's senses and leading them through a fantasy world, which may be a good reason why most current-gen VR simulations are experienced with headphones. Replacing both visual and audio senses in this way requires that they complement each other. If visual and audio do not work together, the illusion of the virtual world will not deliver all it can.

The process of audio design is all too often overlooked in games and simulation design, with many studios leaving audio until the end of a production or skimping on the audio budget. It is a surprisingly common mistake and one that can mean the difference between an amazing project versus an average one. The audio in your experience can make or break it. As well as reinforcing the themes of the experience, audio can guide the player, subtle accents can influence emotion, and music can set a pace and give a game a heartbeat. If you find a good sound engineer to work with you should be extremely nice to them and make sure you give them plenty of time to do their jobs and not rush it!

COMMON TERMS

To be able to discuss the techniques in this chapter, it is necessary to clarify some terms that you may or may not have heard elsewhere. Some terms are specific to games and simulation development, some specific to Unity and some common terms used in audio engineering.

Ambient Sound

Ambient sound is a type of audio that plays in the background, reinforcing the main themes of the scene. This could be something as simple as birds chirping to fill an outdoor scene, or a low rumble inside a spaceship. Ambient audio could also be a dynamically created audioscape consisting of multiple layers of real or synthetic sounds.

Listener

A listener is a Component that is normally attached to a camera rig or character rig, which will act as the ears of a scene. Whatever the listener would "hear" from wherever it is in the space, is what will be played out through the sound hardware of the computer. The standard listener gives a good enough experience, but it is not accurate to how a person would normally hear. You can imagine the standard Unity listener as a single ear pointing forward from wherever it stands in the 3D space. Sound will appear to be coming from a circular radius around its position. A human head, on the other hand, would often have two ears pointing out from each side of the head, making the positional tracking more accurate and easier for a human to distinguish.

Binaural Audio

Binaural audio is the method of recording audio with two microphones positioned in such a way as to represent two ears. Some binaural microphones go so far as to be shaped like ears so as to give a visual representation of how the listener will be spatially positioned in the audio world. When the sound engineer records the sounds, they can see exactly where the listener is and adjust the positions of objects to be recorded to get the desired effect. This system is relatively new to videogames and it is still rare for game studios to employ these types of recording methods due to the high price of quality binaural recording equipment as well as the extra time and effort required to master it correctly.

Mono Sound

Unity refers to single channel audio as mono sound. In this context, the word mono is used as an abbreviation for the term monophonic, which means a sound coming from a single channel of transmission. A mono sound will normally sound as if it is coming directly from in front of the listener when it is played outside of a 3D scene. When you use a mono sound in the 3D world, its attributes like its sound volume, panning, and effects are adjusted based on where it is in the world. You would use mono sounds for objects that emit sound in the 3D world, such as machinery or doors and so on, so that approaching the object will have an effect on how it sounds.

3D Sound

Despite the name, 3D sound in Unity is not linked spatially to the camera, viewer, or listener. It is a sound which is already mastered to have its own 3D space encoded in the audio file itself. If you try to play a 3D sound at a specific point in space, the only thing that will be affected by its spatial positioning will be the volume.

Doppler Effect

If you have ever heard an emergency vehicle go by with its sirens blazing, you may have noticed the way that the pitch of the sound changes depending on how near or far away from you it is. This is known as the Doppler effect and it is caused by the way that sound waves travel. Unity's sound system will attempt to duplicate this effect for more realistic movement in the audio space.

Set the Scene with Ambient Sound

Imagine audio as a series of layers. Often, you are hearing many different layers playing at the same time. As you walk down a city street, for example, you could be hearing cars, birds singing, people talking, distant horns beeping, and an airplane passing by. You may have walked along the street a hundred times before and your focus may be on a conversation you are having with someone else along the way, but those ambient layers of sound help your brain to know and understand the environment you are traveling through. Many of them need to be heard. There are layers of sound that you might never notice until they stopped being there. If just a few of those layers were missing, you will most likely register that there is something wrong with the scene. In a VR experience, the sounds around us have a similar effect in giving our brains extra information about the world we are supposed to be in.

Ambient sound often takes the form of a sound loop that runs in the background of the scene to add a little audio explanation to the location of the action. In the case of a garden, an ambient loop might take the form of birds singing or perhaps a gentle breeze and a nearby lawnmower.

THE AUDIO SOURCE COMPONENT

In Unity, sound is emitted from an Audio Source Component attached to a GameObject. The Audio Listener, usually attached to the camera or an avatar, hears the sound and, in a roundabout way, sends what it hears out to the speakers. The 3D space is an important factor in how the sound will be played back, with panning, volume, and audio effects being applied along the way.

When you apply an AudioSource Component, it has many different properties which directly affect how the engine will process any sounds it will play. AudioSource properties are

Property	Function
Audio Clip	Unity refers to sound files as Audio Clips. The Audio Clip is the sound file that will be played from this Audio Source.
Output	Sounds can be output through either an Audio Listener or an Audio Mixer. We will look at Audio Mixers a little further on, in this chapter.
Mute	Muting the sound means that you will not be able to hear it, even though it will continue to play silently.
Bypass Effects	The Bypass Effects checkbox offers an easy way to turn all effects on/off. When this is checked, effects such as reverb or any filter effects will not be applied to this Audio Source.
Bypass Listener Effects	Listener effects are normally applied to all of the sounds in a scene but this checkbox toggles Listener effects on/off for this Audio Source.
Bypass Reverb Zones	This checkbox turns Reverb Zones on or off. Reverb zones are areas you can set in a Scene that will cause any sound played within them to have a reverberation effect applied.
Play On Awake	When this box is checked, the Audio Source will start playing as soon as the scene starts. Otherwise, you will need to start playback of this source manually.

Continued

Property	Function
Loop	When the Loop box is checked, sound played from this Audio Source will play over and over again in a loop.
Priority	The Priority setting decides how important it is that this Audio Source gets played. (Priority: 0 = most important. 256 = least important. Default = 128.). Audio Sources with a higher Priority rating will be cut first whenever too many sound channels are being used at the same time. For endless audio, such as music or perhaps ambient background sound, you should use a higher Priority. Unity recommends using 0 for music, so that it will not be interrupted when too many sounds are playing at the same time.
Volume	The Volume amount determines at what volume the Audio Source should play the Audio Clip. That is, the volume it should sound like within a distance of one world unit (one meter) from the Listener. Volume is usually affected by distance rolloff, meaning that the sound will get quieter the further away the Listener is from it.
Pitch	You can change the pitch (speed) of playback here. The default is 1, which plays the AudioClip at its original pitch.
Stereo Pan	This value influences the left/right panning of the sound. The panning set here is applied before any of the regular 3D panning calculations are carried out. Values range from −1.0 to 1.0, where −1.0 is full left, 0 is centered, and 1.0 is full right.
Spatial Blend	The 3D engine determines the volume and speaker positions of sounds, based on the positional differences between the Audio Source and the Audio Listener. Spatial Blend determines how much the 3D engine affects this particular Audio Source. If you wanted a 2D sound that will appear everywhere in the Scene, you can set this slider all the way to the left (0). Sliding it all the way to the right will cause the Audio Source to be fully 3D, acting as though it were being emitted from a space in 3D.
Reverb Zone Mix	Sets the amount of the output signal that gets routed to the reverb zones. Unity states that this setting "can be useful to achieve the effect of near-field and distant sounds."
Doppler Level	Determines how much Doppler effect will be applied to sounds played through this Audio Source. See the previous section for a description of the Doppler effect.

Continued

Property	Function
Spread	Spread determines how much 3D positioning affects panning of the Audio Source. To visualize this, imagine the space in your left and right speakers and then think of this value as how much of that space will be used by the Audio Clip. If it was set to zero, the sound will come from wherever it is. Anything above zero means that a portion of extra space will be taken up by that sound. At zero, full panning occurs based on position. At 180, no panning occurs but the sound appears to be all the way, right across, from left to right. Setting this to 360 reverses the panning effect, effectively swapping left and right positional panning altogether so that sound objects on the left will sound like they are coming from the right. In most situations, this value would be 0 for sound effects. Use 180 for audio that needs to sound as if it is coming from the whole environment but still needs its audio volume to be affected by distance from the Audio Source in the 3D space (we will use 180 for the ambient audio we will add in the next section).
Min Distance	When the Listener is within MinDistance, the sound coming from this Audio Source will stay at its loudest. When the Listener is outside MinDistance its volume will begin to drop off based on distance.
Max Distance	If the Audio Listener goes beyond Max Distance (units) from the Audio Source, the volume of the sound will stay at its minimum. Unity describes MaxDistance as: (Logarithmic rolloff) MaxDistance is the distance a sound stops attenuating at. (Linear rolloff) MaxDistance is the distance where the sound is completely inaudible.
Rolloff Mode	How fast the sound fades. The higher the value, the closer the Listener has to be before hearing the sound. (This is determined by a Graph.)

Now that we have a little background information about the Audio Source Component, we can go ahead and set up our ambient audio in the garden scene.

ADD AMBIENT AUDIO TO THE SCENE

Open the Unity project for this chapter. In the Scenes folder, open the scene named game.

We begin adding ambient sound to a VR scene by adding an audio source to the Scene.

Click the Create dropdown button at the top of the Hierarchy. Choose Create Empty. With the new GameObject selected, in the Inspector, change its name to AmbientAudio.

In the Inspector, click the Add Component button. Choose Audio > Audio Source.

Before we go on and set this Component up, we should take a little time to look at the Audio Source Component and its properties.

The Audio Source Component has an AudioClip field at the top of it. To the right of the field is the target icon that lets you choose an audio file. Click the target icon and choose the Morning-Birds_Looping_01 sound.

To position the audio at the bottom of the garden, use the following numbers for the Transform Component's position fields:

X: −4.5

Y: 1.77

Z: 2.07

Making ambient audio in Unity demands a specific approach. If you add an Audio Source to a Scene, the sound will appear to be coming from the location of its GameObject. With a regular Audio Source, viewers can walk around it and it will always appear to be coming from a set location due to its panning and fading. For ambience, we need the audio to sound as though it is all around us, rather than being emitted from just a specified point in 3D space.

In the Inspector, on the Audio Source Component attached to AmbientAudio, change Spatial Blend to 3D (all the way to the right) (Figure 8.1). In the 3D Sound Settings section (you may need to expand this out, using the small arrow next to the heading) change the Spread to 180. This will stop the audio from panning around and should make the ambient audio sound as if it is all around the viewer. Spread defines how much audio panning space will be used by this Audio Source (Figure 8.2).

The garden scene calls for some ambient outdoor sound but I like the idea of the outside sound fading out as we enter the little house. It would work as though the house were shutting out audio in the way a real one might. To get this to work, first we need to set up the minimum and maximum distances on the Audio Source Component and to set how the audio

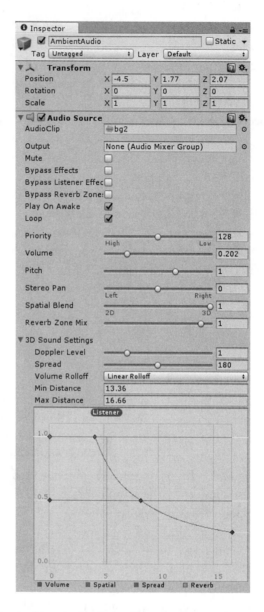

FIGURE 8.1 The AmbientAudio GameObject with its AudioSource Component.

volume falls off over distance. With the Audio Source selected, you can modify the minimum and maximum distances in their respective fields in the Inspector and, as you do so, the Scene view will show a visual representation of the distances (Figure 8.3). The default maximum distance for audio sources is up at 500 units, which is too large for the garden scene we

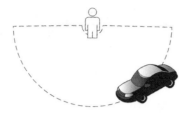

FIGURE 8.2 At the top, a wide spread 180 makes the car audio sound as though it is coming from all around the Listener. A narrow spread makes the car audio take up less audio space and sounds like it is coming from the direction of the Audio Source.

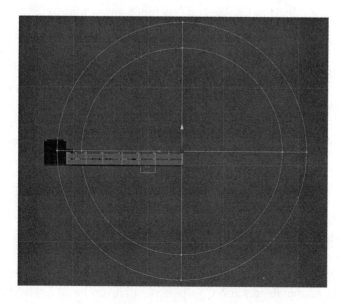

FIGURE 8.3 In the Scene view, the AudioSource is shown with helper graphics to visualize the minimum and maximum distances on the Component.

are working with. We only need the ambient audio for the garden to cover the garden area, going from the bottom of the garden to just outside the door to the house.

Change the Min Distance to 13.36 and Max Distance to 16.66.

Bringing Life to the World with Audio

In the example project, you may have noticed that incoming insects sneak up on you. They are silent. Not very realistic in terms of how insects behave. When the insects are silent like this, they do not seem alive. They are just objects floating silently toward the player. A single audio clip can change this.

It also would work much better as a game if audio gave the viewer a signal as to where to look.

Insects need to buzz continuously when they fly, so this Audio Source will use looping audio. We will add a buzzing sound that runs on a loop to inform the player of an insect. As it gets closer to the Audio Listener (attached to the viewer's camera) the audio will get louder and its position around the viewer's head should become clearer.

One important note is that the choice of sound will affect how easy it is for the player to figure out where it is coming from. Research has shown that high-pitched beep-like sounds make it surprisingly difficult for the brain to figure out where they might be coming from. White noise or other more distinguishable audio is much easier for our brains to pinpoint. Try out different sounds based on the type of effect that you are hoping to achieve. For example, in leading a person through an environment, you might choose not to use beeps or higher frequencies but to go for lower pitched sounds or white noise. When giving the player a warning about something that is not of positional importance, beeping might work well. Think about the effect you are trying to achieve and how the sound makes you feel, before you use it. Good sound design uses both direct and indirect communication for effect.

ADD SOUND TO THE INSECTS

In the Projects browser, find the Prefabs folder and click on it so that you can see its contents. Look for the Insect prefab in that Prefabs folder.

Quick note: Prefabs are files in the project that are made up of one or more GameObjects. The prefabs system is a way to build complex combinations of GameObjects and Components that can be added to the Scene in a single command rather than having to construct them part by part each time you need them. By having a prefab set up for the insect, for example, all we need to do is add an Insect prefab to the game and tell it where to aim. The Insect prefab already has all of the script Components, physics, and Colliders it needs to function. A single line of code adds it to the scene and it is ready to use.

Add the Audio Source Component to the Insect

Click on Insect in the Project browser, so that you can see its Components and properties in the Inspector.

Scroll down to the bottom of the Inspector and hit Add Component. Choose Audio > Audio Source.

On the new Audio Source Component (you may need to scroll down to the bottom in the Inspector to see it) click on the little target icon next to Audio Clip, so that you can choose an Audio Clip to play (Figure 8.4).

Choose the Audio Clip named bzz. Check the Loop checkbox so that the sound will play on a loop.

Next, drag the Spatial Blend slider all the way to the right so that Spatial Blend is set to 1 (3D). This makes sure that the sound will appear to be coming from the direction of its GameObject.

The final thing you need to do to make this work is to check the Play On Awake checkbox. With Play On Awake checked, whenever an Insect prefab is added to the Scene, the buzzing sound will start to play automatically and it will continue to play in a loop until its GameObject is destroyed.

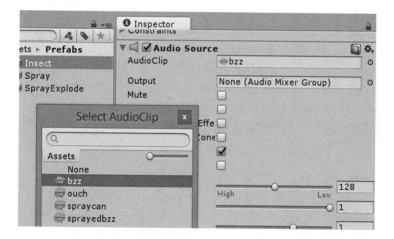

FIGURE 8.4 Choosing an Audio Clip for the Audio Component to play.

Press Play and notice how the buzzing sound's volume and panning changes based on its location in the 3D space. You can now hear where the insects are coming from and hopefully spray them before they sting!

ADD SOUND TO THE SPRAY

When we hit the button to make spray come out of the spray can, it would be nice to make a little sound. The procedure for adding an Audio Clip to the spray is very similar to adding audio to the insect in the previous section. When the spray button is pressed, we have a prefab that will be added to the scene. By adding an Audio Source to the Spray prefab, with its Play On Awake box checked, whenever the spray is added to the Scene it will make the sound automatically. This is the same approach used earlier with the insect prefab.

Click on Spray in the Project browser (in the Prefabs folder).

In the Inspector, click Add Component. Choose Audio > Audio Source. Click on the little target icon next to Audio Clip, so that you can choose the spraycan clip.

This time, we do not need the clip to loop so you can leave that unchecked. Leave the Spatial Blend to 2D. This will mean that regardless of its spatial difference from the Listener, Unity will not do anything to affect its panning or volume. This sound is a short clip that will play whenever the spray appears in the scene and it is just meant to give the player an audio cue that we are spraying from a can.

Check the Play On Awake checkbox.

Add Music

Music can change the game. It can provide atmosphere and help set the pace of the action. It is important to choose the right music for the type of game you are building and the sort of game play you are hoping to achieve. In this section, I want you to do a little experiment where we try two different types of music to see the effect it has on the feel of the Scene. Both music loops work well with the game, but they both set a very different tone for the action.

ADD AN AUDIO SOURCE TO THE CAMERA

Click the Create dropdown button at the top of the Hierarchy. Choose Create Empty. With the new GameObject selected, in the Inspector, change its name to MusicAudio. Over to the Inspector once again to click Add Component. Find Audio > Audio Source.

We will choose the Audio Clip shortly, but I want to set up the other parameters of the Audio Source first. Go through the Audio Source and set the following:

Bypass Effects: Checked.

Bypass Listener Effects: Checked.

Bypass Reverb Zones: Checked.

Volume: 1

Spatial Blend: 0 (Slider on the 2D side)

Doppler Level: 0

Spread: 0

Whimsical and Fun

Set the AudioClip to Whimsical (via the target icon next to AudioClip on the Component).

Grab your VR headset and hit Play to preview the Scene. The tone of the music helps the game to feel light, fun, and perhaps a bit silly.

Fast Paced and Exciting

Now, change the Audio Clip on that Camera Audio Source to FastPaced. Hit Play to preview the Scene again. The tone of the music helps the game to feel fast. There is an urgency to the gameplay now that we did not see when the scene was quiet.

Unity Audio Mixers and Effects

Audio Mixers provide volume level control, audio effects, and the ability to route audio signals into groups. By grouping audio together, you can grab control over the way that certain types of sounds are heard. Grouping all of your sound effects into a single mixer allows you to have many different audio sources and control all of their volume and effects via a single set of parameters. For example, one mixer can control all of the sound effects, with another single mixer to control music; making it easier for a developer to provide volume control sliders for users.

In this section, we will create an Audio Mixers and apply it to sounds and music, so that the music and sounds play through separate channels and we can manipulate them individually.

CREATE AN AUDIO MIXER

Right click on the Sound folder in the Project browser and choose Create > Audio Mixer.

Rename the new Audio Mixer to Main.

Double click your new Audio Mixer to show the Audio Mixer section so that you can see the mixers interface (Figure 8.5).

The Audio Mixer Window

In the Mixers window, you will see several categories; Mixers, Snapshots, Groups, and Views.

Mixers

You can use multiple mixers if you need to, but for most small projects, you will likely only need one. Mixers allow you to route audio and control it along its journey to the speakers.

Snapshots

Changing multiple settings would mean that you had to set each property of a Mixer one by one. Snapshots enable you to take a "snapshot" of all settings and save it. You can then choose a snapshot to load. A good example of how you might use this could be the difference between indoor and outdoor vehicle audio. Engine sounds are very different on the outside of the car than inside. For this, you could have two Snapshots, one for indoor and one for outdoor. By applying different effects and levels to the indoor settings, the engine sounds and road noise could be lower with

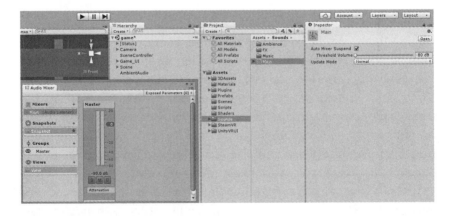

FIGURE 8.5 The Audio Mixer window.

effects applied to make them sound "muffled" as if the sound proofing were doing its job. On the outside Snapshot, the sound could be louder and perhaps with a little more reverb. When the simulation moves from inside the car to outside (such as a camera change, or the viewer physically exiting the vehicle) you could switch to the applicable Snapshot to make the audio sound correct.

Groups

You might think of a Group as an individual channel where you can route whatever sounds you want. By using multiple Groups, you can control the volume and effects applied to whichever sounds you choose to route through them. For example, you might have a Group for sound effects and a Group for music. The music Group could have a different volume to the sound Group so that you can control music and sound volumes individually.

By default, Unity adds a single group named Master to every Mixer and I usually add new Groups that are children of the Master so that whenever settings are changed on the Master group, they carry down to the others. For example, to create a master volume controller slider for an options menu, the master needs to affect all volume levels. Changing the volume level on the Master affects the volume on any child Groups so to create a master volume slider I would make all my sound effect and music Groups children of the Master Group so that they would all be affected by the settings applied to the Master. Like most object systems in Unity, it is hierarchical.

Views

Views are there to help you work with Groups. By using the little eye icons next to each group, you can choose which groups are showing for you to edit in the Audio Mixer window. Views enable you to automate the process of using those eye icons. For example, you could set up a View to show only one set of groups such as those associated with vehicle audio. Another View might be used to only show nature sounds. When you are working with a large number of Groups, the View system will help you work more efficiently with them all.

Setting Up Mixers in the Audio Mixer Window

Audio Groups are shown on the right of the window, as channels (Figure 8.6). Whenever sound is being played through the Group you will

FIGURE 8.6   Click the + icon to add Groups to the Audio Mixer.

see the VU meter showing levels. The dark gray arrow to the right of the VU meter is moveable with the mouse and it points to the currently set attenuation level on this channel. The default is 0 db. This will affect how loud the sound will be output.

Below the VU meter you will find three icon buttons; S, M, and B. Those are (in order)

Solo (S): This will mute audio through any other Groups that are not currently soloed. That is, you will only hear the audio flowing through this Group and all other audio Groups will be silent (unless they are also set to be soloed by having their S button highlighted). When you have a lot of Groups, this is useful to be able to isolate a single Group when balancing and tweaking audio settings.

Mute (M): The mute button will mute all audio going through this Group. Other Groups will continue to behave as normal.

Bypass (B): If effects have been applied to this Group, the Bypass button will bypass the effects system and play the audio dry. This button only applies to the current Group. If there are any parent or child Groups connected to it, they will not be affected. Only the current Group's effects will be bypassed by this button.

At the bottom of the Group mixer, you can add or modify effects. I will not be going into any detail over this part, as it is a varied and complex subject that is beyond the scope of this chapter. If you need more in-depth information on the effects and audio system, the Unity documentation is a really good place to start.

ADDING MIXER GROUPS

Click the + button in the top right of the Groups section. Add two new Groups and name them SFX and Music so that it looks like those in Figure 8.6.

Make sure that the SFX and Music Groups are under the Master Group. You can change their order by dragging and dropping them in this area.

By having the SFX and Music Groups beneath the Master, whenever we change the master volume all of our other sounds will also be affected by the change.

SETTING AUDIO SOURCES TO USE THE AUDIO MIXER GROUPS

Now that we have an Audio Mixer and it has Groups set up for sound effects and music, we need to go ahead and tell the Audio Sources to use them. These are the Audio Sources added as Components to GameObjects earlier in this chapter. The audio will work even without any Audio Mixer set up, but its output will just go direct to the Listener. The only way to change its volume or apply effects and so on will be through code or in the editor, directly applied to this Audio Source. Routing its Output via the Mixer provides global control from a single place.

Let's start by setting up the music. In the Hierarchy, click the Camera. In the Inspector, find the Audio Source Component and click on the little target icon next to Output.

When the Audio Mixers list pops up, choose Music (Master).

Next, the ambient audio. In the Hierarchy find Ambient Audio. In the Inspector, find the Audio Source Component and click on the little target icon next to Output. Set the Output to SFX (Master).

Remember that the insects have sound effects, too. In the Project browser, find the Prefabs folder and click on the Insect prefab. To the left of it is a small arrow to expand out the prefab and show the two other GameObjects it contains:

Insect

Wasp

OuchAudioSource

SprayedAudioSource

When the insect stings the player, the OuchAudioSource will play. When an insect is sprayed, the SprayedAudioSource plays. These two are Audio Source Components attached to empty GameObjects and they need their Outputs set to SFX, too.

Click the OuchAudioSource prefab in the Project browser. In the Inspector, under Audio Source, set the Output to SFX.

Click the SprayedAudioSource prefab. Again, in the Inspector, Audio Source, set the Output to SFX.

Finally, for Insect, we also need to route the buzzing sound through the SFX Audio Mixer Group. Click the Insect prefab. Find the Audio Source and set Output to SFX.

The Spray prefab is the last thing we need to set up. Click Spray in the Prefabs folder and set its Output to SFX on the Audio Source Component.

TESTING AND MIXING AUDIO

Unity's audio system provides a strong interface for editing and setting up audio. You can see audio levels in real-time and even apply audio effects as the audio is playing live. Mixing is done through the Audio Mixer window (Figure 8.7).

When you try out the preview, the first thing you might notice is how much more alive it seems. The ambient audio helps to reinforce the garden visual and, as insects appear, you can hear them approach and know where they are coming from. The insects have character, too. When you spray them, they make a cute little "bzzt" sound as they fly

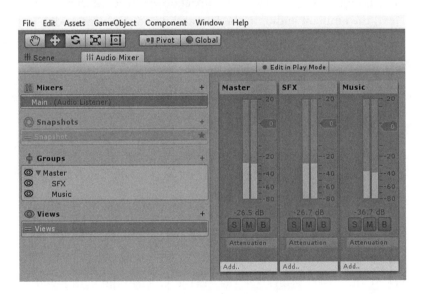

FIGURE 8.7 The Audio Mixer window, shown here docked to the Scene View, displays Audio Mixer Groups with VU meters to monitor and configures sound during game preview.

away. The pitch shifted voice makes it sound small and cute, taking a little more away from the potentially dark theme of spraying bugs. As the bugs never die, they just fly away, the tone is happy and light. Our audio adds to this, taking a lighthearted and fun approach to the garden invaders scenario.

Do not be afraid to experiment. One of the top sound designers in Hollywood, Skip Lievsay, once said that he uses the sound of bacon sizzling for rain sound effects and he mixes lion roars in with car engines to make them more aggressive (Kisner, 2015). It is not just about the sound, but the kind of feeling that a sound evokes when you hear it. For example, perhaps you need a creaky door in a haunted house VR experience. The door needs to creak and all of the doors in your house do not creak, so you cannot use them. Instead, you could recreate the effect in a sound editor package like Audacity (http://www.audacityteam.org/) by sequencing three sounds one after the other. The first sound is the door handle rattle as it is turned. Stage two is the little click sound of the latch opening. The final stage is the creak, which could be recorded from a creaky drawer instead or perhaps something unrelated such as bending a piece of wood to make a creaking sound. The listener may never know that it was not a real creaking door sound used in the haunted house, but the effect could be unforgettable when they hear a creepy old door opening up and they wonder what is going to walk through it! Get creative with sound to create more than just a copy of a sound to something that will help create the atmosphere you want.

We create universes, with their own rules and physics, creatures, and architecture. It is important to try to reinforce not just the visual environment but the themes and tone of the whole experience. By considering more than what is immediately visible, we build a richer and more complete universe for the player to inhabit.

Audio Ducking

Audio Ducking is an effect commonly used by audio engineers to bring down the volume of an audio track so that another audio track is easier to hear. Unity includes a built-in audio ducking effect that we can easily apply to a mixer.

In the Sounds folder of the Project browser, find and double click on the Audio Mixer main. In the Audio Mixer window, you should see the three groups; Master, SFX, and Music.

At the bottom of each mixer group is the Add.. button, for Effects.

Send and Receive

Mixer channels (groups) are able to send and receive data to each other. For audio ducking, the mixer channel you want to have affected by ducking must receive audio from another channel. We will have the Music channel duck based on the output of the SFX channel, so the first thing to do is to add a Send effect to SFX.

In the Audio Mixer view, at the bottom of Music click the Add button and choose Duck Volume. No, this has nothing to do with quacking.

At the bottom of the SFX channel, click Add and choose Send. Over in the Inspector, with the SFX channel selected, you should now see a Send Component. Here, we need to tell Send where its data should be received. Click on the Receive dropdown in the Inspector and choose Music\Duck Volume.

The Send level, also in the Inspector, is important because it determines how "loud" the output from this channel should be sent to its receiver. Slide the Send level all the way to the right, until the number to the right of the slider reads 0.00 dB.

Audio Ducking Settings

To get the most satisfactory effect from audio ducking, you will usually need to do a little tweaking of the values it uses to determine how much input audio it takes for ducking to happen and how it will duck. Guessing these values would be beyond difficult, so Unity has provided a method of setting up the audio as the preview is running so that you get a live audioscape to play around with and you can immediately experience the effect that the settings changes are having.

When you hit Play to preview the scene, the audio views gray out to tell you that you cannot do anything with them in play mode. Additionally, in play mode, two new toggle buttons appear atop the Audio Mixer view and at the top of the Inspector when you have an audio channel selected—both of them are labeled "Edit in Play Mode." Click the Edit in Play Mode when the preview is running and you can change any or all of the audio values and contrary to normal Unity operation, the changes will persist after you hit the Stop button to return to editing.

Through trial and error, I went through setting up values as I listened to how the buzzing noise got louder as an insect approached the player and then how the audio ducking affected the volume of the music. I ended up changing the following values:

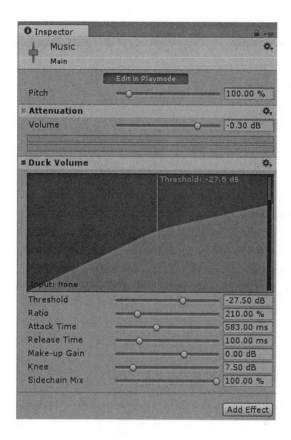

FIGURE 8.8   Audio Ducking settings are set in the Inspector.

Threshold: −27.50

Attack Time: 583.00

Note that in the Inspector, you can drag the white line left or right over the visual representation (Figure 8.8) to set the Threshold. If you press Play to preview, the graph will show the audio input and you will see where the Threshold kicks in versus where the audio levels are from the input.

You can get a really good measure of the Threshold by using the graph.

Other Effects

Just a quick mention of these, as we have been so close to them all. At the bottom of the audio groups in the Audio Mixer, you can find a host of other audio effects inside the Add button dropdown menu. I will not go into detail about them here, but you can play around with things like Lowpass and Highpass filters, Echo, Flange, and Distortion effects—all sorts of really cool effects that you can add to different audio groups for a number of different effects.

SAVE THE PROJECT

CTRL + S to save or FILE > Save Scene.

RECAP

This chapter was all about audio. We began by looking at different types of sounds and then how to set up ambient audio in a Unity scene. The properties of the AudioSource were key to making this work properly. After adding some music to set the pace, we looked at Audio Mixers, how to set them up, and how you can use them to route audio on its way to the speakers. Finally, you got to experience the game scene with all of the audio in place.

HTC Vive Motion Controllers

HOW WE INTERACT WITH THE VIRTUAL WORLD

The way that we interact with the virtual world is one of the most limiting and perhaps disappointing aspects of VR. Our visual and audio senses may be replaced but we are still very limited when it comes to actually moving around, touching objects or picking them up, or having any actual sense or feel for the virtual world. The race is now on to find an intuitive control system that can provide viewers with the feedback and ease of use to feel natural. Those lucky enough to own an HTC Vive will know that the Vive controllers present an excellent way to control and interact with the virtual world and room-scale VR.

HTC VIVE CONTROLLERS

One of the coolest features of the HTC Vive is its out-of-the-box room-scale VR. It was the first in the consumer market to allow viewers to move around and explore the space fully, as if they were actually standing inside it and able to walk around. Most of the games and experiences for Vive are designed for movement and grabbing things in the space—interacting with the VR world you get to inhabit. The wand-like controllers (Figure 9.1) included with the HTC Vive were designed specifically for VR and are very intuitive, offering wireless tracking and force feedback.

When you use the controllers, they are often accompanied by CGI counterparts in the virtual world so that you can easily know where they

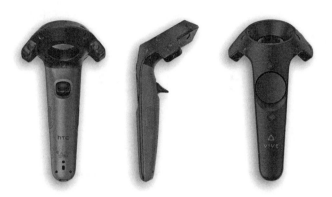

FIGURE 9.1   The HTC Vive controllers are motion tracked and they allow incredible interactions with objects in the VR world. (Courtesy of HTC.)

are and find buttons if you need to. Many games also transform them in-game, visually, to hammers, swords, or whatever it is that the player is supposed to be holding. Thanks to its clever design, the Vive controller is normally easy to operate even when it takes a completely different virtual form to how it is in the real world.

Try Out the SteamVR Interaction System Example Scene

If you have not already tried it, open up the InteractionSystem example Scene in the SteamVR libraries—you can find the Scene in the folder SteamVR/InteractionSystem/Samples/Scenes. The name of the Scene is Interactions_Example. It contains a number of interactive pieces such as UI, objects to pick up and throw, a longbow, and some other bits and bobs. Have a play around with that and meet me back here, once you are done throwing things and shooting arrows.

We will take a quick look at how you can use the SteamVR Interaction System for UI later in this chapter (Interaction System has a great way to use standard Unity GUI with the controllers) but our controller code will work independently of it. We will be putting together a small custom script that will serve for most purposes.

Tips for Designing Room-Scale VR Controls

In this section, you have seen how to use the HTC Vive controllers for manipulating objects in the virtual world. The controllers are an extremely powerful way to interact, offering possibilities for room-scale VR experiences far beyond a standard controller. It is important not just to use the controllers in your experiences, but to try to carefully implement, test, and iterate upon your control systems until they are the most intuitive you can possibly make them. Try out your controls on people and listen carefully to their reactions and opinions.

It may seem as though designing a controller system is as easy as imagining the buttons and assigning behaviors to them, but it is not as straightforward. The only way to truly understand whether your control system works or not is to test it out in VR and try it out. Actual implementation is very different to conceptual design and you may be surprised by how much experimentation and iterative controller design can benefit your experiences.

Try to make your controllers subconsciously blend into the hands of your users. For a successful control scheme to work, your users should not even be aware of the fact that they are using a controller once the basics are mastered. If you find that you need to add giant arrows or screens of tutorials to demonstrate how the control system works, it is most likely that your control system needs more work. A great control system should be as easy to pick up and as transparent to its users as possible.

Take an experimental/jamming approach to controller design. Have fun and take your time refining your controls. Getting a control system right is a hugely rewarding process, but it takes time to do this right and you should allow a good chunk of your project timeline to develop systems that work, to try them out on real people (who both may have used VR before and some who have not) and iterate on your designs until you have the best system you can make. Your virtual world will wow its visitors with their presence inside its majesty—it would be a waste of awesome if your controllers let them down!

On his GamaSutra.com blog, Alistair Doulin mentions that we should never encourage users to bring their controllers too close to each other or the headset (Doulin, 2016). This is a great advice. Try to be aware of how the viewer will use the controllers and keep an eye out for any sorts of situations that might cause them to put either the controllers, or themselves at risk.

You should also consider the room space and how you plan to use it. To be able to support most room-scale users, Doulin recommends a play space of 2×1.5 m or smaller. Try to keep anything that the user will interact with inside this space, too, so that there is less risk of users reaching outside of the bounds to hit obstacles in the real world. If you must go bigger than the minimum recommended space, you should provide a tele-port system to let users still move around even if their physical space is limited.

Research other VR experiences to see how they do things, too. For example, I love the way that Valve's *The Lab* has different worlds inside bubbles that you can pick up and put on your head to teleport to. I do not think I would ever have thought that control systems could be so abstract yet feel so natural to use. The way *The Lab* travels between worlds is one of my favorite examples of off-the-wall thinking turning out to make com-plete sense in VR.

PICKING UP AND DROPPING IN VR WITH THE VIVE CONTROLLERS

This section is focused on making a basic Scene containing a few objects that can be picked up and thrown around (Figure 9.2). The main part of the code that handles picking up and dropping objects is loosely based on the SteamVR_TestThrow.cs, example script that was provided as a part of the SteamVR library prior to version 1.2. After 1.2, you can achieve a similar effect with the SteamVR Interaction System. If you take a lit-tle time to check out the sample Scene in SteamVR/InteractionSystem/ Samples, check out the Throwables GameObject in the Hierarchy and the child GameObjects under that. My method is relatively simplistic,

FIGURE 9.2 The example project for this chapter features a variety of shapes of objects of different weights, sizes, and gravity levels. You can grab them, move, and throw them around the Scene.

compared to the advanced SteamVR example, but it still gets the job done and it should serve as a good solution for most basic interactions.

Adding Vive Controllers to a Unity Scene

Open the example project file for this chapter. We will begin by looking at how to add the controllers to a Scene so that you can see them in VR.

Create a new Scene in Unity, with File > New Scene.

The SteamVR library makes it easy to add controller support, providing a prefab, complete with camera rig, all ready to go.

In the Project browser, find SteamVR > Prefabs and look for the [CameraRig] prefab in there. Drag and drop it out of the Project and into the Hierarchy so that Unity adds an instance of the prefab to the Scene.

In the Hierarchy, expand out the [CameraRig] GameObject to see other GameObjects it contains. Don't worry about digging any deeper in the [CameraRig] hierarchy right now, as we are mainly concerned with the first level down. The basic rig looks something like this:

[CameraRig]

    Controller (left)

        Model

    Controller (right)

        Model

    Camera (head)

        Camera (eye)

        Camera (ears)

The Controller (left) and Controller (right) GameObjects are exactly that; GameObjects that deal with the left and right controllers. Each Controller also renders a visual representation of the controller and all of its buttons and the touch pad. This provides a tangible link between the controllers in the real world and those in the virtual world. Below both the left and right GameObjects is a GameObject named Model. This GameObject is interesting because although it is named Model, it does not actually contain any 3D mesh or model. It has a single script Component attached to it, SteamVR_ Rendermodel, which tells the SteamVR library to load the controller model and build relevant child GameObjects and sub-components that go together to make it function as a fully animated representation of the controller. If you dig around inside the SteamVR folder in the Project browser, you will soon find out that there is no controller model in there, either. That is because SteamVR_Rendermodel gets the model from the local SteamVR installation (the one linked to the Steam client). If you ever wanted to replace the controller models with something else and hide the original ones, you would need to remove or disable the Model GameObject so that SteamVR would not try to do its controller setup.

We can use these Controller (left) and Controller (right) GameObjects to attach custom behaviors to, to make the controllers act differently or react to button presses and such. In this chapter, we will be looking at a script Component for the Controller GameObjects called PickUp.cs. This will allow the viewer to pick up, throw, or drop Rigidbody-based physics objects in the virtual world.

The PickUp.cs Script

The script, as shown here, allows us to use the controller to pick up, drop, and throw objects. The Pickup script in full looks like this:

```
using UnityEngine;

[RequireComponent(typeof(SteamVR_TrackedObject))]
[RequireComponent(typeof(SphereCollider))]

public class PickUp : MonoBehaviour
{
    public string grabbableTag = "GrabbableObject";

    [Space(10)]
    public float throwMultiplier = 1f;
    public float grabRadius = 0.06f;

    [Space(10)]
    public Rigidbody attachPoint;

    SteamVR_TrackedObject trackedObj;
    FixedJoint joint;

    private GameObject theClosestGO;
    private SteamVR_Controller.Device myDevice;
```

```
    void Awake()
    {
        // grab references to things we need..
        trackedObj = GetComponent<SteamVR_Tracked
Object>();
        SphereCollider myCollider = GetComponent<Spher
eCollider>();

        // do a little set up on the sphere collider
to set the radius and make sure that it's a trigger
        myCollider.radius = grabRadius;
        myCollider.isTrigger = true;
    }

    void FixedUpdate()
    {
        myDevice = SteamVR_Controller.Input((int)
trackedObj.index);

        // ---------------------------------------------
        // PICKUP
        // ---------------------------------------------
        if (joint == null &&
myDevice.GetTouch(SteamVR_Controller.ButtonMask.
Trigger))
        {
            PickUpObject();
        }

        // ---------------------------------------------
        // DROP
        // ---------------------------------------------
        if (!myDevice.GetTouch(SteamVR_Controller.
ButtonMask.Trigger))
        {
            DropObject();

        }
    }

    void PickUpObject()
    {
        // if we found a close object, grab it!
        if (theClosestGO != null)
```

```
        {
            joint = theClosestGO.AddComponent
<FixedJoint>();
            joint.connectedBody = attachPoint;
        }
    }

    void DropObject()
    {
        // this function destroys the FixedJoint
holding the object to the controller and resets
theClosestGO
        if (joint != null)
        {
            // if we already have grabbed something,
we keep it locked to the controller
            var go = joint.gameObject;
            var rigidbody = go.GetComponent
<RigidBody>();
            DestroyImmediate(joint);
            joint = null;

            var origin = trackedObj.origin ?
trackedObj.origin : trackedObj.transform.parent;
            if (origin != null)
            {
                rigidbody.velocity = origin.
TransformVector(myDevice.velocity) * throwMultiplier;
                rigidbody.angularVelocity = origin.
TransformVector(myDevice.angularVelocity);
            }
            else
            {
                rigidbody.velocity = myDevice.velocity
* throwMultiplier;
                rigidbody.angularVelocity = myDevice.
angularVelocity;
            }

            // make sure that our max velocity is not
less than the speed of the controller (we want the
object to
            // match the velocity of the controller,
right?)
```

```
                rigidbody.maxAngularVelocity = rigidbody.
angularVelocity.magnitude;

                // reset the reference in theClosestGO
                theClosestGO = null;
        }
    }

    void OnTriggerEnter(Collider collision)
    {
        // when the controller hits and object,
theClosestGO is set to the object and we make a little
buzz
        if (joint == null && (collision.gameObject.tag
== grabbableTag))
        {
            theClosestGO = collision.gameObject;
        }
    }

    void OnTriggerStay(Collider collision)
    {
        // if the controller is inside an object, we
still want to be able to grab it so we keep theClosestGO
set OnTriggerStay
        if (joint == null && (collision.gameObject.tag
== grabbableTag))
        {
            theClosestGO = collision.gameObject;
        }
    }

    void OnTriggerExit(Collider collision)
    {
        // before removing this from the 'possible to
grab' theClosestGO var, we check that it is the current
one
        if (joint == null && theClosestGO != null)
        {
            theClosestGO = null;
        }
    }
}
```

Script Breakdown

We start with the packages, a couple of checks, and the class declaration:

```
using UnityEngine;
[RequireComponent(typeof(SteamVR_TrackedObject))]
[RequireComponent(typeof(SphereCollider))]

public class PickUp : MonoBehaviour
{
```

Above, we use RequireComponent to make sure that the SteamVR_ TrackedObject Component is attached to the same GameObject this script is attached to. Then we check that a SphereCollider is also attached to this GameObject. I have not fully automated the setting up of the SphereCollider by this script, so to use this you will always need to make sure that the Collider Component is already set up correctly on the controller (via the Inspector in Unity). The actual position of the SphereCollider Component should be set up in the Inspector to be at a good point where it will register objects getting close enough to pick up.

The only other thing to note is that the PickUp class derives from MonoBehaviour to use Unity functions.

You may recall from Chapter 3 that the SteamVR_TrackObject class is a script Component attached to the GameObjects that move around with tracked objects from the real world. SteamVR_TrackObject.cs has an Index variable which acts as an ID for the controller hardware—if there is anything we want to do with the hardware, we will need the correct Index to be able to talk to the correct device. Vive controllers are assigned a number dynamically, which means that it could be different each time and hard-coding (the process of using fixed numbers in code) would be unreliable. In this script, we will ask a SteamVR_TrackObject Component for the Index of the controller to monitor its buttons.

```
public string grabbableTag = "GrabbableObject";
```

This script uses Unity tags to tell when an object is able to be picked up. Tags are Unity's system for using strings to identify types of objects. The grabbableTag string (above) should be set up in the Inspector as well as the Tags and Layers interface (NOTE: The example project should have the tags already set up, but for reference you get to the Tags and Layers interface by clicking on Add Tag from the Tag dropdown of the Inspector when a GameObject is selected).

Just a note on string comparisons: String comparisons tend to be relatively slow and it is not advisable to make them regularly (such as in Update or FixedUpdate functions that are called on every frame or more) but in a situation like this, where we only compare when a button is pressed, there should be negligible performance impact.

Variable declarations next:

```
public float throwMultiplier = 1.4f;
public float grabRadius = 0.06f;

public Rigidbody attachPoint;

SteamVR_TrackedObject trackedObj;
FixedJoint joint;

private GameObject theClosestGO;
private SteamVR_Controller.Device myDevice;
```

I will not go into detail over the variables here, as most of them will become clear as we discuss the main body of the script.

As this script derives from MonoBehaviour, Unity automatically calls Awake() when the script is loaded:

```
void Awake()
{
    // grab references to things we need..
    trackedObj = GetComponent<SteamVR_Tracked
Object>();
```

Above, we grab a reference to the SteamVR_TrackObject Component, assuming that it will be attached to the same GameObject as this script so that we can use GetComponent to find it automatically. Next, we look for the SphereCollider:

```
    SphereCollider myCollider = GetComponent<Spher
eCollider>();

    myCollider.radius = grabRadius;
    myCollider.isTrigger = true;
}
```

We grab a reference to the SphereCollider Component with GetComponent() and set its radius and isTrigger property. This controller system uses a SphereCollider to be able to tell when an object is within grabbing distance (Figure 9.3). We do not want the Collider to try to resolve collisions, but we do need to be notified when a collision occurs which is why its isTrigger property is set to true. When an object enters the Collider's trigger area, the engine will automatically call a function, such as OnTriggerEnter(), containing a reference to the object.

Important note: In order for the collision to be registered between an object and the SphereCollider attached to the controller, the object MUST have a RigidBody attached to it. Unity has a requirement that collisions will only register if one or more colliding objects has a RigidBody attached to it. As long as both objects have colliders, it is only a requirement that one of them have a RigidBody attached.

We set the radius in this script, but if you are using anything other than the controller set up in the example project you will also need to position

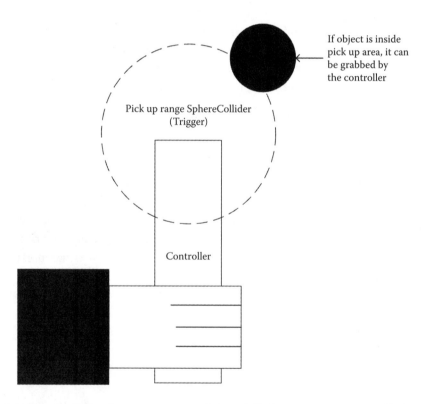

FIGURE 9.3 The pick up system uses a SphereCollider set as a trigger to tell when objects are near enough to be picked up by the viewer.

the SphereCollider manually in the Inspector. In the example project, the SphereCollider will already be correctly placed.

```
void FixedUpdate()
{
    myDevice = SteamVR_Controller.Input((int)
trackedObj.index);
```

FixedUpdate() is another automatically-called function for Mono behaviour-derived classes. The engine calls FixedUpdate() once every physics time step. This is normally the place to put physics-based behavior. In this case, as we will be creating and destroying physics joints based on conditions inside FixedUpdate() this seems like the correct place rather than the Update() or LateUpdate() functions.

myDevice is set up to contain a reference to the controller to which this script is attached. How we get to that reference requires a little explanation: The SteamVR_Controller.Input class is part of the SteamVR library of code you download with the SteamVR package from the Unity Asset Store. It provides publicly accessible functions for dealing with the controller. In the line above, we want to find out which device we are going to be talking to (the controller).

So, we ask the SteamVR_Controller.Input function to return it by passing in our ID number. This will give us a reference to a SteamVR_Controller.Device object that we can then use to track button presses on the controller.

First up, we take a look to see if the trigger is pressed:

```
    if (joint == null && myDevice.GetTouch(SteamVR_
Controller.ButtonMask.Trigger))
    {
        PickUpObject();
    }
```

Above, the first condition, before we talk to the controller, is to see if joint is equal to null. The joint variable is going to hold a reference to a FixedJoint Component that will hold the object to the controller in the physics engine whenever we are holding on to it. When we already have a FixedJoint reference, it means that we must already be holding something with the controller so we do not want to add another and try to hold that, too. Although it may be possible to hold multiple items, this script is intended to only allow the viewer to pick up a single item at a time, one with each controller. If we have no FixedJoint already set up, joint will be null.

Next, we use device.GetTouchDown(SteamVR_Controller.Button Mask.Trigger) to see if the trigger button is pressed. Note that I used GetTouch rather than GetPress. You can actually use either one, but I found that GetTouch registered sooner in the trigger press, so that the user does not have to press the trigger down quite as far down. If you have any problems or doubts about my logic, feel free to change GetTouch to GetPress and try it out for yourself.

device.GetTouchDown will return true if the button has been pushed down during the last update. It takes a single parameter, which is of type SteamVR_Controller.ButtonMask.

SteamVR_Controller.ButtonMask contains all of the inputs available on the controller. Those are

ApplicationMenu: The ApplicationMenu button is the menu button located at the top of the controller.

Grip: The Grip buttons are on the sides of the controller, intended to represent a "squeeze" when you grip the controller's handle.

Touchpad: The Touchpad is that big round bit, near the top of the controller. It works both as a touch-sensitive pad and a button. By using the SteamVR_Controller.device functions for buttons, you can find out when a press occurs. In combination with the GetAxis() function you can find out exactly where the touch was when it occurred. By using the position of the touch button, it is possible to split the Touchpad into many areas/separate functions, as required. For example, in *The Lab* demo the Touchpad is shown split into four quadrants to produce four different colored balloons.

Axis0 (also Axis1, Axis2, Axis3, and Axis4): You can access individual axis of the Touchpad, but the easier method to find out where a touch occurs is with the controller.GetAxis() function. GetAxis provides a Vector2 (2d vector) between (−1, −1) and (1, 1) to tell you where the touch is (top left to bottom right). If you wanted to track a button press on the Touchpad, you could use the standard a button device press function to check the Touchpad and

GetAxis to find out whereabouts on the Touchpad the press actually occurred.

Trigger: The Trigger is the button on the back of the controller.

To recap, in the previous code block, we checked to see if a FixedJoint was not already made and if the trigger button is being pressed. If those conditions are met, a call to PickUpObject() is called to deal with the actual picking up.

```
    if (!myDevice.GetTouch(SteamVR_Controller.
ButtonMask.Trigger))
    {
        DropObject();
    }
}
```

Above, we check to see if the trigger button is not being pressed and drop the object with a call to DropObject() if this condition is met. That is everything for the FixedUpdate() function.

Now that we can tell when the user is trying to pick up or drop an object, we can go ahead and code the functions to do the actual picking up and dropping:

```
void PickUpObject()
    {
```

PickUpObject() begins by making sure that we have an object close enough to pick up:

```
        if (theClosestGO != null)
        {
```

theClosestGO is a variable containing a reference to the GameObject that we think the user is trying to pick up with the controller. It is set further down in the class, inside the OnTriggerEnter() function, whenever an object enters the controller's SphereCollider trigger area. When an object enters our pick up range trigger, theClosestGO will contain a reference to the object possible to be picked up. If we have something in theClosestGO, the code may go ahead and grab it:

```
            joint = theClosestGO.AddComponent<Fixed
Joint>();
            joint.connectedBody = attachPoint;
        }
    }
```

Think back to the FixedUpdate() function, before called this PickUp Object() function, where we checked to see if a FixedJoint was already in action by seeing if the joint variable is equal to null. We wanted to make sure that a FixedJoint was not already holding another object to this controller. Allowing them to pick up more than one gets very messy very quickly, so we only want to allow the user to pick up a single item at a time.

Since we know that the FixedJoint does not already exist, the code above starts out by adding a FixedJoint Component to theClosestGO (the object we want to pick up). It uses the AddComponent() function to do this.

Next, the FixedJoint (a reference we now hold in the variable named joint) is attached to the controller. We do this by setting the connected-Body property of the joint to our attachPoint variable. attachPoint contains a reference to another GameObject that is a child object of the controller. It just acts as a reference point to attach objects to and the Attach Point GameObject is just an empty GameObject with no Components attached to it.

That is all we need to do to attach the object to the controller. The DropObject() function is next:

```
void DropObject()
{
    if (joint != null)
    {
        var go = joint.gameObject;
        var rigidbody = go.GetComponent<RigidBody>();
        DestroyImmediate(joint);
        joint = null;
```

DropObject starts out by checking that joint is not equal to null; that we have a FixedJoint set up and attached to an object. If joint were null, this would be a giveaway that there is no object to drop and we could simply drop out of the function entirely and ignore the call.

When the FixedJoint is found and the condition met, the code above uses DestroyImmediate to remove the FixedJoint from the Scene altogether. Now, you may be wondering why it is using DestroyImmediate and not Unity's standard Destroy function. Good question! The reasoning behind this is that Destroy is always delayed until after the current Update loop completes. This means that any velocity settings may end up being impacted by physics calculations based on the FixedJoint still being attached. By using DestroyImmediate() to remove the FixedJoint right away, the engine's physics calculations will take changes to velocity (coming up in the next code block) as if the FixedJoint was never there.

The Unity documentation warns that you should use Destroy Immediate() carefully and recommends that you always use Object. Destroy() instead. This is because Destroy happens at a safe time whereas DestroyImmediate is likely to cause errors if you are referencing the object being destroyed elsewhere in the script. Since we will only be referencing the variable joint here or when we reset it, the code is safe enough to use.

After the FixedJoint Component is destroyed, the variable joint is also set to null to be safe. The next code block is where we tell the object about the velocity and angular velocity will follow now that it is released from the controller. If we did not pass on the velocity info, the object would be disconnected but it would simply drop to the ground even when we were trying to throw it.

```
var origin = trackedObj.origin ? tracked
Obj.origin : trackedObj.transform.parent;
```

Origin is going to contain the origin point of the controller, but in the line above we carry out a little check to see if there is an alternative origin set on the SteamVR_Tracked Object Component. Why would this be? SteamVR_Tracked Object allows you to set a different origin Transform to use with different shapes or controller meshes. In this demo, we do not change the origin so we can assume that the controller origin point will be that of the parent GameObject. Getting the origin is important when it comes to figuring out our velocities, since it contains Transform information, including scale and rotation, that will be used by our code to transform vectors from local to world space.

To be honest, the ?: operator was new to me prior to looking at this. If it is new to you, let me try to explain. The syntax is

condition? 1st expression: 2nd expression;

The condition can either be true or false. Then, if the condition is true then the result will be whatever is in the 1st expression. If the condition is false, the result will be the 2nd expression. What we do here is to look at trackedObj.origin, to see if it populated or not (i.e., that the variable contains an object reference). If trackedObject.origin contains an object reference, then the result will be our first expression, trackedObj.origin. If trackedObject.origin does not contain an object reference, the 2nd expression, trackedObj.transform.parent, will be the result instead.

As we have not set an alternate origin in the SteamVR_Tracked Object Component (via the Inspector) this expression will always return the value of trackedObj.transform.parent because trackedObj.origin will always turn up empty or null.

The trackedObj.origin check is here so that this PickUp class will be future-proof should you ever choose to use SteamVR_Tracked Object in a different way in the future.

Now that we have the origin for our vector transformations, we can move on to calculate the velocities:

```
if (origin != null)
{
        rigidbody.velocity = origin.
TransformVector(myDevice.velocity) * throwMultiplier;
```

As a security measure (errors are bad, m'kay?) there is a quick null check on origin, to make sure that we actually do have an origin Transform to use.

Next, the variable rigidbody has its velocity set. The variable rigidbody contains a reference to the RigidBody Component on the object to be picked up—the controller does not have a RigidBody attached to it by default.

Calculating the velocity for the object is done by taking the velocity from myDevice (remember myDevice is a reference to an instance of SteamVR_TrackedObject) and multiplying that by the throwMultiplier. throwMultiplier is a float variable I added just to add a little boost to the strength of throws. You can set this to zero to use only the velocity of the controller, but I found that the flat velocity felt underpowered—whether that is a personal thing or because of the scale of the physics simulation I do not know—so I added this as a simple method to make us stronger in the virtual world.

The angular velocity is converted from local space to world space, to preserve how scale affects its calculations:

```
rigidbody.angularVelocity = origin.
TransformVector(myDevice.angularVelocity);
```

The actual TransformVector function, which converts the vector from local to world space, is called on the origin object. Earlier, we made sure that the origin was correct either derived from the SteamVR_Tracked Object Component or just the object's parent. This ensures that the vector we create here will be affected by the origin Transform correctly.

If that origin reference turns out to be null, we then add a fallback to the condition:

```
    }
    else
    {
        rigidbody.velocity = myDevice.velocity
* throwMultiplier;
        rigidbody.angularVelocity = myDevice.
angularVelocity;
    }
```

Both the velocity and angular velocities above are taken straight from myDevice, with no TransformVector to preserve any sort of scaling as we assume that the controller (myDevice) is the object of origin and that its Transform will affect the velocities correctly.

The final part of the velocities puzzle is to set the maximum angular velocity:

```
rigidbody.maxAngularVelocity = rigidbody.
angularVelocity.magnitude;
```

The maxAngularVelocity of the RigidBody, on the object we are picking up, is set to the magnitude of its angular velocity. I realize how confusing this is, but let's dig into it.

In the previous code block, we set the angular velocity of rigidbody. It could be less or more than the currently set maximum angular velocity setting. That would mean, on the next round of physics calculations, the angular velocity would be clamped down to the maximum amount.

To counter this, the line of code above sets the maximum angular velocity to the current angular velocity (set from the previous bit of code) so that when the next physics calculations are done it will not be clamped down slower than it should be. Again, note that this code is called from inside the FixedUpdate() function that is recommended by Unity to be used for physics-based updates. If this code was to be called from any other function, the order that Unity updates everything would come into play. As all of this happens before the physics engine does its calculations for this update, by setting the velocities, changing the maximum velocity, and also removing that FixedJoint—we get the correct result from the physics engine and we are not affected by any changing variables in between updates.

The last part of the DropObject() function resets the reference to the object held in theClosestGO:

```
        theClosestGO = null;
    }
}
```

By resetting theClosestGO, we tell this script that there is no object nearby to pick up. We are, essentially, severing all ties with the object that was just dropped. The rest of the code can then take care of re-populating the-ClosestGO as a part of its regular step. The final part of the PickUp class deals with theClosestGO and keeps an eye out for those collisions, reacting when an object is inside the controller's SphereCollider trigger area:

```
    void OnTriggerStay(Collider collision)
    {
```

OnTriggerStay is called repeatedly by the engine whenever an object is inside of the sphere. The Collider of the object entering the trigger (entering the sphere) is passed into the function for us to use.

We are doing this inside OnTriggerStay so that theClosestGO will always contain an object inside of the trigger area. As we do not want to have to move the controller all the way out of an object and back in again, to reset it after a trigger release, for example, it makes sense to keep the-ClosestGO updated with whatever is inside of the sphere on every update when OnTriggerStay is called by the engine.

```
        if (joint == null && collision.gameObject.tag
== grabbableTag)
```

```
    {
        theClosestGO = collision.gameObject;
    }
}
```

Above, we do a quick check to see whether or not joint is null (telling us that there is nothing already being held by this controller when it is null) followed by a tag check to make sure that the object is in fact one we are allowed to grab. Tags are a nice, straightforward way of identifying objects.

When the above condition is met, theClosestGO is simply set to collision.gameObject. That is; set to the GameObject of the object that entered the sphere and triggered the function to be called in the first place.

The final function in this class helps to reset theClosestGO when the current object leaves the trigger area:

```
void OnTriggerExit(Collider collision)
{
    if (joint == null && theClosestGO != null)
    {
        theClosestGO = null;
    }
}
}
```

I found—when I did not reset theClosestGO when the object left the trigger area—that objects could be held on to even when they were quite far away from the controller. By resetting theClosestGO here in the OnTriggerExit() function, we stop the reference from lingering unnecessarily and allow the rest of the code to take care of resetting theClosestGO when an OnTriggerEnter() or OnTriggerStay() occurs instead.

This PickUp class may be applied to both controllers, as seen in the example project for this section of this chapter. By setting up the tags correctly this is all you need to do to add picking up and throwing/dropping of objects to your own worlds. Just remember to set up the tags on your objects and SphereCollider Components correctly. In the next section, we will look at how to add vibration to the PickUp class for a little feedback to the user. Remember that the example project already has the feedback code in it and it has been separated here to make it easier to explain.

Adding Haptic Feedback

One of the great features of the HTC Vive controller is its ability to pro-vide haptic feedback through vibration. Having a physical event like this makes for a deeper experience, helping immersion, and providing an extra level of connectivity to the virtual world. Users feeling a real-world physical reaction to the virtual world is another way that they can interact with the virtual space.

You can highlight actions in the virtual world with a subtle vibration, and just adding a tiny effect can make a huge difference to the simulation, giving viewers a sense of density in objects, or making objects feel real. In this section, we will take the picking up and dropping example from the previous chapter and add a little vibration feedback.

In the PickUp script from the previous section, we will add in some feedback. The completed, modified PickUp.cs script in full:

```
using UnityEngine;

[RequireComponent(typeof(SteamVR_TrackedObject))]
[RequireComponent(typeof(SphereCollider))]

public class PickUp : MonoBehaviour
{
    public string grabbableTag = "GrabbableObject";

    public float throwMultiplier = 1f;
    public float grabRadius = 0.06f;

    public Rigidbody attachPoint;

    SteamVR_TrackedObject trackedObj;
    FixedJoint joint;

    private GameObject theClosestGO;
    private SteamVR_Controller.Device myDevice;

    private bool isBuzzing;
    private float buzzTime;
    private float timeToBuzz;
    private float buzzStrength;
```

```
void Awake()
{
    // grab references to things we need..
    trackedObj = GetComponent<SteamVR_TrackedObject>
();

    SphereCollider myCollider = GetComponent<Sphere
Collider>();

    // do a little set up on the sphere collider
to set the radius and make sure that it's a trigger
    myCollider.radius = grabRadius;
    myCollider.isTrigger = true;
}

void FixedUpdate()
{
    myDevice = SteamVR_Controller.Input((int)
trackedObj.index);

    // ----------------------------------------
    // PICKUP
    // ----------------------------------------
    if (joint == null && myDevice.GetTouch(SteamVR_
Controller.ButtonMask.Trigger))
    {
        PickUpObject();
    }

    // ----------------------------------------
    // DROP
    // ----------------------------------------
    if (!myDevice.GetTouch(SteamVR_Controller.
ButtonMask.Trigger))
    {
        DropObject();
    }

}

void LateUpdate()
{
    // the only thing we do in this function is to
see whether or not to make the controller buzz
```

```
        // and if we are supposed to do that, we call
TriggerHapticPulse() to make the controller buzz
        if (isBuzzing)
        {
            // increase our timer to keep a track of
buzz timing
            buzzTime += Time.deltaTime;

            // if the buzz is finished, end it below
            if (buzzTime > timeToBuzz)
            {
                isBuzzing = false;
                buzzStrength = 0;
                timeToBuzz = 0;
                buzzTime = 0;
            }

            // do the buzz!
            myDevice.TriggerHapticPulse(500);
        }
    }

    void PickUpObject()
    {
        // if we found a close object, grab it!
        if (theClosestGO != null)
        {
            joint = theClosestGO.AddComponent<Fixed
Joint>();
            joint.connectedBody = attachPoint;

            // give a little buzz to the controller to
register the pick up
            DoBuzz(1, 0.2f);
        }
    }

    void DropObject()
    {
        // this function destroys the FixedJoint
holding the object to the controller and resets
theClosestGO
        if (joint != null)
        {
```

```
            // if we already have grabbed something,
we keep it locked to the controller
            var go = joint.gameObject;
            var rigidbody = go.GetComponent<Rigidbody>
();

            DestroyImmediate(joint);
            joint = null;


            var origin = trackedObj.origin ?
trackedObj.origin : trackedObj.transform.parent;
            if (origin != null)
            {
                rigidbody.velocity = origin.
TransformVector(myDevice.velocity) * throwMultiplier;
                rigidbody.angularVelocity = origin.
TransformVector(myDevice.angularVelocity);
            }
            else
            {
                rigidbody.velocity = myDevice.velocity
* throwMultiplier;
                rigidbody.angularVelocity = myDevice.
angularVelocity;
            }


            // make sure that our max velocity is not
less than the speed of the controller (we want the
object to
            // match the velocity of the controller,
right?)
            rigidbody.maxAngularVelocity = rigidbody.
angularVelocity.magnitude;
            // reset the reference in theClosestGO
            theClosestGO = null;
        }
    }


    void OnTriggerStay(Collider collision)
    {
        // if the controller is inside an object, we
still want to be able to grab it so we keep theClosest
GO set OnTriggerStay
```

```
        if (joint == null && (collision.gameObject.tag ==
grabbableTag))
        {
            theClosestGO = collision.gameObject;
        }
    }

    void OnTriggerExit(Collider collision)
    {
        // before removing this from the 'possible to
grab' theClosestGO var, we check that it is the
current one
        if (joint == null && theClosestGO != null)
        {
            theClosestGO = null;
        }
    }

    void DoBuzz(float strength, float time)
    {
        timeToBuzz = time;
        buzzStrength = strength;
        isBuzzing = true;
    }
}
```

Modifying the PickUp Class to Include Feedback
For vibration, we add a few extra variables to the start of the script:

```
private bool isBuzzing;
private float buzzTime;
private float timeToBuzz;
private float buzzStrength;
private float targetBuzzStrength;
```

I will explain the variables as we work through the rest of the code. The next addition to the PickUp class is a LateUpdate() function. LateUpdate() is called automatically by the game engine at the end of each update cycle and we tap into it here to keep tabs on whether or not any controller vibration should be happening.

To make the controller buzz, we need to access the TriggerHapticPulse() function inside an instance of the SteamVR_Controller.Input class.

We hold a reference to the instance for this controller, in the variable named theDevice. The TriggerHapticPulse() function, in this code, takes a single parameter in microseconds. That is, in millionths of a second. The function is designed to be called repeatedly for the duration of the vibration you want to make, which complicates the code a little bit because we need to build our own timer system. That is what we do here in the LateUpdate() function:

```
void LateUpdate()
    {
        if (isBuzzing)
        {
```

The isBuzzing variable is a Boolean that will be set to true whenever we want the controller to vibrate. You will see where it is set in the DoBuzz() function further down in the script, but for now just accept that it will be true only when we need to vibrate.

```
            // increase our timer to keep a track of
buzz timing
            buzzTime += Time.deltaTime;
```

My timer code works by adding the deltaTime (i.e., the time between this and the previous frame) to a variable named buzzTime. This only gets added whenever isBuzzing is true, which means it acts as a clock that we can then check against to see how long the buzzing has been going on:

```
            // if the buzz is finished, end it below
            if (buzzTime > timeToBuzz)
            {
                isBuzzing = false;
                buzzStrength = 0;
                timeToBuzz = 0;
                buzzTime = 0;
            }
```

timeToBuzz is set in another function (DoBuzz() further down in the code) and contains the amount of time we want the vibration to go on for. Above, we compare our timer buzzTime to timeToBuzz to know when the buzz should end. If more time has elapsed than that shown in timeToBuzz, isBuzzing is set to false and the other values we use for vibration are zeroed.

Finally, it is time to make a buzz:

```
        myDevice.TriggerHapticPulse(500);
    }
}
```

myDevice contains a function named TriggerHapticPulse(). I briefly mentioned this at the start of the section, so that you would understand why we were building a timer system. That is, TriggerHapticPulse() takes a single parameter in microseconds—millionths of a second. As we are going to be repeatedly calling this each LateUpdate() until our timer reaches timeToBuzz, I have set the amount of time to an arbitrary number of 500. This should be enough of a vibration to tide us over until the next time it is called, but if you see any issues with the severity or frequency of the pulse you can always come back here and experiment with different values if you like.

Right at the bottom of the class is now a function named DoBuzz(). This is here just to provide an easy way to set the variables that make our vibrations happen:

```
void DoBuzz(float strength, float time)
{
    timeToBuzz = time;
    buzzStrength = strength;

    isBuzzing = true;
}
```

The above function makes it nice and easy to make the controller vibrate when we need it to. Instead of messing around with the variables each time, we can just cause a vibration by calling DoBuzz(<strength of vibration>, <duration in seconds>).

USING THE SteamVR INTERACTION SYSTEM FOR USER INTERFACE

After version 1.2 of the SteamVR library, Valve provides an amazing way to work with the Vive controllers and gives us all the source code to do it with. In this section, we will build a very simple interface with Unity's GUI system and then set it up to use the Interaction System so that you can use the interface with the Vive controllers. Nothing fancy; just basics.

Create a New Project and Import SteamVR

Make a new Unity project and import the SteamVR libraries the same way we did back in Chapter 3.

Create a New Scene and Add a Player Prefab

Create a new Scene via the menu File > New Scene.

In the Hierarchy, find the Camera and right click on it to bring up the GameObject menu. Choose Delete to get rid of it.

In the Project browser, find the folder SteamVR/InteractionSystem/Core/Prefabs. Inside that Prefabs folder you should find an object named Player.

Drag the Player prefab out of the Project browser and drop it into the Hierarchy.

Make a Simple UI Canvas and Button to Try Out

Right click in an empty space in the Hierarchy and choose UI > Canvas. The Canvas needs a little set up (Figure 9.4). With the Canvas highlighted in the Hierarchy, set the following properties in the Inspector:

X: −0.93

Y: 1.2

Z: 0.96

Width: 1

Height: 1

Pivot X: 0.5

Pivot Y: 0.5

Rotation:

X: 0

Y: −45

Z: 0

Right click Canvas in the Hierarchy and choose UI > Button. The button will appear, but most likely absolutely huge! We need fire up the shrink

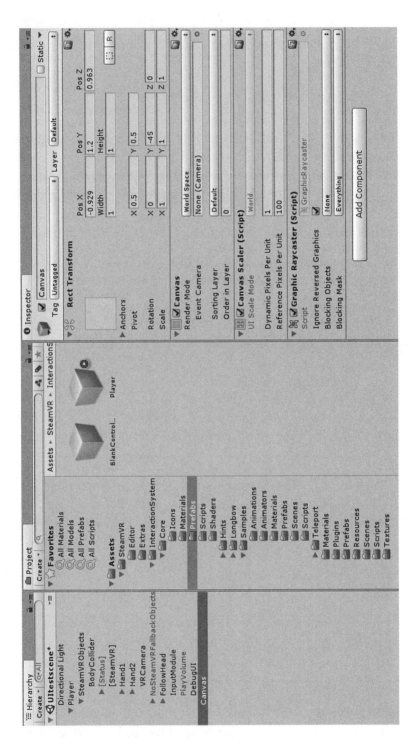

FIGURE 9.4   The Canvas is set to World Space so that it shows up in VR.

ray and fix that. OK, there is no shrink ray but we need to change the button scale properties in the Inspector.

Click the Button to highlight it, then over in the Inspector enter the following values into its Transform Component, in the Scale section:

X: 0.005

Y: 0.005

Z: 0.005

The button should shrink down to a more reasonable size, now.

To work with the Interaction System, the button will need an extra Component. In the Inspector, scroll down so that you can see the Add Component button.

Click Add Component and from the menu, choose Scripts > Valve.VR. InteractionSystem > Interactable.

The SteamVR system will use Unity's collision system to find out when the controller is near to, or intersecting, with the button. In order for that to happen, the button will need a standard Unity Collider adding to it.

Click Add Component again, from the menu choose Physics > Box Collider.

In the Inspector, find the Box Collider Component and change its Size properties:

X: 160

Y: 30

Z: 30

In the Scene panel, you should see that the Box Collider now surrounds the button. The area covered by the Box Collider will be the area that activates the button whenever the controller is within it.

To make the effect of the button obvious, we should change the highlight color to something darker. Right now, by default, it will likely be set to white. Find the Button Component in the Inspector and click the box next to Highlight Color. Choose a nice darker color from the color picker, like a nice red.

Try It Out in VR

Press Play in the Unity editor, switch on your Vive controllers, and make your way over to the button. Hold out a Vive controller so that it is inside the Box Collider area and the button should highlight in the color you chose from the Inspector.

This is how easy it is to work with standard Unity UI Components and SteamVR! You can build UI in exactly the same way as you might in a regular Unity game. As long as you add the Interactable Component and a Box Collider, the Interaction System will take care of triggering Unity's UI standard functions in a regular way.

USING VIVE CONTROLLERS FOR TELEPORTING AROUND THE VIRTUAL WORLD

As of version 1.2.0, the SteamVR Unity package contains everything you need to add teleportation to your game using the controllers, complete with a nice graphical arc to show the location of the teleport, as well as a cool overlay that shows where it is possible to teleport to. As if that wasn't enough, they also take care of input (press the top of the touch pad) and include nice teleport sound effects!

Create a New Project and Import SteamVR

Make a new project in Unity and import SteamVR libraries (see Chapter 3 for full instructions on that).

Create a New Scene and Add a Player Prefab

Create a new Scene via the menu File > New Scene.

In the Hierarchy, find the Camera and right click on it to bring up the GameObject menu. Choose Delete to get rid of it.

In the Project browser, find the folder SteamVR/InteractionSystem/ Core/Prefabs. Inside that Prefabs folder you should find an object named Player. The Player prefab is an alternative to the [CameraRig] set up you have seen elsewhere in this book. The Player rig contains not just a SteamVR camera but Vive-specific Components to help jumpstart your virtual world interactions.

Drag the Player prefab out of the Project browser and drop it into the Hierarchy. You may recall from the previous section ("Using the SteamVR Interaction System for UI") that the Player prefab is a replacement for the [CameraRig] set up we have used elsewhere in this book. We need to use this set up to be able to use the teleporting system the way that the makers of SteamVR intended.

Now that we have the player rig, we need to add in the code to allow teleportation. In the Project browser, find the folder SteamVR/ InteractionSystem/Teleport/Prefabs.

In that Prefabs folder, click and drag the Teleporting prefab out of the Project browser and into an empty space in the Hierarchy so that it gets added to the Scene.

Perhaps surprisingly, that is all we need to do to enable teleportation with the Vive controllers. The next step is to tell the teleportation system where we will be allowed to teleport to.

Right click in an empty space in the Hierarchy, to bring up the menu. Choose 3D Object > Plane from the menu.

In the Hierarchy, you should see the new Plane GameObject appear. Click on Plane to highlight it, then over in the Inspector click the Add Component button.

From the Component menu, choose Scripts > Valve.VR.Interaction System > Teleport Area.

The Teleport Area Component will take care of changing the plane and telling SteamVR that we can use it to determine that it is an area capable of being used by the teleporter. It will also hide the plane and change how it is displayed in the Scene during playback. For that reason, when you use this system in your own virtual worlds, you should add planes that are completely separate to your world geometry to preserve it.

Essentially, we are good to go. That said, when I built this example I added in a few cubes here and there so that I had a few visual reference points in the Scene to move around.

Add in a cube to the Scene. That is, right click on an empty space in the Hierarchy and choose 3D Object > Cube.

Click the new Cube GameObject in the Hierarchy. In the Inspector, change the position values in the Transform section to:

Position:

X: 3.14

Y:

Z:

Beam Yourself Up!

Grab your controllers and headset and give this a go. Inside, you can press the touch pad to show the teleport arc. When it is pointing to a safe teleport point, it will be shown in green and when it points to an area not allowed for teleporting the arc will show up in red. Try pointing at the side of the cube, then down to the ground, to see the differences between the arc graphic on allowed and disallowed teleport areas. The teleportation script will automatically take into account any standard Unity Colliders that might be in the way, and you will not be allowed to teleport on top of, or inside, any obstacles.

RECAP

In this chapter, we looked at one way to use the Vive controllers. We looked at picking up and moving objects around, building a re-usable picking up and drop class. Then, we went on to see how to use the haptic feedback system to help add a little more physical interaction to the experience. After that, we looked through using the SteamVR Interaction System to have Vive controllers operate standard Unity UI. In the final section, it was the SteamVR teleportation system we got to work with.

There is much more you can do with the controllers from here, and we have only just scratched the surface of what these controllers can do. Using the principles outlined in this chapter, you should be able to go on and start to make controls that are not only easy-to-use, but fit seamlessly into your virtual worlds. Whether you change the controller images to look like hands, blasters, or anything else—keep experience immersion and presence in the back of your mind and you should not go far wrong.

CHAPTER **10**

Using Hands for Input Systems

T HERE ARE A FEW developing solutions for using your hands as control systems in the virtual world.

LEAP MOTION VR

The Leap Motion is a device to bring hands and gesture control to computers. As VR began to grow in popularity in tandem with its development, more and more developers found themselves trying to get Leap working with VR to use as an input method. It was not long before the lovely folks at Leap Motion started solving the problems themselves, firstly by allowing the device to work in a "face-forward" orientation suitable for VR and then building their own library of code to help developers with interactivity.

In this section, we will grab the example project and add the right Leap-related libraries to it, to make it work. The example project is a simple piano keyboard (Figure 10.1) that you can play with your hands. There is nothing particularly complicated about this, but we will take a quick look at the script which detects the key press and plays the sound, with the main focus remaining on adding the libraries to get up and running quickly with Leap Motion.

Early hand-based interaction with virtual objects was cumbersome and somewhat difficult, as developers tried to mix simulation physics with human expectation. For example, pushing against an object on the ground, to get a grip on it, only works when the object actually exists.

215

FIGURE 10.1   The Leap Motion piano example.

Doing this in the virtual world normally ends up with the object getting pushed into the ground mesh, often ending up with the object getting catapulted off into the distance as the physics engine attempts to correct the collision. Another example might be grabbing an object tighter to pick it up, causing fingers to actually enter the object in the virtual world, and again causing unforeseen physics consequences.

Leap Motion became aware of this and are solving these problems in a really intelligent way. Leap now have their own library designed exclusively for Leap Motion, called the Interaction Engine. Interaction Engine is a layer that exists between Unity and real-world hand physics. To make object interactions work in a way that satisfies human expectations, it implements an alternate set of physics rules that take over when your hands are embedded inside a virtual object. The results would be impossible in reality, but they feel much more satisfying and easy to use.

The Leap Motion VR Mount Kit

Although you can do the same job with a USB extension cable and some tack, the Universal VR Mount is the best way to attach a Leap device to your headset (Figure 10.2). The Leap Motion VR Mount Kit contains a USB 2.0 cable suitable for extending Leap Motion's possible distance from the PC to around 15′. It also contains a nice, curved mount track piece, and some custom 3M adhesive to stick it safely to your headset.

When I tried the DIY tack approach, the device kept falling off my headset and I ended up trying to hold it in my mouth. This is both dangerous and extremely silly-looking (as if we do not already look silly enough in our headsets) so I do not recommend it at all. The Leap Motion is a great device but I can tell you that it does not taste all that nice. If you can, order a Universal VR Mount from Leap, instead.

FIGURE 10.2   The VR mount kit provides a stable solution for attaching the Leap Motion device to a VR headset.

Downloading Leap Motion Orion Drivers and Software

To start the journey, you need to download the Leap Motion Orion software. This is an alternative software set from the original desktop-based Leap Motion—if you have the desktop software already installed, it may be a good idea to uninstall it before going ahead.

Head to https://developer.leapmotion.com/get-started and hit the green download button. When this has finished downloading, run the installer. This should install the necessary drivers and the Leap Motion control panel app that will sit in the taskbar to show the current status of the device and give you instant access to configuration and so on. Plug in your Leap Motion's USB cable. This software will take care of the Leap device and the change in orientation once it is mounted to the front of your headset. After successful setup, you should see a new icon in the Windows taskbar, which looks like a little green leap device.

Connect the Headset and Try Out the Visualizer

Hook up the Leap Motion to your headset (using tack or the Universal VR Mount—whichever) and right click on the new Leap icon in the Windows Taskbar. Choose Visualizer from the menu. The first time you try this out, it makes for a pretty crazy experience. The Leap Motion device works like a camera mounted to the front of the VR headset. Hold out your hands in front of the headset, so that you can see them in your camera view. Within seconds, a skeleton arm and hand should appear overlaid on top of the camera feed (Figure 10.3). This is what Leap Motion is tracking.

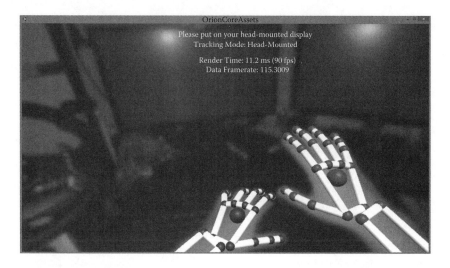

FIGURE 10.3   The Leap Motion visualizer shows the view from the Leap and any hands being tracked.

Now you can pretend you have those Mechanoid hands you may have always dreamed of!

Once you have had a good play around with the visualizer (I found this demo kept me amused for much longer than it probably should have) we can go ahead and download the Unity libraries needed to develop with.

Download Leap Motion Unity Packages

Leap Motion provides a whole bunch of assets and code examples for us to play around with. For this project example, we will use the Leap Motion Interaction Engine and the Hands Module (just for fun).

To be able to use the device, forward-facing from the headset, we need to grab the Unity Assets for Leap Motion Orion from https://developer. leapmotion.com/unity—look for the large green Download Unity Core Assets button. This is what you need to talk to the device, but the Interaction Engine is a separate library of code designed to make interactions easier.

Grab the Leap Motion Interaction Engine files from the Add-on Modules section below the main download button link. Scroll down to find Leap Motion Interaction Engine and download the file.

Setting Up the Unity Project for Interaction Engine and Leap Motion

Open Unity. Find and open up the example project for this section of this chapter. Find the Unity Assets for Leap Motion Orion SDK you downloaded in the previous section. The file is a .unitypackage format file containing all you need, and when you double click on it Unity should go ahead and extract the files straight into your project for you. It will ask for confirmation in Unity, so hit OK and let Unity import.

Next, find the Leap Motion Interaction Engine .unitypackage and double click that file, too, so that Unity extracts it into your project. With both of the unitypackage files imported, your project contains everything Leap Motion needs to work but we still need to grab the SteamVR libraries.

Note that also on the developer.leapmotion.com/unity page, in that add-on packages section, are some cool extras such as hands and touch UI prefabs. Well worth exploring for future projects!

Import the SteamVR package from the Unity Asset Store. If you have already downloaded SteamVR from the asset store, you will only need to re-download it when Valve updates the files, you delete them manually from Unity's cache folder or you reinstall your system and wipe out the files. Unity should just grab them from your hard drive and import them without re-downloading. After the confirm box, let Unity import them and we are ready to get to work.

Hands-On in the Virtual World

Open the example scene. Adding the Leap Motion hands to the Vive camera rig can be done relatively quickly and painlessly. The LMHeadMountedRig prefab, provided as part of the Leap Motion libraries, contains everything you need to add hand support to your simulation, but it is set up with the assumption that you will be using Unity's built-in support for VR rather than the SteamVR library. We have a small amount of work to do to get it to play nice with SteamVR's camera rig.

Find the SteamVR folder in the Project browser, open it up and look inside the Prefabs folder. Drag the [CameraRig] prefab out of the SteamVR > Projects folder and into an empty space in the Hierarchy, to add [CameraRig] to the current Scene.

In the Hierarchy, find the little arrow next to [CameraRig] and hold the ALT key on the keyboard as you click the arrow. This should expand out all of the child objects under that main [CameraRig] GameObject (Figure 10.4). Normally, when you click on the arrow it will only expand to show the level below—holding down ALT unfolds everything below it. Find the Camera (head) GameObject.

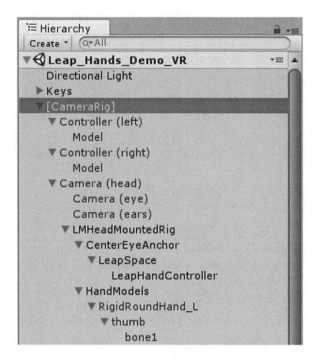

FIGURE 10.4   ALT + Click on the expand arrow to expand all levels below the GameObject.

Find the Leap Motion > Prefabs folder and drag the LMHeadMountedRig prefab into the Scene, but drop it on top of the Camera (head) object so that LMHeadMountedRig becomes a child of Camera (head).

Next, expand LMHeadMountedRig out to show its child object CenterEyeAnchor. We need to remove the Audio Listener, as SteamVR will be dealing with the audio listening. Click CenterEyeAnchor and, over in the Inspector, look for the Audio Listener Component. Right click Audio Listener and choose Remove Component.

Next, we need to do the same to remove the Camera Component, since SteamVR will be dealing with cameras, too. Right click Camera in the Inspector and choose Remove Component.

The piano itself is already in the Scene, so you should now be able to put on your headset and hit Play to try out the Scene in VR.

That was everything you needed to do to set up Leap Motion for VR, but in the next section we will take a look at how those piano keys are detecting the finger hits.

Programming to React to Piano Key Presses

In the example, the hands that Leap Motion uses are made up of a rigged model (rigged in a similar fashion to how a regular character model would be constructed), Rigidbodies and Colliders. The Colliders move around when you move your fingers, providing collisions between your fingers and the virtual world. As they are regular Collider Components, other Rigidbodies will react to the collisions and we can use standard Unity functions to detect intersections such as OnTriggerEnter, OnTriggerStay, and OnTriggerExit.

For the piano example, I chose to use OnTriggerEnter so that there would be no issues with fingers pushing or moving the gameObjects we use for keys.

The complete script for the piano key behavior looks like this:

```
using UnityEngine;

using System.Collections;

[RequireComponent (typeof(AudioSource))]

public class KeyTrigger : MonoBehaviour {

    private bool locked;
    private AudioSource mySrc;
    private Transform myTR;

    void Start()
    {
        mySrc = GetComponent<AudioSource>();
        myTR = GetComponent<Transform>();
    }

    void Update()
    {
        Vector3 tempVEC = myTR.localPosition;
        if(mySrc.isPlaying)
        {
            tempVEC.y = -0.4f;
        } else
        {
            tempVEC.y = 0;
        }
```

```
        myTR.localPosition = tempVEC;
    }

    void OnTriggerEnter ( Collider collision )
    {
        if ( locked )
            return;

        mySrc.Play();
        locked = true;
        CancelInvoke("Unlock");
        Invoke("Unlock", 0.25f);
    }

    void OnTriggerStay(Collider collision)
    {
        if ( !mySrc.isPlaying )
        {
            mySrc.Play();
            locked = true;
        }
    }

    void Unlock()
    {
        locked = false;
    }

}
```

Script Breakdown

The script begins with:

```
using UnityEngine;
using System.Collections;

[RequireComponent (typeof(AudioSource))]
```

Above, the standard Unity packages followed by a RequireComponent statement. RequireComponent checks that the GameObject this script is attached to will have an AudioSource Component attached to it. If one is not already attached, it will be added automatically.

Next up, we start the class itself:

```
public class KeyTrigger : MonoBehaviour {

    private bool locked;
    private AudioSource mySrc;
    private Transform myTR;

    void Start()
    {
        mySrc = GetComponent<AudioSource>();
        myTR = GetComponent<Transform>();
    }
```

Three variables to hold a reference to the AudioSource, a reference to the Transform Component and a Boolean type variable to keep a tab as to whether or not the key is locked. We lock the key for a short time after a press, to avoid repeat calls when the hand or finger stays within the collider trigger area.

The Start() function just sets up those references, using GetComponent to find the AudioSource and Transform Components attached to the same GameObject as this script.

Next, the Update() function—quick reminder: Update() is called automatically by Unity every frame:

```
    void Update()
    {
        Vector3 tempVEC = myTR.localPosition;
        if (mySrc.isPlaying)
        {
            tempVEC.y = -0.4f;
        } else
        {
            tempVEC.y = 0;
        }
        myTR.localPosition = tempVEC;
    }
```

What happens in Update() is that the key's localPosition is updated so that it looks like the key has been pressed down whenever its audio is playing.

tempVEC holds the localPosition, taken from our Transform cached in myTR. Since you cannot set x, y, or z values directly we need to grab the whole vector then modify it and copy the values back into the Transform Component at the end of the function.

The condition asks is mySrc (the AudioSource) reports that its .isPlaying property is true. isPlaying will return true whenever the AudioSource is playing its audio clip. If isPlaying is true, we set the .y of tempVEC to −0.4f. This is just an arbitrary value I came up with through trial and error. Setting the y of the key's localPosition to −0.4 will make it look as though the key has been pressed down.

The above condition continues on with an else statement—whenever isPlaying is not true—where the .y of tempVEC is set to 0. This will put the key back at its original y position, making it look as though the key has moved back up after being pressed.

After the conditional statement, the Transform (myTR) gets its localPosition updated to tempVEC, to reflect the changes we made to its y position.

To actually detect the hit between the hand and the key, we use OnTriggerEnter:

```
void OnTriggerEnter ( Collider collision )
{
    if ( locked )
        return;
```

When the isTrigger property is checked, on a Collider Component (such as a Box Collider, Sphere Collider, or similar), the Unity engine will automatically call functions that we can tap into, to tell when a Collider enters the trigger area. Above, we catch the call that will be made when a Collider first enters the trigger area. The engine passes in some information about the collision, too, in the form of a Collider type parameter. We do not actually use this information, but we need to make sure that the function matches the format that Unity is expecting to find, otherwise Unity may throw an error.

When the hand first enters the trigger area, the first thing we need to do is make sure that the key is not locked already. In the code above, we start with that—by checking to see if locked is true. If locked is true, we just drop right out of the function without running any more code, with the return statement.

Since we now know that our key is not locked, the next part of the code can get on and start the audio playing:

```
mySrc.Play();
locked = true;
```

You will probably remember that mySrc contains a reference to the AudioSource attached to the same GameObject as this script. In the Scene, I have already set the audio clip that the AudioSource Component will use, via the Inspector. Each key plays a different sound sample containing a different piano note. The first version I made only used a single sound and I attempted to set the pitch to change the note. By the time I had driven myself completely bonkers adjusting the pitch up and down to try and get the notes in key, I figured doing it this way (with one sound sample per note) would just be much faster and probably sound better in the long run, too, since there would be no speed change. To play the audio, it is just a simple call to the AudioSource's Play() function.

After the sound starts, we set locked to true to stop repeat calls getting through without a small amount of time. To unlock the key, we just need to set locked to false a little later on. This happens in a function in the same class, named Unlock, which we call next via the Invoke command:

```
    CancelInvoke("Unlock");
    Invoke("Unlock", 0.25f);
}
```

In the code above, you may wonder why I am calling CancelInvoke when there should be little or no chance of duplicate Unlock calls based on the status of the variable locked—it is pure force of habit. I prefer to use CancelInvoke before any Invoke statement when I know that I only ever want a single call to be scheduled. It is there purely for safety and I am aware that it may be unnecessary, at this point. I use the phrase "at this point" because future-proofing code is always a good idea. By covering this Invoke statement, I know that in the future the way this function might change but the way Invoke is called here should always be safe.

The actual schedule call is the last part of the OnTriggerEnter() function above. Invoke takes two parameters, first the function we want to call and then the time in seconds when it should be called. When another

Collider enters the trigger, that statement schedules the Unlock() function to be called 0.25 seconds later.

As well as catching trigger enter calls, we keep the audio going (looping) if the collision continues. An ongoing collision will cause OnTriggerStay to be called each update:

```
void OnTriggerStay(Collider collision)
{
    if ( !mySrc.isPlaying )
    {
        mySrc.Play();
        locked = true;
    }
}
```

If the trigger continues to intersect with another Collider (a finger is pressing the key down) then we only want to react if the audio has stopped. If audio is stopped, we just need to call.Play() on the AudioSource to get it going again.

We start the code block above with a check to see if the .isPlaying property of mySrc is false. If it is false, mySrc.Play() will restart the audio. Also inside that same condition, locked is reset to true.

The final part of the class deals with unlocking the key:

```
void Unlock()
{
    locked = false;
}

}
```

Above, the Unlock() function just sets locked to false. You may recall that Unlock is called after being scheduled by the Invoke function earlier in the class.

Potential Issues

The only issue I saw was dealing with the smallest objects not firing Trigger functions—Unity 5.4 appears to not like it when two colliders are extremely small and may not register. Hopefully this will be addressed in future versions—it is also hard to know where the bug comes from. It could be the finger colliders, Unity libraries, or PhysX—there are a lot of places where the problem could be happening. If you experience any sorts of problems and you need to use Triggers, you may need to make objects a bit bigger for the collisions to register correctly.

If you are having tracking issues, find the Leap Motion taskbar icon and use the Visualizer to make sure that everything is working correctly outside of Unity. You may need to re-calibrate the device, which can also be done through the Leap Motion taskbar app.

NOITOM PERCEPTION NEURON MOCAP

Perception Neuron is cutting-edge motion capture technology using individual sensors called Neurons. The Neuron houses an Inertial Measurement Unity (IMU) with a gyroscope, accelerometer, and magnetometer. Neurons are placed around the body in areas that need to have motions captured, such as on legs, arms, or fingers, then the input is sent via either WiFi or USB to the PC.

The Perception Neuron appeared on the crowd-funding site Kickstarter back in August, 2014. Fast-forward to 2016 and the Perception Neuron motion capture suit has been widely adopted in the 3D animation industry as a low-cost, high-quality method for capturing movement for 3D animation. As VR is sweeping the tech world, some developers are looking at the Neuron system as an input method for VR. Noitom, aware of the potential, are also working on something called Project Fingertip. Certainly worth keeping an eye on this space to see where it leads.

What we can cover here in this section, in terms of hand tracking, is relatively simple. Full room-scale tracking of a Neuron based glove is beyond the scope of this chapter because it calls for some very complex translations due to the differences in orientation of the capture versus orientation of the headset in the virtual world. The example I present here is just a very simple method of getting live input into Unity to get the ball rolling. Later in this chapter, I will also look at using a full body suit but only theoretically, to demonstrate what it should take to get working and one approach to doing so, not a final solution.

Installation and Downloads
Install Axis Neuron

Download the Axis Neuron Standard download from https://neuronmocap.com/downloads.

This contains an application named Axis Neuron that you will use to get your PC to talk to the hardware.

Set Up the Motion Capture Suit

The set up procedure will vary depending on how many Neurons you have. You can use just a few or many, depending on how much of the body you want to capture motion from. Having a complete motion capture suit is the ideal situation so that you can move an entire avatar around, but for the demonstration here I will be using a single hand for a simple demonstration in this book.

Neurons are provided inside a special container to protect them both from physical damage and magnetization. Always keep Neurons well away from strong magnetism and/or magnetic fields. If they are magnetized, it is possible for Neurons to be de-magnetized and recalibrated, but it is certainly something to try to avoid (Figure 10.5).

Suiting Up   Perception Neuron can work with either WiFi or USB. For USB mode, there is a USB port on the top of the Hub that should be connected to your PC via a USB cable. The lower USB port on the Hub is only for power. On the bottom of the Hub is a small plug to connect the main cable into your suit.

The Hub has a small belt clip on the back. Use this to attach the Hub to your belt, or a similarly located area.

FIGURE 10.5 Perception Neuron. The Neurons must be treated with extreme care when they are outside of the protective carrying case.

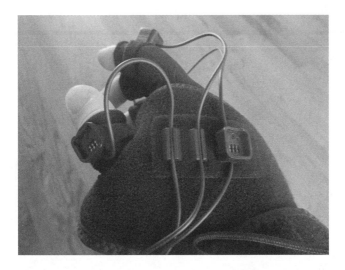

FIGURE 10.6   The Neurons slot into their small housing at various points along the suit or glove.

Plug the Neurons into the glove (Figure 10.6) and body straps.

Once the suit is all up and ready to go, connect the Hub to your computer via USB cable and start the Axis Neuron software.

Open Axis Neuron   The main Axis Neuron interface will show a skeleton when connected, or an empty environment if the connection is not yet made (Figure 10.7). The Axis Neuron application is used for motion

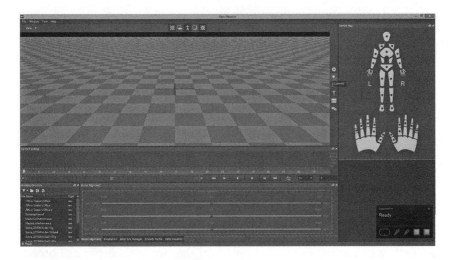

FIGURE 10.7   The Axis Neuron main interface.

FIGURE 10.8   The Axis Neuron configuration toolbar.

capture, but we need to set it up so that Unity will be able to tap into the input from the hardware.

The application must be connected to the hardware first. To connect to the hardware, click the Connect button from the configuration toolbar icons to the right of the main window (Figure 10.8). Note that all of the icons have tooltips; if you are unsure as to what any of the icons are for, hover the mouse over it for 2 seconds and a tooltip should appear to tell you what it is.

Once a connection is established, you should see a skeleton in the main window. It may move with you, but you will need to go through calibration next to make sure it is correctly aligned with your movements.

In Axis Neuron, go to the Skeleton icon on the configuration toolbar to the right of the main window. Click it to show the calibration window. If you have calibrated the system already, you may not need to calibrate every time you start the application as it stores the last set up. Try out the skeleton preview. Move around a little, flex, and see how it looks. If you try out the skeleton preview and it looks okay, there is no reason to re-calibrate. It is only if you see faults or misalignments in any of the motions that you need to go ahead with recalibration. That said, for absolute accuracy you should calibrate often to account for any magnetic interference or changes in the Neurons.

Next, we need to tell the Axis Neuron that we want it to send broadcast data that Unity can pick up on. Click on File > Settings. Click the

Broadcasting section on the left of the window. Find the BVH section and check the box labeled Enable. The other settings should be okay in their default state. Close the Settings window, but leave Axis Neuron open in the background. The Axis Neuron application will talk to the Neurons and relay the information into a real-time data stream that Unity will read into. We need to keep Axis Neuron open for the motion capture data to transfer into our virtual world.

Play with the Example Project

In the example project for this chapter, I have included a few little buttons to press. The rotation is locked, so it is similar to being inside a vehicle with a robot arm, but it is a fun little example all the same.

The way it works is that I have attached a small cube (Figure 10.9) to the index finger of the right arm.

When the cube's Collider enters the button, the button script detects it and spawns an object. It is a really simple example, but you can see how easy it would be to expand this out and add interactivity to more parts of the body.

The camera rig is not ideal, as the arm is disconnected, but if you have a full Perception Neuron suit you could easily track the entire body. In the next section, I will show you how I set up the camera in an empty project.

Set Up a Unity Project

Make sure that you have Steam running in the background along with SteamVR. You can start SteamVR from inside the Steam client at any time by clicking on the VR icon on the top right.

If you have not already downloaded the Perception Neuron Unity SDK, grab that now from https://neuronmocap.com/software/unity-sdk.

Open up Unity and create a new project (call it whatever it you like—NeuronTest perhaps—it is not too important as long as you can remember what you called it!).

Extract the Perception Neuron.zip SDK file into a folder you can find easily, then open it up in a Windows file browser. Inside, there should be a file named PerceptionNeuronUnityIntegration.unitypackage. Double click this file and Unity should attempt to open it.

You should then see a number of folders in the Project browser in Unity. Find the Scenes folder and double click the TestNeuron Scene it contains.

The Scene view should show two skeletons. Press Play in Unity to preview the scene. You should see the skeleton match your motions.

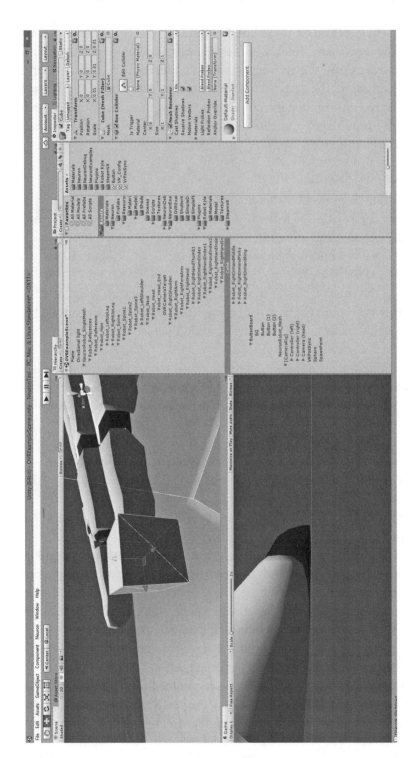

FIGURE 10.9   A small cube, attached to the index finger, acts as a trigger to activate buttons.

Once you are done playing with the skeletons, we need to download and install the SteamVR libraries from the Unity Asset Store.

Click the menu Window > Asset Store and type SteamVR into the search bar. Click the SteamVR item that appears in the search results, then download it, and Import the SteamVR library into the project. When the SteamVR settings window pops up to tell you that some settings need changing (as it always does!) click the Accept All button.

In the Project browser, find the folder NeuronExamples > OVRExample and open up the Scene named OVRExampleScene. It is intended to be used with a specific HMD but we can modify it to work with SteamVR.

First, delete Camera from the Scene. In the Project browser, inside SteamVR > Prefabs find the [CameraRig] prefab and drag it into an empty space in the Hierarchy.

Select [CameraRig] in the Hierarchy so that you can see it in the Inspector. Click the Add Component button and add Scripts > Neuron OVR Adapter. This script Component will position the camera rig at the location of a Transform positioned at the head of the robot.

Type OVRCameraTarget into the search bar at the top of the Hierarchy. This should show the OVRCameraTarget GameObject so that you can drag it out of the Hierarchy and into the Inspector's Bind Transform field, in the Neuron OVR Adapter Component.

The final piece of the puzzle here is to use the VR_Config class you may have seen elsewhere in this book. The VR_Config class tells SteamVR to use its Sitting tracking configuration so that the Camera can be positioned correctly. It also provides a button to reset the view. Press R on the keyboard to tell SteamVR where your idle/sitting position is. In this demo, the reset view button may be the biggest help for Vive users to make sure that your HMD is aligned with the robot.

With [CameraRig] selected in the Heirarchy, click Add Component and either add the VR_Config script to the [CameraRig] GameObject if you have it from previous examples, or add the following script as a new one (Add Component > New Script, and name it VR_Config):

```
using UnityEngine;
using System.Collections;
using Valve.VR;

public class VR_Config : MonoBehaviour
{
```

```
public enum roomTypes { standing, sitting };
public roomTypes theRoomType;

void Awake()
{
    SetUpVR();
}

void SetUpVR()
{
    SetUpRoom();
}

  void SetUpRoom()
{
    var render = SteamVR_Render.instance;

    if (theRoomType == roomTypes.standing)
    {
        render.trackingSpace =
ETrackingUniverseOrigin.TrackingUniverseStanding;
    }
    else
    {
        render.trackingSpace =
ETrackingUniverseOrigin.TrackingUniverseSeated;
    }
    Recenter();
}

void LateUpdate()
{
    // here, we check for a keypress to reset the
view
    // whenever the mode is sitting .. don't
forget to set this up in Input Manager
    if (theRoomType == roomTypes.sitting)
    {
        if (Input.GetKeyUp(KeyCode.R))
        {
            Recenter();
        }
    }
}
```

```
void Recenter()
{

    // reset the position
    var system = OpenVR.System;
    if (system != null)
    {
        system.ResetSeatedZeroPose();
    }
}
}
```

Save the script (CTRL + S) and return to Unity. With the script attached to [Camera Rig] you can now set it up in the Inspector. Choose The Room Type dropdown and choose Sitting.

Grab your headset and glove, then hit Play to preview the scene and try it out.

At the moment, the biggest issue is keeping the headset in the correct position to make the arm movements seem natural. With a fixed camera, this is possible, but due to the way that Axis Neuron captures the data in a pre-calibrated direction we are unable to move around with just an arm. A better solution would be to use an entire body suit, so that you can move around and do it the other way—locking the camera to the body suit, instead.

Using a Full Body Perception Neuron Motion Capture Suit

The code in this section is sort of theoretical, in that I have been informed it works, but it is not something I have been able to test personally. At the very least, the concept is here. What it should do is to lock the camera to the head of the skeleton. It moves the skeleton around with the camera. The body rotation should match up with that of the Perception Neuron suit if motion capture has been calibrated correctly.

In the Scene from the previous section, click the Create button at the top of the Hierarchy and choose Create Empty to add an empty GameObject. Rename it to BodyPos. With the new empty object selected, click Add Component in the Inspector and choose New Script. Name the script BodyPos. Thanks to the user kkostenkov for posting his original VRPosSync script on the Perception Neuron forum.

Add this script:

```
using UnityEngine;
public class BodyPos : MonoBehaviour
{
    public Transform viveCameraEye;
    public Transform robotHead;
    public Transform robotHips;

    void LateUpdate()
    {
        Vector3 headPelvisOffset = robotHead.position
- robotHips.position;
        robotHips.position = viveCameraEye.position
- headPelvisOffset;
    }
}
```

Once you have the script set up, save it (CTRL + S) and return to Unity.

In the Inspector, first set up the viveCameraEye field in the Inspector. Find the [CameraRig] GameObject and expand it out so that you can see its child objects. Expand out the Camera_head GameObject. Under Camera_head, drag the Camera_eye GameObject into the Inspector to the Vive Camera Eye field on the BodyPos GameObject's BodyPos Component.

The robotHead and robotHips are joints belonging to the robot mesh. They are buried in the Hierarchy under other joints, so use the search bar at the top of the Hierarchy to find them, in turn, then drag each one into the Robot Head and Robot Hips fields of the BodyPos Component in the Inspector.

With the references set, that is everything we need to set up for the skeleton to follow the Vive headset around the room. That said, you may need to remove the NeuronOVRAdaptor script, if you added that to the camera rig in the previous section. To do this, click on the [CameraRig] GameObject, then check in the Inspector to see if NeuronOVRAdaptor is attached or not. If it is, you can just uncheck the checkbox in the top left of the Component, to disable it.

Put all the gear on and give that a go. Hit Play to preview the Scene.

Potential Issues

Error in Unity

If tracking is not getting through to Unity, you may notice an error in the console, when you hit Play to preview the scene—[NeuronConnection] Connecting to 127.0.0.1:7001 failed.

FIGURE 10.10   Settings with for Broadcasting in the Axis Neuron application must be correct for motion capture to work in Unity.

If you see an error about the connection to Neuron Connection failing, double check that you still have Axis Neuron open in the background and that it is connected to the Perception Neuron. You should be able to switch over to the Axis Neuron window and move the skeleton around in real-time. If this is all okay, check the settings in Axis Neuron to make sure that Broadcasting is set up correctly. To do this, in Axis Neuron go to File > Settings and select Broadcast on the left of the Settings window. Check that the BVH section is right (Figure 10.10).

View Obscured by Robot Head

One potential issue is that your view may be obscured by the head of the robot. A quick solution is to scale the head joint down to zero, so that the models head is effectively squashed. The downside to this approach is that the OVRCameraTarget GameObject (used by our code to position the camera rig) will then also be affected by the scale. OVRCameraTarget will not be positioned correctly and due to the scale of 0,0,0 you will find it will not be moveable. To remedy this, change the parent of OVRCameraTarget to the Robot_Neck GameObject, instead. You may have to tweak the position of OVRCameraTarget a little bit, just to move it away from the neck and up to where you would expect the line of sight to begin.

RECAP

This chapter was the most experimental yet, featuring some examples of working with two cutting-edge solutions for input. We started with the Leap Motion and its VR Mount Kit, then went on to see how to implement the technology into a relatively basic Unity project. After playing around with the virtual piano for a while, we went on to visit Noitom's Perception Neuron system with a single glove set up. Despite it being designed for full body motion capture in the animation industry, the Perception Neuron can be used as a way to monitor hand movements for VR. We looked at getting set up to watch input from inside Unity and considered the theory behind using a full suit.

The future of VR depends on the continued development and evolution of methods for interacting with the virtual world. For all of our senses to be fully engaged, technology needs to keep pushing toward mimicking our everyday movements and gestures. Until then, it is up to us, as developers, to push the boundaries of what we have and to keep things moving forward. When you are finished waving your hands around, in the next chapter we will be looking at using the SteamVR camera rig in a different way. In Chapter 11, we look at the extra configuration required for seated VR experiences.

Handling the Camera Rig for Seated or Static VR Experiences

I T GOES WITHOUT SAYING that there is more to VR than room-scale experiences or teleporting around the virtual world. Some games need to take place inside vehicles, or perhaps even stay in the same seated spot. By default, SteamVR assumes that the experience is going to be room-scale whenever room-scale VR is available and it takes a little configuration to change that.

Room-scale VR allows the viewer to move freely around the entire play space defined during the SteamVR set up procedure. If room-scale technology is not plugged in, or you are using non room-scale VR such as out-of-the-box Rift or HDK, SteamVR will place you in a very small area but still allow for movement within the space. If you only have a non room-scale VR system to test with, you should most likely stick to a seated configuration.

In this chapter, we will look at two example situations where a sitting down configuration is required; driving a simple vehicle and following a character avatar around in third-person view.

As a side note, anecdotal evidence suggests that VR sickness is reduced when the viewer has fixed visual reference objects, such as sitting inside a cockpit. If you are working on some kind of flying experience, you may want to consider the idea of having a cockpit or some sort of fixed surround within the main field of view, to help viewers have a stable reference and a more comfortable experience.

DRIVING A SIMPLE VEHICLE IN VR

The first example scenario for a seated configuration is of driving a simple vehicle (Figure 11.1), where the camera is attached to the vehicle and moves around with it.

Open the Example Project

Open the example project for this chapter. In the Project browser, find the Scenes folder and, inside that, choose the Scene named main.

The camera is inside of the vehicle already. It is a space vehicle, by the way, from the future. A 1980s future where things are all sort of grid-like and neon. Buttons are far too big, because that is what buttons from the future looked like in the 1980s.

When you look at the Game View, you can see that the Camera is correctly located inside the vehicle, in the driving seat but if you were to hit Play to preview the Scene, the view may move away from its default location, especially if you are using room-scale VR. This is because SteamVR is calibrated for a non-seated experience. Under normal circumstances, making the Camera a child object of the Vehicle GameObject would mean that the view moves with the vehicle and remain in the correct place. With SteamVR we need to tell it to stay in one place, by switching the tracking space to seated mode.

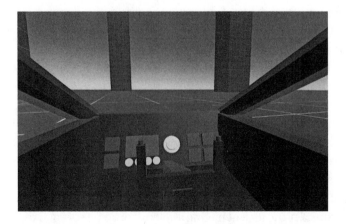

FIGURE 11.1   Driving a vehicle in VR, inside the cockpit, calls for a seated tracking configuration.

Setting Sitting or Standing Calibration in Code

We can choose which mode of operation SteamVR will operate in via the SteamVR_Render class. It is a Singleton, which means we can access it via.instance from anywhere in the code. In this section, we build a simple script Component that will set SteamVR to sitting or standing depending on which one you choose in the Inspector. With a seated experience, it is also important to provide the functionality for re-centering the view whenever the viewer presses a button or key on the keyboard. The most common reason for resetting is that sometimes the viewer is not quite in the right position when the simulation starts. Perhaps they were still putting the headset on after loading the simulation, for example. When that happens, the default position is incorrect for their headset and it needs to be reset.

Click on the Main camera GameObject in the Hierarchy. You will find it as a child object of Vehicle, so you will need to use the little arrow next to Vehicle to expand out the view.

With Main Camera highlighted, click the Add Component button in the Inspector. Choose New Script and name the script VR_Config. Make sure C Sharp is selected in the Language dropdown and click Create and Add. In the script editor, add the following script:

```
using UnityEngine;
using System.Collections;
using Valve.VR;

public class VR_Config : MonoBehaviour
{
    public enum roomTypes { standing, sitting };
    public roomTypes theRoomType;

    void Awake()
    {
        SetUpVR();
    }

    void SetUpVR()
    {
        SetUpRoom();
    }

    void SetUpRoom()
```

```
    {
        var render = SteamVR_Render.instance;

        if (theRoomType == roomTypes.standing)
        {
            render.trackingSpace =
ETrackingUniverseOrigin.TrackingUniverseStanding;
        }
        else
        {
            render.trackingSpace =
ETrackingUniverseOrigin.TrackingUniverseSeated;
        }

        Recenter();
    }


    void LateUpdate()
    {
        // here, we check for a keypress to reset the
view
        // whenever the mode is sitting .. don't
forget to set this up in Input Manager
        if (theRoomType == roomTypes.sitting)
        {
            if (Input.GetButtonUp("RecenterView"))
            {
                Recenter();
            }
        }
    }


    void Recenter()
    {
        // reset the position
        var system = OpenVR.System;
        if (system != null)
            system.ResetSeatedZeroPose();
    }
}
```

Script Breakdown

```
using UnityEngine;
using System.Collections;

using Valve.VR;
```

SteamVR_Render is a part of the Valve.VR packages, so we need to tell Unity about it along with the other standard packages in the code above.

```
public class VR_Config : MonoBehaviour
{
    public enum roomTypes { standing, sitting };
    public roomTypes theRoomType;
```

The script we are building here only requires a single variable to hold the selected room type. theRoomType is a public variable, making it visible in the Inspector. I could have opted for a simple integer for theRoomType or perhaps even a Boolean to say whether we are standing or not. Instead, I chose an enumerator, above, so that the variable displays nicely in the Inspector. Unity will show the value of theRoomType as a nice, neat, drop-down menu containing the text from roomTypes; standing and sitting.

```
    void Awake()
    {
        SetUpVR();
    }

    void SetUpVR()
    {
        SetUpRoom();
    }
```

The Awake() function calls to SetUpVR(). Since we always want to future-proof the code, the SetUpVR is a function intended to be used for generic VR setup. If there are any more things to be set up for the VR simulation to work the way we want, I would call them from SetUpVR() rather than doing them inside SetUpVR(). So, here, for example, I call SetUpRoom(). For this particular VR experience, SetUpRoom() is all we need to do to be set up and ready to go.

```
void SetUpRoom()
  {
     var render = SteamVR_Render.instance;
```

SetUpRoom(), declared in the code block above, is a private function designed to only be called from inside the VR_Config class.

A local variable named render is set up to hold the SteamVR_Render instance. This provides a link directly to the active SteamVR_Render Component running in the current Scene.

The next part of the code deals with setting the experience type:

```
     if (theRoomType == roomTypes.standing)
     {
          render.trackingSpace =
ETrackingUniverseOrigin.TrackingUniverseStanding;
     }
     else
     {
          render.trackingSpace =
ETrackingUniverseOrigin.TrackingUniverseSeated;
     }

     Recenter();
  }
```

Above, based on the value of theRoomType, we set a property of SteamVR_Render named trackingSpace. render.trackingSpace requires an ETrackingUniverseOrigin enum value (which would have been declared elsewhere in the Steam code in the same way we declared the roomTypes enum at the start of this class). ETrackingUniverseOrigin has three possible values:

TrackingUniverseRawAndUncalibrated: This setting is not calibrated for either standing or sitting. What happens with regard to the space and how the view interacts with it, under this setting, may be unpredictable. Valve recommends that TrackingUniverseRawAndUncalibrated should probably not be used.

TrackingUniverseSeated: Using the TrackingUniverseSeated setting means that SteamVR will function a lot better with the kinds of positions and movements which happen in a seating position.

Note that there is no specific seated calibration procedure in the SteamVR setup. If the system is calibrated to room-scale, it will intelligently figure out seated parameters as required. Also note that the seated setting does not "lock" the player into place, but instead uses settings that are more suited to a seated position. You will still be able to get up and walk away from the seated position and it is up to the developer to solve this issue, if you like (for example, pausing the simulation if the player steps too far away from the center point).

TrackingUniverseStanding: SteamVR will use the standing settings, which are more suited to standing or room-scale VR experiences.

Once the tracking type is all set, there is a quick call to Recenter(), which will re-center the view. We will look at the Recenter() function a little further down in the code, first up is the LateUpdate() function:

```
void LateUpdate()
{
    if (theRoomType == roomTypes.sitting)
    {
```

LateUpdate() is a function called automatically by Unity at the end of every update cycle. It is useful to provide viewers with a method to reset the view at will, for whatever reason. Room-scale, standing VR does not require resetting, as it is always assumed that the space will always be the space configured during SteamVR's initial set up procedure. For that reason, we only bother checking for a re-center key hit when the room type is sitting.

```
        if (Input.GetButtonUp("RecenterView"))
        {
            Recenter();
        }
    }
}
```

Input.GetButtonUp takes a string to say which virtual button to check. The RecenterView button has already been set up in Unity's Input Manager (to get to the Input Manager inside the Unity editor, hit Edit > Project Settings > Input).

When the button up is detected, Recenter() is called.

Re-centering, or resetting, the view is especially useful when you are dealing with seated experiences that call for the player to match a certain position inside the virtual world. The seated position is known as a zero pose, as it is the pose that we assume the viewer will be in when they are at our zero world position. For example, imagine a virtual racing car driver sitting in the seat of a virtual racing car. Her head is resting against the headrest in the virtual world and the camera rig, in the Scene, starts out positioned where the virtual racing driver's vision would be. In the real world, however, the viewer's head position may not be in the correct position for this. When the simulation starts, if the positions are not in alignment the VR camera will show a view from somewhere other than the virtual racing driver's head. By resetting the view, the virtual camera will be re-positioned to its original location in the Scene. The viewer's head should now match the virtual racing driver's viewpoint. That is, the camera will start out in the correct place for driving.

The next part of the code deals with the actual re-centering of the view:

```
void Recenter()
{
    // reset the position
    var system = OpenVR.System;
    if (system != null)
        system.ResetSeatedZeroPose();
}
}
```

Recenter() is another local function intended only to be called from within the VR_Config class.

Above, we start out with a local variable named system, to store a reference to OpenVR.System.

OpenVR is another class belonging to the Valve.VR namespace. It provides a number of system-level commands and properties such as resetting the view or accessing hardware features such as haptic feedback.

If the variable system is null, we know that it has not initialized correctly and we do not want to try to call it in this state as Unity will raise an error. Instead, just in case there has been any sort of problem during the initialization of the OpenVR class, there is a quick null check.

The command to reset the view is system.ResetSeatedZeroPose(). When this is called, the view will immediately reset. The default position of the camera in the Scene will tie to the current position of the headset.

Parenting the Camera to the Vehicle

OK, so I cheated a little bit here. In the example files you will find that the Main Camera is already a child object of the Vehicle. May seem an obvious observation, but it is important to note that you can do this. Parenting the camera to a vehicle will work even with a room-scale VR experience, but unless you are simulating a room-sized moving platform then you probably will not want to do this. With the tracking system set to use the Seated universe, the calibration makes a lot more sense for an application like this.

The vehicle could be just about anything you want the viewer to ride or follow. For example, it could be a carriage of a train, a motorbike seat, or perhaps an empty GameObject that is placed in a location you want the camera to be. In the next section, we will parent the camera to an empty GameObject and move it around so that the viewer follows a character avatar around a simple arena environment, as it fights off an invasion of robots.

WHAT IS THIRD PERSON AND IS VIRTUAL REALITY REALLY THE RIGHT PLACE FOR THIRD-PERSON VIEWS?

The initial thinking about VR, and how it fits into full-vision headset hardware, was that it would be a replacement for reality, attempting to simulate the viewpoint of the viewer in an alternative computer-generated universe (known as a first-person viewpoint). Despite this commonly perceived notion of what VR is, a growing number of experiences take place outside of a body and present alternative views of the virtual world.

Another viewpoint seen in a lot of videogames, such as *Gears of War*, *Tomb Raider*, or *Uncharted*, is the third-person view. Usually, this means that the camera sits behind a character being controlled by the player and follows it around. We refer to this view as a third person, most likely inherited from the terms used in explaining the point-of-view of books. In literary terms, a third-person point of view is a form of storytelling where a narrator uses terms like "she" or "he" to explain what is happening, as opposed to the first-person terms like "I" or "me."

EXTERNAL CAMERA FOR FOLLOWING THE VEHICLE

In this section, we look at using the camera with another type of control script from outside of the vehicle (Figure 11.2). This could be any camera

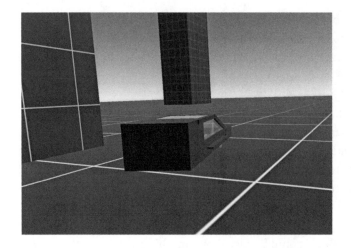

FIGURE 11.2 The follow rig trails behind the vehicle as it moves around the Scene, with the viewer taking on the role of the camera.

script you need to use; for example, if you have your own custom camera control script the same principles shown in this section may be applied to get things going.

We start by opening up the same Unity project from the previous section, if you don't already have it open.

Open the Example Project

Open the example project for this chapter. In the Project browser, find the Scenes folder and, inside that, choose the Scene named main_followcam.

Set Up the Camera Rig

The Scene needs a camera. Expand out the SteamVR folder in the Project browser. Inside the SteamVR folder, there is a Prefabs folder. Click on that to show its contents in the preview. Inside Prefabs you should see [CameraRig], [Status], and [SteamVR].

Grab the [CameraRig] prefab out of the Project browser and drop it into the Hierarchy.

Add a Camera Script

In the Hierarchy, highlight the [CameraRig] GameObject. In the Inspector, click the Add Component button and choose Scripts > VR_Config. The VR_Config script is the same configuration script from the previous section in this chapter. It allows us to choose which type of tracking calibration the SteamVR system should be using. On the VR_Config Component, choose Seated from the The Room Type dropdown menu.

Next up, we need to add a script to move the camera rig around the scene and follow the vehicle. Again, in the Inspector choose the Add Component button and find Scripts > Camera Controller.

The Camera Controller script is very basic:

```
using UnityEngine;
using System.Collections;

public class CameraController : MonoBehaviour
{
    public Transform cameraTarget;
    public Transform lookAtTarget;

    private Transform myTransform;

    public Vector3 targetOffset = new Vector3(0, 0,
-1);

    void Start()
    {
        // grab a ref to the transform
        myTransform = transform;
    }

    void LateUpdate()
    {
        // move this gameObject's transform around to
follow the target (using Lerp to move smoothly)
        myTransform.position = Vector3.
Lerp(myTransform.position, cameraTarget.position +
targetOffset, Time.deltaTime);
        // look at our target object
        myTransform.LookAt(lookAtTarget);
    }
}
```

The Camera Controller script uses Vector3.Lerp to move the camera around and Transform.LookAt to point the camera in the right direction. To use a follow camera in your own projects, you will probably need something far more complicated. For now, though, this script will do the job of moving around the camera rig.

Normally, you might be directly moving around the GameObject with the Camera Component attached to it, or perhaps moving around an object the camera is attached to. When you are using SteamVR, the object you want to move is [Camera Rig].

In the Unity editor, click the [Camera Rig] GameObject if it is not still selected from earlier. In the Inspector, notice the two fields in the Camera Controller Component, Camera Target, and Look At Target.

This scene is almost the same as the one you saw in the previous section, except the vehicle now has a couple of extra empty GameObjects attached to it as children.

Expand out the Vehicle object in the Hierarchy so that you can see its child objects. The two additions for this scene are CameraMount and LookPoint. The camera will follow close to the CameraMount object as it looks in the direction of LookPoint.

Drag the CameraMount GameObject out of the Hierarchy and drop it into the Camera Target field in the Inspector.

Drag the LookPoint GameObject out of the Hierarchy and drop it into the Look At Target field in the Inspector.

Save

Save the project with File > Save Project.

Preview the Scene

Grab your headset and press Play to preview the scene, but if you are at all susceptible to VR sickness I recommend that you keep your time in the simulation down to just a few seconds. The way that the camera moves is not exactly optimized for a comfortable experience. In the next chapter, we will discuss this further and investigate a better camera movement method.

RECAP

In this chapter, we looked at the principles behind taking control of the camera away from the viewer and its implications. To be able to move the camera around with a vehicle, we also needed to reconfigure the SteamVR calibration to be suited to a seated position. By modifying the tracking, the camera can appear where we wanted it to be instead of being based upon its position in the room-scale VR space.

We also looked at the importance of having a re-center button to reset the view for a seated viewer whenever the calibration was out of sync with our simulated viewpoint.

We looked at a third-person approach to gameplay in the VR world and scripted a simple camera. After setting up a third-person camera to follow around the vehicle, we observed that it is not at all optimized for comfort and that VR calls for an approach to camera movement that might lessen the impact of its movement on the symptoms of motion sickness. We then saved our work (yes, I am sure you have gotten the message now about saving your work regularly but I will continue to push the issue as I know how important it is to do so!). In the next chapter, we will look a little deeper in to motion sickness and some of the strategies developers have recently formulated to try and reduce or avoid it.

CHAPTER 12

Virtual Reality Sickness

I F YOU ARE GOING to be building VR, it may be a benefit to understand how much of an issue VR sickness currently is and why. There is a lot of misinformation. VR sickness is something that could seriously inhibit widespread adoption. At such an early stage in VR evolution, we are all ambassadors for the virtual world and our experiences may very well help to shape its future. It is every VR content creator's responsibility to try to lessen or find workarounds for VR sickness if we are going to see this current generation of VR succeed.

This chapter is not about forcing you to build VR experiences in a particular way, or even saying that you should not create experiences that may make people feel ill. Honestly, if you want to go ahead and target the groups of people who are not affected by sickness and you want to spin the camera around 360° at high speed; you should go ahead and do that because there will be people who can enjoy it without an issue, but providing the option to turn on or off sickness prevention systems could be a great selling point for your game, and we need to understand that everyone is different and people are affected differently by VR sickness. For that reason, I am providing problems and solutions in this chapter so that you may consider the options.

Room-scale VR experiences do not suffer from the same kinds of simulation sickness problems as seated or automated moving experiences, so if your development is centered around only room-scale VR you might even be able to skip this entire chapter with no consequence. But if you do intend to automate movement or gaze in any way—it might just help to know what you are up against.

This chapter is text-heavy. I have tried to collect my findings, through various research papers, websites, articles, and conversations, into something more readable than academic. I want to give you as full a picture as possible into why it is we think these things are happening to our virtual visitors and you will come away from this book with theory and practical methods to make VR experiences more comfortable. I begin by asking the most obvious question.

WHAT IS VIRTUAL REALITY SICKNESS?

VR sickness is also known as simulator sickness or cyber sickness. It may invoke a range of symptoms such as sweating, nausea, sickness, headaches, and drowsiness, and other symptoms similar to those experienced by motion sickness sufferers who get sick in cars, boats, or planes.

Despite years of research, we still do not know what causes it. The most popular theory is that VR sickness is caused by a mismatch between what a viewer actually experiences versus what the viewer's brain thinks it is experiencing. This is known as cue conflict theory (Kolansinski, 1995). Cue conflict theory, in summary, is when the brain thinks that the input (sight, sound, and so on) is not real or correct. The mind is normally able to tell when something with the body is not right and then attempt to correct it and it performs "safety checks" to make sure that the body is in a healthy state. The detection system looks for cues or clues to abnormalities, such as tying movement and sight together to build up a body of information that can confirm that what you are experiencing is correct. When the cues do not match up, it is then believed that the brain switches into a defensive mode that might normally be triggered when the body is under attack. A rejection system kicks in as the brain attempts to rid the body of any poisons, through bodily fluid (sweat secretion and/or vomiting depending on severity).

Personal Experience

The first VR development kit I used made me feel sick within minutes of using it. The sickness would last anything from an hour or right up to a full day after taking off the headset. I began to wonder if I would ever be able to stay inside the headset for more than just a few moments at a time and over time it just seemed to get harder and harder. Over time, it was as if my brain started to associate the headset with feeling sick. I hardly needed to switch it on before the symptoms kicked in and even the smell of the headset plastic would make me start to feel ill. The word from researchers is that you can build up a tolerance to VR sickness over time, which is what people commonly refer to as "finding your VR legs," but that never happened to me. Despite starting small, every day spending short bursts of time in VR, I was never able to extend my time. I also tried travel sickness meds and homeopathic treatment. After months of trying, I decided to skip the next development kit and wait for the consumer versions to see if any significant improvements would have been made. And, thankfully, they had.

The difference is amazing between the Rift development kit 1 (DK1) and the consumer headsets. I still struggle with some types of movement and there are some games that can put me out for a long time, but there are many more VR experiences I can play now with little or no sickness at all.

My own experiences led me to believe that the primitive resolution display and slower refresh rates of the development kit were the main contributors. Research suggests a similar theme, but we need to be careful about making assumptions which rely on our own experiences. Not everyone is affected in the same way.

VR Sickness Symptoms and Cues

VR visitors are affected in different ways and by different situations. Some people exhibit all the signs and symptoms, whereas others only experience a few or, in some cases, none at all. Kennedy and Fowlkes noted that simulator sickness is polysymptomatic (Kolasinski, 1996). That is, no single symptom appears in a greater quantity across their test subjects, there is no dominant symptom, and VR sickness symptoms are extremely difficult to measure.

Humans experience the world in very different ways. If cue theory is to be believed, the cues may work under an entirely different set of parameters dependent on the person. The way one person moves could vary dramatically from a disabled person, for example, which may mean a difference in the perception of cues. There are so many potential cues, with influence levels varying from person to person, combined with individual physical factors, that there are a huge number of variables we need to factor in. This is by no means an exhaustive list, but here are just some of the variables in play:

Vection

It is well known that a camera system involving a lot of movement is likely to induce VR sickness. According to research, it may be associated with something known as vection. The best way to describe vection is to imagine sitting in a car, looking out of the window. The car beside yours slowly moves forward, but you get the feeling that your car is rolling backward because your brain misread the cues.

Vection is the illusion of peripheral movement and it has been found to be a strong contributor to VR sickness. Hettinger et al. in 1990 hypothesized that vection must be experienced before simulation sickness occurs (Kolasinski, 1996). They took 15 subjects. Ten were reported as sick. Subjects reported either a great deal of vection or none at all. Out of the five subjects who did not report vection, only one felt ill. Out of the 10 subjects who reported vection, eight reported feeling sick.

I believe that it is also important to note the widely reported lack of motion sickness experienced by those in room-scale VR. Moving around in VR, rather than being moved around, produces dramatically less symptoms of VR sickness.

Field of View

A wider field of view produces more vection. Andersen and Braunstein (1985) found that reducing the field of view helped to reduce ill-effects, even in cases where the vection illusion was increased. A reduced central visual field meant that only 30% of subjects experienced motion sickness.

More recently, in 2016, researchers at Columbia University, Ajoy S. Fernandes and Steven K. Feiner tested a method of reducing field of view dynamically to reduce sickness (Fernandes and Feiner, 2016). They used Unity to adapt an existing VR demonstration so that whenever the viewer moved around the scene, the field of view would be lessened by an overlay. The actual visible world would grow less and less, the longer the viewer moved around in the virtual world. When the viewer comes to a stop, the field of view would be returned to normal. By reducing the field of view in this way, their hypothesis was that the restrictor helped subjects have a more comfortable experience and be able stay in the virtual world longer. Also, surprisingly most subjects also reported that they hardly even noticed the changing field of view restrictor as they moved around.

Inter-Pupillary Distance

There has been a lot of emphasis placed on IPD recently, but there is actually little scientific evidence to suggest that it is a contributing factor of VR sickness per se. An incorrectly configured IPD on the headset may however cause eye strain, which is of course undesirable and will make for an uncomfortable experience regardless. Elsewhere in this book, we looked at measuring IPD correctly.

Illness

It probably goes without saying that certain illnesses may be exacerbated by virtual reality. The inner ear may be affected by many medical conditions including colds, flu, or ear infections. Any sort of issue in the ear can directly affect how the brain interprets balance, and how vection might affect a viewer. Tiredness and other illnesses will also play a role in its effect.

Motion

The way that the viewer is moved around inside the virtual world will produce different experiences. Faster movement speeds may produce more of a sense of motion, leading to more feelings of sickness. The way that a person perceives motion is important here, too. Some people are better at rotational movement than others, for example. Forced movement is also a problem. People do not tend to enjoy having their view moved around automatically for them, as it tends to move in a way that may not be natural to them which can, in turn, cause nausea.

Age

Many articles about VR sickness will quote age as a factor, along with gender, but there is no actual proof to back up this claim. It may just stem from studies on motion sickness, which has shown that people between the ages of 2–21 are more likely to experience it. Rather than blindly quoting motion sickness studies, I believe that more research is required in VR specifically. Most currently reported findings on age or gender as factors of sickness in VR should be taken with a pinch of salt.

Frame Rate

Developing comfortable experiences for VR calls for maintenance of a constant frame rate throughout the entire experience. Higher spec hardware is called for, due to relatively recent findings leading to a better understanding of how important frame rate is to a comfortable experience. For example, lower-spec hardware might be perfectly capable of rendering at 40 frames per second in a VR device but frame rate glitches become much more obvious to the viewer and present much more of an issue when they crop up. A frame rate hiccup at 40 fps can mean that frames get dropped and VR sickness cues are triggered. Rather than risking this, it is better for

VR experiences to run at 90 fps so that glitches are much less apparent and much less of an issue. In their quest to keep the PlaystationVR platform at a high quality, Sony will not certify games for their system if they drop to a frame rate less than 60 fps. To avoid uncomfortable experiences, senior staff engineer Chris Norton stated "If you submit a game to us and you drop down to 30 or 35 or 51 we're probably going to reject it" (Hall, 2016).

Depth Perception

Ironic though it may be, the people with the best vision for VR may be the ones most prone to experience motion sickness. People with good depth perception will experience more of a sense of vection in the virtual world, which may increase susceptibility to sickness (Allen et al., 2016).

Rate of Linear or Rotational Acceleration

Acceleration needs to make sense to the viewer. For example, the camera used in Chapter 11 may cause problems for sufferers of VR sickness. The smoothing out of the acceleration and deceleration is unnatural when it is applied to human movement. We do not slowly decelerate when we focus on an object, so why would doing the same in VR make any sense to a viewer? In Chapter 13, we will look at building a better camera for VR.

As with all of these cues, the type of movement affects people in different ways. One of the most basic methods for reducing its effect is to move relatively slowly. Not so much that you are edging around the environment, but to try to avoid zooming around at high speed rates. Removing acceleration smoothing may go some distance to help, too. A more abrupt start and stop may not be visually the nicest effect, but in VR this is a good compromise when trying to reduce sick users.

Positional Tracking Errors

When the tracking hardware fails, or the headset moves out of view of the base stations it can make for an uncomfortable experience as the view wanders randomly away from where it is supposed to be. At the time of writing, I have yet to see a VR experience that tries to keep tabs of this. It may be worth considering programming a system to look out for unexpected movements or movements that fall outside of a particular threshold.

Sitting versus Standing

Some people are naturally steady on their feet, others not so much. This can have an impact on the virtual experience.

CAN WE SOLVE IT?

The answer to this is difficult. Unless we can pinpoint exactly where it is that VR sickness begins, treating it would be similar to fixing leaks in a pipe that just keeps springing new holes. Fix one, find another. That is not to say that it is impossible. It may well turn out that a particular technical issue is causing people to get sick—for example, I do not know what sort of an impact new technologies such as the new Near Eye Light Field headset will have for sufferers (I will look at Light Field VR some more in Chapter 15). Initial findings seem to suggest that the ability for Light Field VR to have the eye focus more naturally may actually eliminate VR sickness. Unfortunately, the Light Field technology is still in its early prototype stages and the verdict will be out for a while. We just have to wait and see.

Shutting down the inputs or sensory synapses causing VR sickness may be another option, though I doubt the ethics or viability of surgery to accomplish this. Perhaps a medical solution is on the horizon? Assuming that VR sickness is caused by cue conflict—the most common theory—manufacturing any kind of catch-all solution is marred by the fact that there are so many possible cues, and they vary from person to person. At the time of writing, there is no medical solution and even traditional medical motion sickness cures have limited success in VR.

Although we do not yet have the answers, we can at least reduce the impact of VR sickness with technical solutions and workarounds. I think that it is important for developers to keep an eye out for advancements or new theories on this subject, as we still have a lot to learn about it. Sharing knowledge is important as we all try to move forward into this new entertainment medium. The rules of VR are not written and we, the early adopters, are ambassadors of VR. The potential for the virtual experience falls far beyond simple games or walk-arounds and there is potential for VR to change the world for the better. We need to work together and share our findings, working to keep VR as an open platform away from corporate interest, to make it a better place for the future.

RECAP

In this chapter, we have focused on VR sickness and looked at some of the most current research findings to help understand what it is we are up against when it comes to VR's worst enemy. Although I have added my personal experience to this chapter, it is important to remember that the way one person experiences virtual reality may be completely different from the next. Humans are complex creatures made up of many different components that may be differently sized, have varying sensitivity, or even limited functionality. Variation between just a few of the components we use to judge depth, distance, or balance can mean that one person's comfortable experience may be another person's VR barf-o-rama.

I touched briefly on why there is not, as yet, a medical solution to the problem but how we can try to create more comfortable experiences through sharing our findings and implementing workarounds.

In the next chapter, we will look at some practical methods and Unity implementations to help create VR experiences more comfortable for people susceptible to sickness.

CHAPTER 13

Hands-on, Practical Techniques for Reducing VR Sickness in Unity

USING A UI OVERLAY FOR FIELD OF VIEW REDUCTION

Researchers at the Computer Graphics and User Interfaces Lab of Columbia University found that the effects of VR sickness were reduced by controlling the range of visibility, based on how much the user is moving around in the virtual world (Evarts, 2016). They used a mask in front of the camera, to provide a view similar to looking through a hole in a piece of card (Figure 13.1). When the user moved around, the mask was scaled down so that the viewing hole grew smaller. When the user stopped moving, the hole returned to its original scale and, as a result, the field of view restored. You may have seen a technique very similar to this used in the Google Earth VR application (available free on Steam) where the view is masked out whenever you fly around. Google do not use so much of a transition as we do in this section, but the effect of reducing the field of view is the same.

Another example of the masking system in the real world can be found in the VR game *Eagle Flight* (published by Ubisoft). It uses a number of carefully researched and tested methods to allow players to fly through Paris as an eagle without making them feel ill. Without these systems in place, the experience would likely be unplayable by most VR sickness

FIGURE 13.1 The example project for this chapter uses a mask image to reduce the field of view during movement.

sufferers. In this section, we will look at one way to implement a similar system to display an image in front of the camera that will reduce visual range whenever we move around.

Open the Example Project

Open the example project for this section of this chapter. It contains a Scene named main, which you can find inside the Scenes folder in the Project browser. Open the Scene.

The FOV Mask

The objective of the mask (Figure 13.2) is to provide a visible area in the center and to mask off the rest of the screen. We will scale the image up or down, depending on the movement speed of the object we are tracking, which will reduce or increase the size of the hole in the center and, as a result of that, the visible area for the viewer.

To create the image, I used a program called Paint.Net which is amazing free software, provided under a Creative Commons license, for editing and creating art. You can download it from http://www.getpaint.net/download.html. If you can afford it, please do donate if you find it useful because the developers rely purely on donation to fund future development.

The image is 1024 pixels in width and 1024 pixels high. To make it, I used the Paint Bucket tool to fill the entire image with black. Next, I used

FIGURE 13.2   The image used for masking the field of view.

the Paintbrush tool with a large sized brush with a (very) soft edge to create a white circle in the center of the image. To make a brush soft, you just set the Hardness level right down. To get the circle size right, it was trial and error all the way! When it was too small, it did not matter how I scaled it inside Unity—I could see that the area was too small. When it was too large, the effect was almost unnoticeable without scaling down the image so much that its edges became visible. If you decide to make your own mask image, play around with different sizes to see what works for you.

Finally, I exported the image as a .PNG format image and imported it into Unity to use as the overlay. In Unity, the shader used to make this image transparent is a Multiply shader normally used for particle effects. In the shader's dropdown of a Material, it can be found under Particles > Multiply.

In the example project, click the Canvas GameObject in the Hierarchy and you can see that the Plane Distance is set to 0.31. The trick here is to position the image just far enough from the camera so that it does not get distorted by its projection across both eyes, but close enough to the camera to avoid clipping other 3D objects in front of the camera.

Programming the Dynamic Scaling Script

You can find this script attached to the MaskImage GameObject in the Hierarchy in the main Scene. The script in full looks like this:

```
using UnityEngine;
using System.Collections;

public class MaskScaler : MonoBehaviour
{
    public Transform objectToTrack;
    [Space(10)]

    public float maskOpenScale = 4f;
    public float maskClosedScale = 1f;
    [Space(10)]
    public float minSpeedForMovement = 2f;
    public float maskSpeed = 0.1f;

    private float moveSpeed;
    private Vector3 lastPosition;
    private float theScale;

    private Transform myTransform;
    private Vector3 myScale;
    public float multiplier = 100f;

    void Start()
    {
        // grab some info we are going to need for
each update
        myTransform = transform;
        myScale = transform.localScale;

        // set the default value for the scale
variable
        theScale = maskOpenScale;
    }

    void FixedUpdate ()
    {
        // figure out how fast the object we are
tracking is moving..
        moveSpeed = (( objectToTrack.position -
lastPosition ).magnitude * multiplier);
        lastPosition = objectToTrack.position;

        // here, we check to see if the object is
moving and if it is, decreases scale to shrink the
visible area
```

```
        if ( moveSpeed > minSpeedForMovement &&
theScale > maskClosedScale )
        {
            theScale -= maskSpeed * Time.deltaTime;
        }

        // here, we check to see if the object is NOT
moving and if so, increases scale to expand the
visible area
        if ( moveSpeed <= minSpeedForMovement &&
theScale < maskOpenScale )
        {
            theScale += maskSpeed * Time.deltaTime;
        }

        // finally, we set the localScale property of
our transform to the newly calculated size
        myTransform.localScale = myScale * theScale;
    }
}
```

Script Breakdown

The script derives from MonoBehaviour, so that we can tap into the Start() and FixedUpdate() functions Unity will call automatically. The packages we use are just the standard ones Unity includes with all new C# scripts:

```
using UnityEngine;
using System.Collections;

public class MaskScaler : MonoBehaviour
{
```

The next part of the script contains all of the variable declarations:

```
    public Transform objectToTrack;

    public float maskOpenScale = 4f;
    public float maskClosedScale = 1f;

    public float minSpeedForMovement = 2f;
    public float maskSpeed = 0.1f;
```

```
private float moveSpeed;
private Vector3 lastPosition;
private float theScale;

private Transform myTransform;
private Vector3 myScale;
public float multiplier = 100f;
```

The Start() function has a little setup in it:

```
void Start()
{
    // grab some info we are going to need for
each update
    myTransform = transform;
    myScale = transform.localScale;

    // set the default value for the scale
variable
    theScale = maskOpenScale;
}
```

The Start() function above grabs a couple of references. The Transform Component on this GameObject has a reference to it held in the variable myTransform. myTransform will be used in the main part of the script when we need to modify the scale. myScale contains the original scale of the transform, which I store so that the scale is not hard-coded into the script. If you need to scale your mask in some sort of nonuniform way, it should work just fine because we are using a multiplier against the original scale rather than forcing a scale directly. When we multiply the original scale, its aspect ratio will remain the same.

Our calculations all take place in the FixedUpdate() function because the vehicle updates take place in FixedUpdate and we need to get to its numbers before they change as a part of the update process:

```
void FixedUpdate ()
{
    // figure out how fast the object we are
tracking is moving..
    moveSpeed = (( objectToTrack.position -
lastPosition ).magnitude * multiplier);
    lastPosition = objectToTrack.position;
```

If you look in the Inspector at the MaskRawImage GameObject, you will see that there is a reference to the vehicle in our Mask Scaler Component. The first part of the FixedUpdate() function figures out the current speed of the object we are tracking. It finds the speed by taking the current position of the object and subtracting the last position of the object. This gives us a vector between the position at the time of the last update and this update, so we enclose this in brackets and use .magnitude to find out the magnitude that these two vectors create. The next part uses a variable named multiplier. This is, admittedly, a bit of a necessary hack. When I worked out the speed of my vehicle originally, I found that scientific notation kicked in as the magnitude approached zero. This is likely due to the small scale of the environment and the movements through it. I hit upon a few rounding errors, so to rectify this I decided to use a multiplier that would bring up the speed to more manageable values. If you decide to go ahead and use this script, you should look to see whether or not this sort of multiplier is still required.

Above, the last part of the code block above stores the position in lastPosition so that we can use it to figure out the position difference the next time FixedUpdate() is called.

The next code block deals with changing the current scale based on whether or not the object is moving:

```
        if ( moveSpeed > minSpeedForMovement &&
theScale > maskClosedScale )
        {
            theScale -= maskSpeed * Time.deltaTime;
        }

        // here, we check to see if the object is NOT
moving and if so, increases scale to expand the
visible area
        if ( moveSpeed <= minSpeedForMovement &&
theScale < maskOpenScale )
        {
            theScale += maskSpeed * Time.deltaTime;
        }
```

Above, moveSpeed is compared to minSpeedForMovement to see if we are moving at a speed over the threshold set in minSpeedForMovement. theScale is then compared to maskClosedScale so that we stop it from growing too big when we stretch out its scale. If the two conditions are met, theScale is incremented by maskSpeed * Time.deltaTime. You can adjust how fast or slow the mask will change size by adjusting the value of maskSpeed in the Inspector.

The second condition in the code block above deals with increasing the scale—this is pretty much the opposite condition to the one just before it. Here, we check that moveSpeed is less than or equal to the movement speed threshold in minSpeedForMovement.

Finally, with theScale worked out we can multiply the original scale held in myScale and set the .localScale on the Transform Component (via the reference in myTransform):

```
    myTransform.localScale = myScale * theScale;
}
```

That is the end of the MaskScaler.cs script. In the Scene, you will find it attached to the MaskRawImage GameObject, which is a child object of the Canvas GameObject.

Try Out the Example

Press Play to preview the Scene.

Remember that you may need to re-center the camera. The VR_Config script (attached to the [CameraRig] GameObject) takes care of this, when you press R on the keyboard.

When you drive the vehicle around the Scene, the field of view will change dynamically depending on your movement. When you stop moving, the view should open up with no limitation. It may well have the same effect if you kept the field of view restrictor on the screen at all times, but it is a nicer effect to size it dynamically. One of the great things about VR is to be able to look around and admire the environment—taking in its scale, lighting, and majesty is an amazing experience. As most of the VR sickness triggers involve movement or vection, standing still is the only time that some viewers can truly enjoy the environment without feeling ill, so removing the field of view restrictor whenever the viewer stands still makes sense as something to improve the experience for them.

Another advantage of the dynamic field of view system is that you may even be able to make it happen in such a way as to go mostly unnoticed. If you can tweak the settings and size of the mask, you may be able to lessen the impact of VR sickness quite unnoticed. The researchers at Columbia University were able to find a balance that meant several of their test subjects did not even notice when the field of view closed down.

I played around with the settings here quite a lot, but I did not really reach the same level of quality as that reported by the researchers. My time was limited, but perhaps you can manage to find a nice balance (feel free to let me know if you do—I am on Twitter and I would love to hear about it).

Here's how it works

1. A Canvas shows the mask image, just in front of the camera used for VR rendering.

2. The MaskScaler script Component is attached to the image. The MaskScaler will track the movement of the vehicle GameObject in the Scene.

3. The vehicle moves around. The MaskScaler script figures out how fast the vehicle is moving and changes the scale of the mask image if it finds that the vehicle is moving. When the vehicle moves, the mask gets smaller which, in turn, lowers the visibility in the scene—growing the amount of screen covered in black and shrinking the transparent circle in the center.

4. When the vehicle stops moving, the mask scales back toward its original size (which lets the entire view be visible).

In *Eagle Flight* (Ubisoft), they use an FOV mask with settings much stronger than mine. If you see the mask in a video, in stills, or anywhere outside of VR it may appear to be extremely obvious but it is not always the case. When you are involved with the action, immersed in the experience, you would be surprised by how strong you can make the mask before it becomes obtrusive. For the masking system to work, it needs to mask. So, do not be afraid to push it a little further by reducing its transparency to a more obvious level.

A THIRD-PERSON CAMERA SUITABLE FOR VR

As we have seen in games like *Lucky's Tale*, by Playful Inc., it is absolutely possible to make a fun and comfortable third-person experience in VR that can be enjoyed by just about everyone; including people who might normally get sick from VR. In their Virtual Reality Developers Conference talk, in March 2016, Dan Hurd and Evan Reidland from Playful Inc., outlined their approach to designing the levels and camera systems for *Lucky's Tale* (Hurd and Reidland, 2016).

One of their key observations was the importance of getting the camera movement just right. Some VR sickness symptoms may be triggered by the character stopping in place but the camera continuing to move. If the camera does not appear to exist in the same context as the player, moving in the same way, it appears to cause some kind of disconnect between the two, leading to an uncomfortable feeling for the viewer.

The research carried out by the Playful team is significant. It reinforces again that rules need to be in place, certain consistencies between what we see and what we expect to see, to make for a comfortable VR experience. The way the camera moves around and follows its targets has a significant impact on the comfort rating of the experience.

The Playful Inc. developer Evan Reidland outlines a camera system for third-person VR. They used a velocity-based linear follow camera, which is in a set position back from the main character. In this section, we build a camera based on their findings.

Note: If you suffer from VR sickness, you should sit down before trying the example project for this chapter. The camera moves around a lot and it may cause nausea and you may feel unstable on your feet. If you do begin to experience dizziness or sickness, remove the headset and take a break immediately.

Open and Try Out the Example File

Open the example project for this chapter. The example here is a game demonstration of a third-person arena game. Several robots spawn into the arena and the main character can move around and fire a blaster to blow up the robots. The graphics are taken from Unity's demonstration project, the same AngryBots project, and the majority of the game code can be found in my book *C# Game Programming Cookbook for Unity 3D* (Murray, 2014). The way that the game works is not important here, it is provided purely to give you a sense of how the camera works in a real environment like a VR game project. We will only be looking at the scripts applicable to the camera and VR.

In the SCENES folder, there are two Scenes named game_LBS and start_LBS. To try out the game, open the start_LBS Scene and hit Play with your headset on. Remember that you can reset the camera to its correct position at any time, by pressing the R button. Use a game controller or arrow keys on the keyboard and Z to fire the blaster.

Programming

In the Project browser, open the scene named game_LBS in the SCENES folder. This is the main game scene, where we can take a look at how the camera is being moved around and so forth. The script in this section is applied to an empty GameObject acting as a parent object to the camera itself. This allows us to easily offset the position of the camera from the target—the target being our character running around the virtual world.

The movement code is based on Playful's advice that we use the characters velocity to determine the camera speed, linking them together for cohesion. The key here is to make sure that the camera stops and starts as we expect it to, and not to follow the player around uniformly. When the player stops moving, we want the camera to stop moving too. This is counter to what you would normally see in game camera behavior. Normally, the camera movement speed would be independent of the player speed, following the target around the environment at a given speed of interpolation. Instead, we use the player speed to tell the camera how quickly to move or when not to move.

In the Hierarchy, find the GameObject named CameraParent.

Click on CameraParent so that you can see it in the Inspector. Right click on the VR_Cam Component in the Inspector and choose Edit Script from the dropdown menu.

Here is the script in full:

```
using UnityEngine;
using System.Collections;

public class VRCam : MonoBehaviour {

    private Vector3 deltaPosition;
    private Vector3 targetPosition;
    private Vector3 currentPosition;
    private Vector3 targetVelocity;
    private Vector3 currentVelocity;

    public float targetSpeed = 2;
    public float maximumVelocity = 10;
    public float acceleration = 20;

    public Transform followTarget;
```

```
    private Transform myTransform;
    private Rigidbody myRB;

    void Start()
    {
        myTransform = GetComponent<Transform>();
        myRB = GetComponent<Rigidbody>();
    }

      void Update ()
    {
        currentPosition = myTransform.position;
        targetPosition = followTarget.position;

        // grab deltapos
        deltaPosition = targetPosition - current
Position;
        targetVelocity = deltaPosition * targetSpeed;

        // clamp velocity
        targetVelocity = Vector3.ClampMagnitude
(targetVelocity, maximumVelocity);
        currentVelocity = Vector3.MoveTowards
(currentVelocity, targetVelocity, acceleration *
Time.deltaTime);

        myRB.velocity = currentVelocity;
    }

    public void SetTarget(Transform aTransform)
    {
        followTarget = aTransform;
    }
}
```

Script Breakdown
The script starts with:

```
using UnityEngine;
using System.Collections;

public class VRCam : MonoBehaviour {
```

The class derives from MonoBehaviour, as we will update movement within the Unity-called Update() function. As you can see in the code above, we do not need to use any packages other than the standard packages added automatically by Unity (UnityEngine and System. Collections).

The variable declarations are next:

```
private Vector3 deltaPosition;
private Vector3 targetPosition;
private Vector3 currentPosition;
private Vector3 targetVelocity;
private Vector3 currentVelocity;

public float targetSpeed = 2;
public float maximumVelocity = 10;
public float acceleration = 20;

public Transform followTarget;

private Transform myTransform;
private Rigidbody myRB;
```

I will explain the variables as we continue through the script. Next, the Start() function takes care of a little set up:

```
void Start()
{
    myTransform = GetComponent<Transform>();
    myRB = GetComponent<Rigidbody>();
}
```

Nothing unusual in the code above. We just grab references to the GameObject's Transform and Rigidbody Components so that they can be used further down in the script. You will see myTransform and myRB appearing in the Update() function below. The Update() function is the core of our class, where all of the position calculation takes place:

```
void Update ()
{
    currentPosition = myTransform.position;
    targetPosition = followTarget.position;
```

To find the current velocity of the player, we need to know where both of our main objects are, in the 3D space. currentPosition holds the position of the camera and targetPosition holds the place of the target object that we want the camera to follow around.

```
// grab deltapos
deltaPosition = targetPosition -
currentPosition;
targetVelocity = deltaPosition * targetSpeed;
```

Delta position is basically the difference in position between where we are and where we want to be, expressed as a Vector. In the code above, we get to the delta position by subtracting the current position of the camera from the position of the target.

To find out how quickly we want to move the camera around, a value to store in the targetVelocity variable, the next line takes deltaPosition and multiplies it by the targetSpeed variable. targetSpeed is a float used by the developer (us) in the Inspector, to tweak the camera speed. deltaPosition contains the direction we want to move in, targetSpeed contains the speed we want to get there at.

```
// clamp velocity
targetVelocity = Vector3.ClampMagnitude
(targetVelocity, maximumVelocity);
```

The movement needs to be clamped to a maximum, so that it does not go too fast. As developers, we need control over the maximum speed to be able to make sure that the experience stays comfortable. Zipping the camera around the scene at high speed would be a sure fire way to require barf bags.

To clamp the motion, here we use Vector3.ClampMagnitude which takes a vector to represent the original vector you want to clamp, and a float to represent the maximum length of vector for the ClampMagnitude function to return. The magnitude (the length from point to point) of the vector returned by Vector3.ClampMagnitude will be at the value in maximumVelocity. maximumVelocity is public so that the developers can alter this value in the Inspector easily.

```
currentVelocity = Vector3.MoveTowards
(currentVelocity, targetVelocity, acceleration *
Time.deltaTime);
```

currentVelocity is calculated inside the Vector3.MoveTowards() function. The Unity documentation describes MoveToward as moving a point in a straight line toward a target point. We take the currentVelocity and move toward the targetVelocity at a maximum distance of acceleration * Time.deltaTime. The variable acceleration is a float type variable, set by us earlier in the variable declarations or via the Inspector, to control the movement effect.

Unity gives access to its timing system via the Time class and Time. deltaTime is the time between this frame and the last frame. By multiplying our acceleration value by the Time.deltaTime, it provides a time-friendly value that will retain steady movement regardless of computer speed or any potential glitches in frame rate. This value is used to tell Vector3.MoveTowards how far to move each time this code runs. The vector returned by MoveTowards is held by currentVelocity, which is used in the next line to set the velocity of our rigidBody:

```
myRB.velocity = currentVelocity;
}
```

The last part of the script is the SetTarget() function:

```
public void SetTarget(Transform aTransform)
{
    followTarget = aTransform;
}
}
```

The SetTarget() function is there specifically to fit in with the game-specific code. The game code spawns the player into the scene and then needs a method to tell the camera about the player object, so that the camera can follow it around the scene as the game is played. The GameController script finds the main camera GameObject and uses GameObject. SendMessage (a Unity-provided function) to call the SetTarget() function, passing in the Transform of the player as a parameter. The variable followTarget is set to the transform passed in by the game code and the camera can then follow it around.

The Third-Person VR Camera Rig

With a script in place on the CameraParent GameObject, we should take a little look at the Inspector to revise the structure and see how it looks in the editor (Figure 13.3).

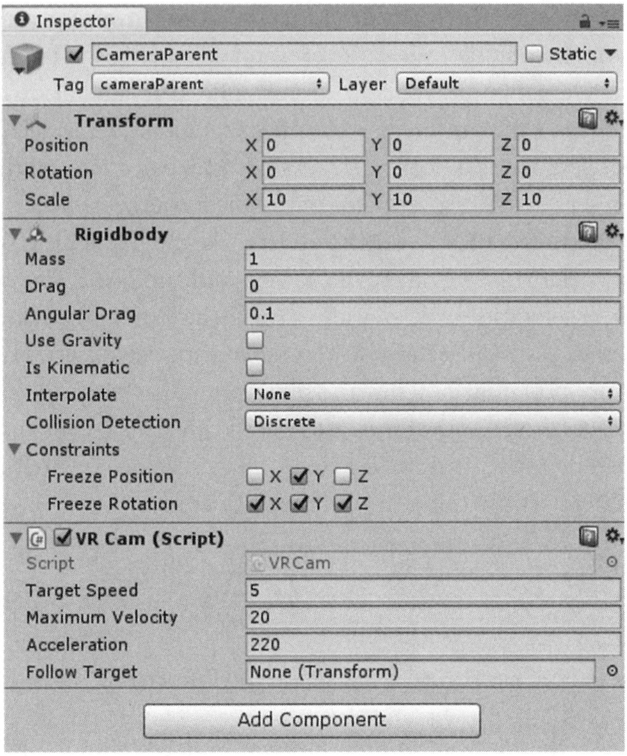

FIGURE 13.3 The third-person camera component in the inspector.

The VR Cam Component has three parameters. Those are

Target Speed: This is the speed we are consistently trying to get to.

Maximum Velocity: This is a limit on how fast the camera can actually move around.

Acceleration: The camera can gather up speed slowly or quickly toward its target speed. If the acceleration value is too low, you may find that the camera sometimes overshoots its target and takes too long to accelerate back in the opposite direction to follow its target.

By changing the parameters on the VR Cam Component, you can achieve a number of different effects to suit your game. Lower acceleration will make for slower transitions between stasis and movement. If you have slower moving targets, lowering the target speed will help to bring down the speed of the camera without affecting the transition speed and so on.

CameraParent moves around and [CameraRig] moves with it. If you were to expand the CameraParent GameObject out in the Hierarchy, you would find the standard SteamVR prefab [CameraRig] in there as a child object. All of the movement control is on CameraParent and there is no movement specific code on [CameraRig] at all.

In the next part of this chapter, we take a look at something a little unusual: a fake nose.

A FAKE NOSE? HOW DOES IT SMELL?!

One of the more bizarre sounding theories is that a virtual nose can reduce VR sickness. David Whittinghill, an assistant professor in Purdue University's Department of Computer Graphics Technology says that the virtual nose can reduce the effects of simulator sickness by 13.5% (Venere, 2015). Dr. Whittinghill says "You are constantly seeing your own nose. You tune it out, but it's still there, perhaps giving you a frame of reference to help ground you."

In this part of this book, I will provide you with a virtual nose (Figure 13.4) and show you how to apply it to your VR simulations.

It does not always need to be a nose, as we know it. The VR game *Eagle Flight* (Ubisoft) uses a shape similar to a nose to reduce motion sickness as players fly around the open skies of Paris. Instead of a literal nose, the developers chose to position a beak (you are, after all, playing as an eagle) where the player's nose might normally be. The beak substitute nose is believed to help players in exactly the same way as a regular nose shape might. If you are unsure about using a big schnozzle, perhaps try another similar shape to see if you can achieve a similar effect.

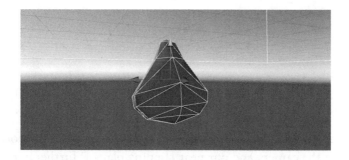

FIGURE 13.4 The virtual nose sits in the center of the view, barely visible.

Open the example project for this chapter. Import the SteamVR libraries the same way you did back in Chapter 3.

In the SteamVR folder, in the Project browser, inside the Prefabs folder drag in the [CameraRig] GameObject and add it to the Hierarchy.

Type Camera into the search box at the top of the Hierarchy, so that you can see all of the GameObjects with Camera in the name.

Leaving Camera in the search box, next look to the Prefabs folder and drag the Nose into the Hierarchy on top of the Camera(head) GameObject so that the nose becomes a child object of Camera(head). We will need to reposition the nose a little, but it will now move around with the camera as though it were attached to our face. Clear out the search box at the top of the Hierarchy and click Nose to highlight it.

In the Inspector, set the following values for the Transform of the Nose GameObject:

Position:

X: 0

Y: −0.09

Z: 0.05

Rotation:

X: −105

Y: 0

Z: 90

Scale:

X: 10

Y: 10

Z: 10

The camera will clip the nearside of the nose because it is positioned so close to the camera and our near clipping plane is further out, at 0.05.

Click on the Camera (eye) GameObject and, in the Inspector, change the Near Clipping Plane (on the Camera Component) to 0.02.

The nose color may not be to your liking, or for that matter match the color of your avatar's nose. To change the nose color, find the Materials folder in the Project browser. Click the NoseSkin material. In the Inspector, to the right of the word Albedo is a little color swatch (a square of color). Click on the color swatch to show the color picker and choose your new nose color. As this Material is already applied to the nose in the prefab, the nose in your Scene should update automatically as you select colors.

Grab your headset and hit Play to test out the Scene. You will notice that it is not quite possible to focus on it. That is the intended effect. It is supposed to work in a similar way to the visibility of a regular, real nose, in that we are constantly aware of its presence but unable to actually look at it in detail. Inside the VR headset, you should be able to see the nose if you close one eye and look at it, but it should not be too visible when you look straight ahead.

Some may find this whole nose business distracting whereas others may find it helps, so perhaps the best way to implement a virtual nose is to allow viewers to switch it on or off. The nose provided with this book is what I like to think of as a starter nose. It is usable enough to demonstrate the concept, but you could probably source a much nicer nose elsewhere. Feel free to also implement nose customizations, too, such as skin color and/or texture selection. I found that the nose in my own tests became less visible when I used darker colors, so you may want to experiment with the colors to find the least noticeable nose effect. Again, we only need it to be there not to be the perfect in-focus representation of a real nose. The virtual nose is there to help try to trick the brain into having one of its regular reference points back. You could also try out a few different nose shapes and sizes, too, so that people can choose how prominent the nose will be in their view.

RECAP

In this chapter, we looked at building a third-person camera that should make for more of a comfortable experience for viewers. Following on from that, we looked at another technique for reducing the effects of vection by reducing the field of view with an overlay. The final part of this chapter looked at adding a virtual nose. It may seem a little outlandish, but research suggests that it can make a difference in some subjects.

This brings us back to a point made in the previous chapter, in that we may not be able to stamp out VR sickness for everyone but we can at least provide some tools to lessen its effects. Something as silly sounding as a virtual nose may be just the right cue for someone out there to feel more comfortable, so it is worth consideration if your simulation is going to be out in the public domain where you do not know who will be experiencing it. The shape of the nose, its color, and visibility may have different effects for different people. Try to sniff out the best solution and do not blow it when you pick the nose.

In the next chapter, we take a brief look ahead to the future and wonder where things might be going from here.

Polish and Optimization

CUSTOMIZING THE STEAMVR COMPOSITOR

You may notice sometimes that the VR world switches out of your Unity project or turns white when the computer gets busy, such as when it is loading complex Scenes or doing some heavy calculations. This is caused by something known as the Compositor. The Compositor is in charge of synchronization, distortion, prediction, and other issues that would otherwise be a huge challenge to get working nicely for comfortable VR experiences. By default, the Compositor will show an empty world when the computer gets busy, but we can actually set it up to display a skybox instead. The skybox uses a system known as cube mapping to project six images in a cube around the camera, to create the illusion of a surrounding world.

The images it uses for the skybox can be generated from inside your own Unity 3D environment, to provide a much smoother transition and to help keep the user immersed inside your experience without breaking theme.

In this section, we will use a simple test environment to try out the procedure and see how it works.

Create a SteamVR Skybox for the Compositor

Open up the example project for this chapter, then import the SteamVR libraries as we did back in Chapter 3: Download the SteamVR API for Unity from the Unity Asset Store.

In the Scenes folder, open Sky.

Create an empty GameObject (click the Create button at the top of the Hierarchy and choose Create Empty). Name/re-name the empty GameObject to Skygen.

With the new Skygen GameObject selected, in the Inspector click the Add Component button. Choose Scripts > SteamVR_Skybox.

The SteamVR_Skybox script is awesome. One click should be all it takes to get the job done. Click the Take snapshot button (Figure 14.1) to have Unity build the skybox images for you. In the SteamVR Skybox Component, the image fields (Front, Back, Left, Right, Top, and Bottom) will be populated with some newly generated images.

The Take snapshot button will take a full 360 view of the scene, from the Main Camera. If you have added the [CameraRig] to your scene, or any other lead camera for that matter, it will use that. Whichever camera is dominant.

Grab the headset and hit Play, to preview the Scene. You should be able to look around as normal, but if you hit Pause in the Unity editor you will see that the SteamVR Compositor takes control of rendering and displays the skybox. There are a few small differences, usually in the shadows, but you should be able to see that the skybox is working.

The images generated by the system are simple 2D captures from each direction around the camera (Figure 14.2). Skyboxes are a traditional method used in videogame graphics to create the illusion of a sky around a 3D environment. The generated images are used to form a box that the Compositor renders around the view, creating the illusion of an environment in the same way a 360 video or panoramic photograph might work.

You can find all of the images that this system generates in a folder named sky, which will appear in the Project as a subfolder in whichever folder your Scene resides in. In this demo, that is Scenes > sky. You could re-use these images for other purposes, like effects for simulating reflection and so forth, if you wanted to.

The flat skybox is good, but you can also choose to use a stereoscopic rendering to create an illusion with depth. This makes the view look more realistic, but it will take significantly longer to do the rendering. The stereoscopic image generation procedure only builds two images, but they are two panoramic pictures that are offset for left/right stereoscopic view (Figure 14.3).

Stop the preview. We need to clear out the previous set of images before generating new ones.

In the Project browser, delete the sky folder (Find it in Scenes > sky, right click on sky and choose Delete).

FIGURE 14.1   A test scene with the SteamVR_Skybox Component added to generate a skybox for the Compositor.

FIGURE 14.2   SteamVR_Skybox Component generates a series of images to use when your Unity simulation's renderer is busy.

Click on the Skygen GameObject again, if it is not already highlighted. In the Inspector, click the Take stereo snapshot button. Give it a little time to render.

Headset on, hit Play to preview the Scene again. Pause the engine and take a look around.

You can use this technique in any environment, or just use the code to generate a different type of surround for the Compositor to use. It does not have to be your game, it could just be a mock-up of an environment with some text on it, for example.

FIGURE 14.3 The two stereoscopic images for the Compositor vary greatly in format from the regular six images used for cube mapping.

OPTIMIZING FOR VR

VR calls for the hardware to do a lot more than just render a single image for a monitor or TV screen. For VR, two images need to be rendered for the headset. The images also need to be updated quickly, to keep up with the speeds needed for comfortable experiences as our motion tracking hardware tries to keep up with a user's movements. At its current level, the quality of experience we would all strive to achieve is pushing the limits of the hardware we have and it is important to optimize the experience as much as possible. One of the most difficult parts of VR development is cramming everything into the simulation without destroying performance. Keeping the frame-rate high, responding quickly to input and providing smooth, intuitive interfaces are the key to providing a comfortable nausea-free VR experience for your users. It can sometimes be difficult to achieve, but Unity provides some tools to help make it happen and with a little caution it is possible to deliver really high-end experiences.

The Rendering Statistics Windows (Stats)

Your journey to optimization starts with the Stats window (Figure 14.4) which is accessible by the toggle button in the top right of the Game view. The information shown in the stats window contains

CPU—Main: This is the time that it takes to process and render a single frame of the Game view. This timer does not include time taken by the editor to do its thing—only how much time it took to put together a frame of the Game view.

Render Thread: This is the time taken to render a single frame of the Game view, without processing. This is only how long it takes to render.

Batches: This tells us how many objects have been batched together in terms of sending their data to be rendered.

Saved by Batching: This number is how many render passes have been saved through the process of batching. It is a good indicator of how much the batching optimization process is helping in your Scene.

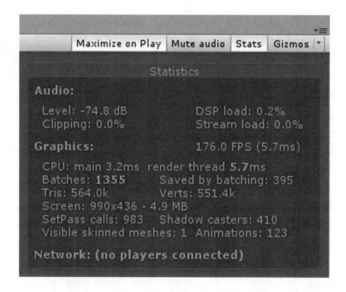

FIGURE 14.4   The Stats window shows running statistics in the Game view.

Tris and Verts: Triangles and vertices make up the entire 3D world. Although rendering technology is extremely good at dealing with them, you should always be wary of pushing the tris and verts counts too high.

Screen: This is the current resolution of the Game view, along with the antialiasing level and memory usage.

SetPass: The number of rendering passes. A high SetPass number will impact performance negatively.

Variable Skinned Meshes: This is the number of skinned meshes being rendered in the Game view.

Animations: The number of animations running in the Scene.

The Performance Profiler

To pinpoint exactly where the engine is working the hardest—where the CPU cycles are being spent—you can use the Profiler (Figure 14.5). As the application runs, the profiler collects information about all of the elements—scripts, shaders, audio, and so on—to display information about how they are using system memory, CPU cycles, and more useful tidbits you can use to figure out how to improve performance.

You can open up the Profiler window through the menu Window > Profiler. This is the Profiler in its most basic mode. With the Profiler window open, Unity will record performance data and display it on the graph (Figure 14.6).

Profiler Modes

Record   Start or stop performance data recording. Performance will be profiled whenever this button is checked and the Profile window is active (either open or hidden behind another tab, but not closed).

Deep Profile   The profile will record many different aspects of the simulation but if you wanted to get in-depth and have the editor record levels from all scripts and objects you will need to enable Deep Profiling. Deep Profiling monitors everything going on in the application, and you can enable it by clicking on the Deep Profile button from the bar of buttons at the top of the Profiler window. The downside to deep profiling is that you will be unable to do very much when it is happening due to the amount of resources and memory that the profiling process will take. Your project will very likely drop down to just a few frames per second as Unity times every single line

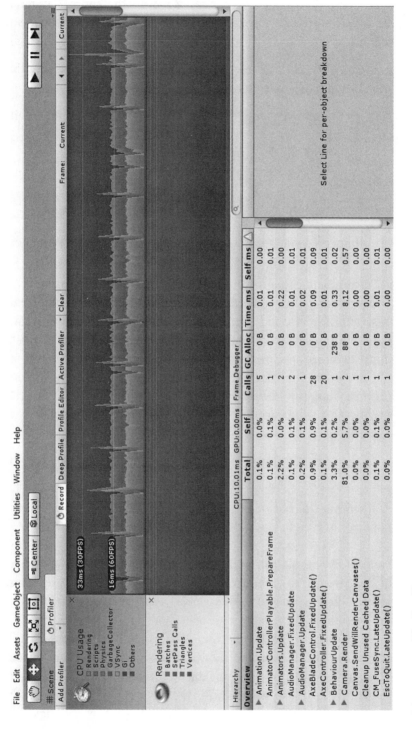

FIGURE 14.5   The Profiler.

FIGURE 14.6   The buttons across the top of the Profiler allow you to customize and choose the level of profiling.

of code being executed and every element being rendered or manipulated by the engine.

Profile Editor   This toggles whether or not to include the Unity editor in the performance data recording. Under normal circumstances, you can leave this unchecked but if you decide to use or build editor plugins or extensions, it can come in super-handy to make sure everything is behaving as expected.

Active Profiler   For SteamVR, as it stands right now there is no real reason for you to have anything to do with this one. It allows you to attach the profiler to different devices—useful for mobile or console development where you might want to profile your application running on the actual device rather than in the editor.

Clear   Clears the Profiler window of all recorded performance data.

What Do the Squiggles Tell You?

The Profiler window takes the form of a timeline, showing performance data recorded by any active profilers. You can click on the timeline and drag around to see the data recorded at specific times along the timeline.

The list down the left side of the window is the available profilers, with the currently selected category highlighted—the currently selected category will take over the timeline. Profilers in the profiler list are active and recording whenever the profiler is recording, but the data shown in the graph belong to the currently selected profiler only.

Profiler Types

The different available profilers:

CPU: The central processing unit (CPU) is the processor inside the computer.

GPU: The graphics processing unit (GPU) refers to the processor on the main board of the graphics card.

Rendering: The Rendering Profiler sheds light on how much time is spent doing the actual rendering and how the time is being spent.

Memory: The amount of memory your simulation uses can affect performance when it gets too high. When the memory is full, the computer system may end up being forced to move things around to accommodate new assets and so on, which can waste precious CPU cycles.

Audio: The performance impact of a few sounds may be small, but once your audioscape gets more complicated it can begin to affect things more. The Audio Profiler lets you know about the sounds in play and how they affect memory, CPU usage, and so on.

Physics: Overloading the physics engine will slow things down. The Physics Profiler lets you know some useful statistics about what the physics engine is up to and how all of the physics objects are behaving.

Physics 2D: Unity is also used for 2D games. The 3D and 2D physics are dealt with by two different physics engines inside the one engine, so profiling the 2D physics needs to be done separately by the Physics 2D Profiler.

Network Messages: When you are making multiplayer or networked projects, the Network Message Profiler will help to determine where and how network resources are being spent.

Network Operations: When you are making multiplayer or networked projects, the Network Operations Profiler provides profiling of network-specific functions like synchronized variables and Remote Procedure Calls (RPCs).

You can drag and drop the Profilers to re-organize them, remove them (e.g., to focus on specific areas without the performance overhead of unwanted profilers), or add new profilers from the Add Profiler button.

Example Usage

To demonstrate how the Profiler works, I will present a basic fictitious scenario.

Example 1: Rendering—In this example, I have the Deep Profiling toggle button set on so that the Profilers will record performance data at a deep level. I look at the graph in the CPU profiler (Figure 14.7) and I can immediately see that the majority of the graph is shown in green or

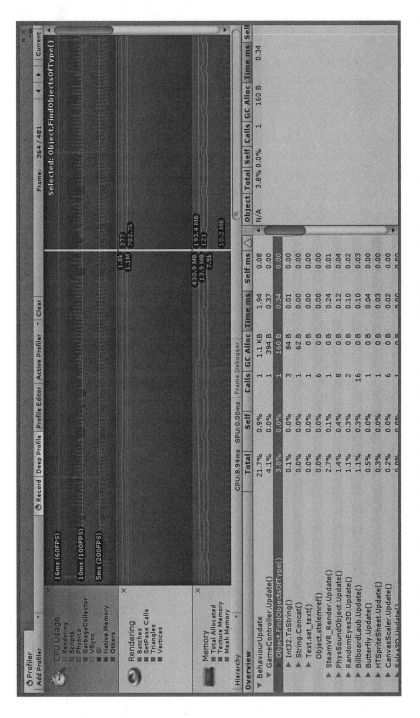

FIGURE 14.7   The Profiler graph here shows that BehaviourUpdate is top of CPU usage in the overview.

blue. As per the key to the left of the graph, we can see that green is the Rendering and blue is Scripts. Down under the graph is the overview. It is ordered by CPU usage by default, with the maximum CPU use at the top. Here, I can see that BehaviourUpdate is top of the list. This tells us that updating the scripts is the biggest bottleneck.

Expanding out BehaviourUpdate in the overview, I then find that GameController.Update() is at the top. This lets me know that my GameController script might need some improvement. I can then go on to expand GameController.Update and, at the top inside there, it says Object. FindObjectsOfType() at the top. The FindObjectsOfType() function is one built-in to Unity that we use to find GameObjects, but it can be quite a performance muncher when it is called frequently or in the wrong place. Looking in my GameController script I see, inside the Update() function, the following statement:

```
targetCount = FindObjectsOfType<TargetController>().
Length;
```

As FindObjectsOfType() gets called every time unity calls Update (which is every frame), it is making a substantial hit on my performance (NOTE: In Unity 5.5, the actual impact that FindObjectsOfType has on performance is substantially less than in previous versions, but I would still advise against using it in an update function like this). I move it out to the Start function, since my number of targets never changes I can do a count there instead. To see what happens, I re-run the Profiler and I can see that BehaviourUpdate is no longer at the top of the overview (Figure 14.8) and this simple fix has given the game a significant performance boost—BehaviourUpdate's CPU usage now down from 21.7% to just 6.8%.

After fixing up the GameController script, the Profiler now tells me that my biggest performance hit is no longer caused by the scripts—now, the biggest CPU eater is in rendering but that is an issue for another day! Perhaps batching will help?

Batching

When the renderer puts images together to display on the screen, it has to process each piece of geometry, lighting information, all of the shaders and textures, and send all of the relevant information to the display system. The CPU deals with all of the maths processing inside the PC as a GPU works on the graphics card to deal with the graphics-specific

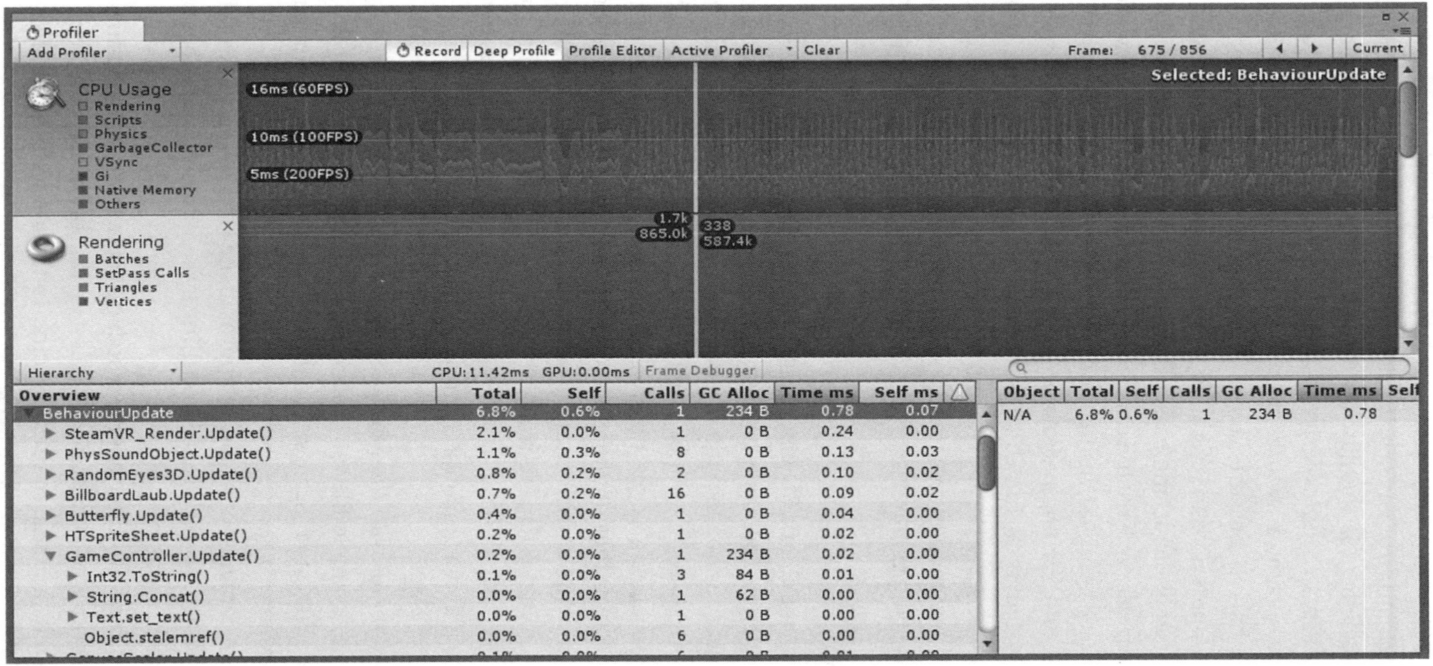

FIGURE 14.8 The Profiler after moving FindObjectsOfType() out of the main Update function.

processing. The two combined are extremely powerful and capable of some amazing things, but VR is extremely demanding for both of them. A huge challenge for the hardware is in moving the massive amounts of data to support the experiences we are trying to achieve—all those meshes, shaders, and textures take up a lot of bandwidth. In the game engine, we have a measure known as rendering passes. For the record, Unity developers used to refer to draw calls for performance, which have been replaced by rendering passes. Put simply; a rendering pass count is how many times we have to send information about objects to be drawn to the GPU. Keeping down the rendering pass count is vital to reducing bandwidth and keeping performance at a good level. Unity provides a batching system built-in, which can combine multiple draw calls into a single call whenever they share common features such as using the same material. When meshes remain in a single place, they can also be grouped together as static geometry.

Occlusion

Sometimes, not all of a 3D environment's nonmoving objects will be visible to the viewer. There may be obstacles between objects and the camera, or the camera may be looking in another direction. So why render them all, even when they may not be visible?

Occlusion culling is the process of skipping the rendering of static objects whenever they are not visible to the camera, whether that means out of the camera's visibility range or hidden behind other object(s). Unity's occlusion culling system has been refined down to a really straightforward set up process that will help you to squeeze out some extra frames per second with just a small amount of work.

Try Occlusion Out with the Example Unity Project

Open up the example file for this chapter in Unity: Chapter13_Project_Occlusion. Find the Scenes folder and open up the Scene named occlusiontest.

The main camera sits inside an approximate circle of 3D cubes (Figure 14.9). We will set up the occlusion culling system to hide any cubes out of the view of the camera.

First, we need to tell the engine which objects are static. Occlusion culling only works with static objects. Click on one of the cubes in the Scene view so that it shows up in the Inspector. In the top right of the Inspector is a checkbox labeled Static. Check the box.

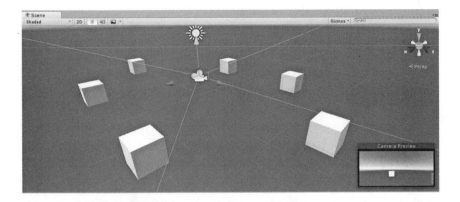

FIGURE 14.9   In the example project for this section, the main camera is surrounded by cubes.

Repeat the procedure for all of the remaining cubes. They all need their Static checkboxes setting to true for this to work. Note that if, for whatever reason, you only want to set the object to static for occlusion purposes only, use the Static dropdown menu to select individual static properties.

The Occlusion Panel

The Occlusion panel will give you access to everything you need for setting up. Open the Occlusion panel via the menu Window > Occlusion Culling. The Occlusion panel will open as an extra tab over the Inspector.

At the top of the window is a small section for Scene filtering. The available options are All, Renderers or Occlusion Areas, and the default setting is All. In that Scene Filtering section, click Occlusion Areas and you should notice that the GameObjects shown in the Hierarchy will disappear, as the editor filters out any type of object that is not an occlusion area. Since there are no occlusion areas set up at the moment, the Hierarchy will be empty.

Occlusion areas are used to tell Unity which areas to use in culling. This means you can pick and choose which areas should be affected by it. You do not actually need any occlusion areas if you intend for occlusion culling to affect the entire Scene. There is nothing to stop you from just hitting the Bake button in the Occlusion panel and letting Unity calculate occlusion data for the entire scene. We will cover adding an occlusion area here, anyway, since it may not always be the case that you will want to cull the entire Scene.

Adding Occlusion Areas

Click the Create New (Occlusion Area) button, in the Occlusion panel (Figure 14.10). In the Scene view, a new green cube should appear—this is a visible guide to the Occlusion area and it can be dragged and dropped around, re-sized and such, just like a regular GameObject.

The Occlusion area widget has handles on each of its faces, which can be used to resize it easily. You can just use the regular object move mode to drag them around. Grab the handles on the side faces and pull them out, so that the area covers all of the cubes around the camera (Figure 14.11).

The occlusion area will be used to calculate visibility data, which is then used at runtime to decide which models are visible and which ones are not and, in turn, which objects to render, and which ones not to. If your camera finds its way outside of the occlusion area, the occlusion culling will not work. You need to make sure that anywhere the camera might go, is covered by the occlusion area.

Bake the Occlusion Cells

Back in the bottom right of the Occlusion panel is a Bake button. Click Bake to have Unity go ahead and calculate all of the occlusion data. The Scene window will change. These are the data cells that Unity's occlusion

FIGURE 14.10 The Occlusion panel appears as a panel in the same part of the editor as the Inspector.

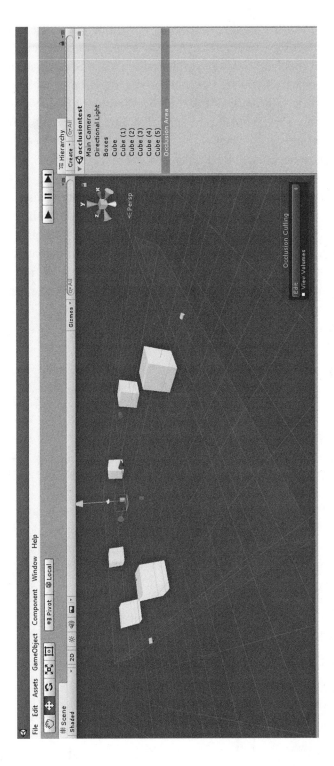

FIGURE 14.11   The occlusion area widget needs to cover all the objects to be included for occlusion.

culling system uses to create something known as binary trees. Binary trees can be a complex subject beyond the scope of this sentence, so we will leave it at that here. You can easily find some good information about binary trees online, if you are interested in digging deeper.

Try out the demo project: Check that the Maximize On Play checkbox, above the Game view, is not checked and that the editor layout shows both the Game view and Scene view at the same time. We want to be able to see the culling as it happens in the Scene view, but still be able to see what the camera sees in the Game view.

Press Play to preview the Scene. The camera will rotate based on the mouse position. Move the mouse left or right and notice how the cubes in the Scene view appear and disappear, depending on their visibility.

Occlusion culling is least useful for game environments that are combined into single large meshes, and most useful when you are making an environment with separate objects that may be easily hidden or rendered. Unity's terrain system will also be affected by occlusion culling, which helps a lot when trying to generate frame-rate-friendly scenes featuring terrains.

Quick Code Tips

The most important code tip I can pass on is to cache all of your object references that are accessed with GetComponent() in regularly called code or functions like Update(), FixedUpdate(), or LateUpdate(). If you are referencing transform or GameObject repeatedly, you may end up negatively impacting performance. It is a lot more efficient to declare variables to store references in.

Here, we will compare two versions of the same mouse rotation script from the "Occlusion" section of this chapter. The script is added to the camera as a Component and acts to rotate the camera around about its y axis based on the mouse position.

The bad way:

```
using UnityEngine;
using System.Collections;

public class MouseMove : MonoBehaviour {

    void Update () {
        Vector3 tempVec = transform.eulerAngles;
        tempVec.y = Input.mousePosition.x;
```

```
        transform.eulerAngles = tempVec;
    }
}
```

The good way:

```
using UnityEngine;
using System.Collections;

public class MouseMove : MonoBehaviour {

    private Transform myTransform;
    private Vector3 tempVec;

    void Start () {
        myTransform = GetComponent<Transform>();
    }

    void Update () {
        tempVec = myTransform.eulerAngles;
        tempVec.y = Input.mousePosition.x;
        myTransform.eulerAngles = tempVec;
    }
}
```

In the two scripts above, the first thing you may notice is that there is a bit more work involved in caching the references. That may be off-putting and when you are working to get things done quickly, the bad way may look like a more attractive proposition. Sure, it may be easier, but the performance hit will soon show up in Profiling and it is worth getting into the habit of doing things the good way.

In the bad way, we use the command transform to find the Transform Component attached to the same GameObject as this script.

Prioritize Where in the Update Cycles Your Code Runs
When using MonoBehaviour-derived classes, there are a number of functions that will automatically be called by the game engine at different times in its update cycles. For performance, you should put a little thought into where you code runs—as an example, you might not need UI updates to run in a function that gets called at a fixed frame rate and it would likely be more efficient to do it in LateUpdate, after everything else is done.

There are a huge number of automatically called functions (Unity calls these Messages) which you can go through in the Unity MonoBehaviour documentation at https://docs.unity3d.com/ScriptReference/Mono Behaviour.html but the most commonly used functions are

Awake()—When the script instance is being loaded, Awake() is called. This makes it the best place for initialization that does not rely on other GameObjects (since other GameObjects may not have been initialized at this stage).

Start()—This is called before any updates are called, at the start of the Scene after the script instance has loaded. It will only be called once by Unity.

Update()—The Update() function is called every frame. You cannot rely on the timing of it, so you either need to implement your own timing or avoid updating positions or physics here.

FixedUpdate()—called every fixed frame rate frame.

LateUpdate()—Called after all Update functions have been called, this is useful for updating things that occur after main updates or potential physics updates. For example, camera code is likely best placed in LateUpdate because cameras usually look to objects that might have moved during the main loop. Sometimes, you may find that placing camera following code anywhere other than LateUpdate will cause juddering.

OnEnable()—This function is called whenever the object becomes enabled and active.

OnDisable()—This function is called whenever the object is disabled.

As a rule, I generally stick to only using FixedUpdate() for physics updates such as applying forces and such. If code can possibly go into either Update() or LateUpdate(), I would rather it go there and run less than run as much as FixedUpdate().

Geometry and Modeling

As mentioned earlier in this book, VR is extremely demanding in terms of hardware requirements and how hard your PC will be pushed by rendering the virtual world. As we are at such an early stage of VR, the types of experiences we are aiming to achieve are right at the top end of what most computer hardware is capable of dealing with. Most VR-spec graphics cards will be pushed to render what we accept as normal on desktop systems, in a virtual world alternative. Anything we can do to reduce the load, within a reasonable compromise of quality if we have to, is going to be a big help.

Materials

Texture atlasing is the process of using a texture map which contains several different textures combined into a single image (Figure 14.12). The large multi-texture is mapped to more than one surface or 3D object differently, reducing the number of times that the CPU is required to send texture data to the GPU and reducing draw calls. Reducing draw calls will, in turn, improve performance.

Sadly, texture atlasing is not just a case of combining textures. It calls for the way that the 3D models are UV mapped to be tiled to suit. A 3D artist should plan to UV map in this combined way before texturing, as it is harder to re-texture a model for an atlas after it has been textured for individual image mapping.

FIGURE 14.12   A texture atlas combines multiple textures into one, saving memory and helping to increase performance. (Courtesy of Kenney Game Assets—www.kenney.nl.)

Level-of-Detail (LOD)

As a 3D model moves further away from the camera, its details are less visible. There is little point in rendering a highly detailed model when it is so far away that all of its details will be lost, so LOD provides a solution. Many videogames use a process known as LOD to draw different versions of models based on their distance from the main camera. Usually, each model is the same shape but containing different detail levels where, as you get closer the more detailed meshes are used and as you move further away the less detailed meshes are used. This takes a degree of strain off the processing—possibly reducing the number of meshes, reducing the number of triangles that need to be drawn, the draw calls, and possibly the total texture sizes required to render the current camera view.

LOD calls for the 3D artist to produce multiple versions of the same mesh, but the performance boost in complex games is huge. Most commercial games employ some kind of LOD system—if you have ever played any 3D games from the early 2000s you may have seen something called "popping in" where the switches between levels of details are very obvious and create a sort of popping effect as the environment around the main camera constantly changes. Nowadays, we usually employ some kind of fading effect to use transparencies and fade between meshes of different levels of detail—often with smart use of fading, the correct distances, and clever positioning, it is possible to almost completely hide the switching process from the viewer.

Unity has a built-in option for LOD grouping. To take advantage of it, you first need to create a set of meshes with names ending in _LOD followed by a number—for example, CAR_LOD0, CAR_LOD1, CAR_LOD2, CAR_LOD3, and so on—for as many LOD levels you want to provide. Unity assumes that 0 is the most detailed model, with LOD numbers increasing with lower detail models in the higher numbers.

When you import a sequence of meshes like this, an LOD group for the object with appropriate settings will be created for you automatically. When you add the main model to the Scene, it should already have an LOD Group Component attached to it (Figure 14.13) but if you need to, you can add an LOD Group Component via the Add Component button in the Inspector. You can find it under Rendering > LOD Group.

LOD Groups are used to manage level of detail (LOD) for GameObjects. With the LOD Group Component, you can change where the LOD models get switched out and add a fade effect between the transitions.

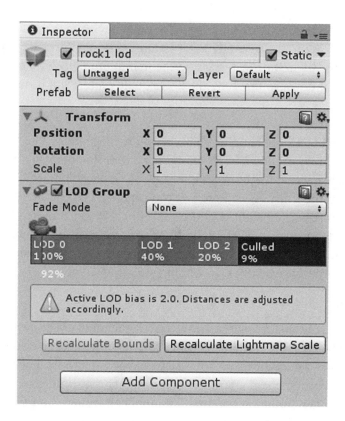

FIGURE 14.13   The LOD Group Component configures how the LOD system will choose which mesh to render.

There are also two global LOD settings that can be found in the Quality Settings menu inside the Unity editor Edit > Project Settings > Quality. In quality settings, there are two settings applicable to LOD. These are LOD Bias and Maximum LOD Level:

LOD Bias   The LOD Bias setting determines how LOD system will decide which level to use when it needs to decide between two levels. A lower bias leans toward less detail and a higher number more than 1 leans toward using the higher quality levels.

The Unity documentation provides the example where setting LOD Bias to 2 and having it change at 50% distance (set on the LOD Group Component), LOD actually only changes at 25%.

Maximum LOD Level   Models below the maximum LOD level are not included in the build, which means we can customize the LOD system for the type of device you are building for without having to rebuild or change your higher-end device-ready LOD set up. Lower-end devices might not require the highest detail levels and the maximum LOD level means you can drop it down so that only the lower quality levels will be used in the build.

Automated LOD If building the separate meshes seems like too much work, you may want to look at purchasing one of the automated solutions. One such solution might be Simple LOD by Orbcreation, which is available from the Unity Asset Store and can generate LOD meshes and carry out automatic set up with very little work. There are a few other LOD solutions and tools available on the Unity Asset Store, such as Automatic LOD by Ultimate Game Tools—it really depends on budget, what you are looking for, and what exactly you are hoping to achieve.

RECAP

At the start of this chapter, we investigated a method of generating a skybox for SteamVR to use during transitions. By keeping the viewer inside our virtual world, albeit within a static skybox that only looks like our virtual environment, their imaginations might be suspended in our world a little longer. To keep our virtual visitors comfortable and our experiences high quality, visiting Unity's profiler is a good way to find out how to make things run smoother. We looked at the profiling performance with the Profiler in this chapter, and also looked at something called occlusion. Occlusion means that the game engine only has to draw what is visible, saving precious processing time by leaving out any 3D geometry that need not be drawn. After looking at the occlusion system, we also covered some coding tips and finished off with a few hints and tips on keeping the geometry efficient.

All game projects go through some sort of optimization and polish phase and your VR projects should follow suit. If your VR experience is going out to the public, or it will run on unknown systems, you can never be quite sure how near or far that system will be from the minimum specifications recommended by the headset manufacturers. Other factors than the hardware itself often come into play, such as other programs that may be running in the background or any CPU-intensive background tasks that might be running as a part of the operating system. It is our job, therefore, as VR developers, to try to optimize our experiences as much as possible without compromising too much visual fidelity. The frame rates should be as high and as smooth as possible and it may take some work to get there, but it will be work that your audiences will appreciate in the long run. At the very least, you should look into profiling to make sure that there is nothing silly happening to cause your simulations to run at a speed less than optimal. If you can, try to always schedule polish and optimization time at the end of your project. Make sure that you are not still adding features at this stage, however. The project should be 100% feature complete for final optimization, but there is nothing stopping you from scheduling in multiple optimization sessions throughout development. Running the profiler, checking the occlusion, and double-checking code for more efficient approaches is something that should ideally be scheduled several times throughout the entire production. I am realistic and I understand that doing this weekly would probably be unacceptable in a production environment, but you should at least factor it into the development schedule, for example as production milestones, if that is how you are working. In VR, keeping the frame-rate up is utterly vital. With the current generation of technology, optimization is key to achieving that.

CHAPTER 15

Further Possibilities and a Final Word

THE FUTURE

The future is now, but there is another future tomorrow and it has some really cool technology in it! On the horizon, there are a few ways the technology makers are heading in their efforts to improve and build upon our virtual experiences. In this section, we will close this book with a little view to the horizon to see what is in the near future for VR.

Wireless Headsets

VR headsets which use mobile phones for the display have proven their place in the market and one of the biggest advantages they have over their desktop counterparts is the lack of cables to connect them to a computer. Mobile headsets such as Google Cardboard offer a wireless experience with no restriction on distance or location. People can use mobile VR anywhere—it is frequently used on public transport, outdoors, and in shared public spaces such as coffee shops or restaurants. As the range of room-scale VR systems increases and VR experiences are based in larger environments, this type of freedom is growing increasingly important as users need to be able to roam freely without being tied to a computer.

Cables present several problems for VR experiences; they are restrictive to movement and provide extra weight to the headset, they take away from the immersion of the experience by keeping the viewer grounded in reality and the cables are also easy to trip over, which means the user needs to be constantly aware of the cable position. HTC recently opened up pre-orders for a wireless peripheral for the Vive called TPCast and Oculus has given the world a sneak peek of a wireless headset that may end up going to market sometime in the future. It looks as though the next step for desktop computer-driven VR may be to remove the cables and go fully wireless like their mobile counterparts.

The Visus VR (http://www.visusvr.com/) already offers a glimpse of the future as it takes an alternative approach to the problem by using a mobile phone as a screen with the desktop computer providing the actual graphics and processing. The headset houses the mobile device and has a dedicated wireless tracking system built-in. As the mobile is only used for display, the minimum spec is lower than regular mobile VR.

Backpack Laptops

Sending data over wireless networks offers a number of challenges that may be hard to solve for longer ranged VR experiences. Several computer manufacturers are providing a solution in the form of a laptop, powerful enough to run VR, designed to run in a backpack. A backpack computer, such as the MSI VR-One, can hook into a VR headset—avoiding the need for trailing wires. Rift cameras need to be connected by USB cables, so they are not really an option for this but when a backpack laptop is combined with technology like Lighthouse (Valve's inside-out positional tracking system used by the Vive), it can provide a full desktop computer-driven VR experience without the need for cables of any kind.

Warehouse-Scale Experiences

VR company WorldViz is taking motion tracking to the next level. Their technology allows users to walk around in a space the size of a warehouse and still be tracked by a motion-sensing system. Their tech is perfect for larger scale experiences, such as VR theme parks and VR arcade experiences like laser tag in VR.

So far, we have looked at ways to expand the play space and take VR away from being tethered to a computer. As well as expanding the scope of the virtual world, hardware makes are making significant improvements in our interactions with the virtual world.

Eye Tracking

Some experts suggest that eye tracking will substantially improve VR. Tracking pupil position and gaze direction will help developers to anticipate what the viewer is trying to accomplish. VR hardware with eye tracking may be able to provide a performance boost by rendering what you are looking at in high detail, but only using lower quality rendering everywhere else. This works in a similar way to how the brain processes images through a human eye. It may also lead to more realistic experiences with image effects to recreate focus and depth of field around the user's gaze.

Light Field VR

Nvidia and Stanford University have come up with a way to make VR a more comfortable experience. According to researchers (Kramida and Varshney, 2016), vergence–accommodation conflict can cause problems with how our eyes focus in the virtual world. The subject is complicated, but to summarize it; our eyes use real-world distance for focus and when it is not there, the eyes cannot act in their natural way and that can cause eye strain or even act as one of the cues that may aggravate VR sickness. Light Field VR allows the viewer's eyes to respond more naturally and rest at focal cues, reducing strain and allowing eyes to work much closer to how they would focus on objects in the real world for a more comfortable experience.

In November 2013, Nvidia researchers Dr. Douglas Lanman and Dr. David Luebke published a paper at the ACM SIGGRAPH Asia illustrating the company's prototype near-eye Light Field display (Lanman and David, 2013).

Right now, the Near Eye Light Field VR headset is still in an early prototyping phase and the version shown at Virtual Reality Los Angeles Expo (2016) was not ready for commercial sale. Price and exact specifications are still yet to be announced at the time of writing.

SparseLightVR

Microsoft Research found an inexpensive way to expand the field of view in a VR headset by using an array of LEDs around the lenses. The LEDs are lit as though they are giant pixels, but as they are right at the limits of what our eyes see, the changes in color and brightness are enough for our brains to feel more comfortable and to reduce VR sickness. It is, according to Microsoft Research, as though the headset's view is much wider. It will be interesting, as tech develops, to see if VR headset manufacturers will begin to incorporate this system in the interim, or opt to wait for larger screens. For more information on this, you can watch a YouTube video: https://www.youtube.com/watch?v=af42CN2PgKs.

Khronos VR

Already, we are seeing a fragmentation of the VR market. Multiple proprietary runtimes and drivers mean more work for developers to see their experiences on a spread of devices. Many industry leaders such as Razer, Valve, and Google are working together to bring Khronos VR to life. Khronos VR is initiating the development of a standard way for VR applications to connect to VR hardware. For developers, this could be a huge help. At the moment, we have to rely on some tricks and hacks to be able to run content intended for specific headsets. Although still in early development, if Khronos VR is adopted it will lead to more choice for VR consumers and better support across the board. Visit khronos.org for more information.

FINAL WORD

Since the first page, this has been a crazy awesome journey. If you have been playing along with the projects in this book, you will have gone right from setting up the hardware and downloading software all the way through to looking at cutting-edge technologies such as Leap Motion. I like to think that this book has what you need to get up and run with VR development using SteamVR, whether that is taking just a few pieces or taking it all. One of the reasons I chose to use SteamVR libraries over other specific hardware-provided systems is the flexibility it offers and quality of the software, giving you the widest possible audience and widest number of devices at the lowest cost. Using the SteamVR system means that we only need to manage a single codebase for multiple devices and device types. With its full integration with the Steam store, OSVR compatibility, Steam social network and download client, SteamVR makes for a feature-rich, wide-reaching environment already geared up for solid, social experiences.

Now that we have reached the end of this journey, I hope that you go on to take what is in this book and venture out there to bring your VR ideas to life on your next adventure. The virtual space is a place without rules, which makes it the perfect place to get a little crazy and try something different. All of the rules and conventions we have established in videogames and simulations are there to be built upon or completely rewritten for VR. Do not think for a second that the conventional approach is the best or only way to do something. In the virtual world, it is all unknown. If something feels natural, regardless of what it is or how silly it seems: you should pursue it and see where it goes. Ten years from now, a simple crazy idea you have today could become a convention of interaction in the future. Get wacky and aim for great experiences rather than following the herd!

Feel free to let me know what you create, because I would love to hear about it. Find me on Twitter @psychicparrot and give me a shout! Create, explore, have fun, and please always take good care of yourself and everyone else.

Have fun making games!

Jeff.

References

3Dfx Interactive 3D chipset announcement. *Google Groups.* Last modified November 26, 1995, accessed April 11, 2017. https://groups.google.com/forum/?hl=en#!msg/comp.sys.ibm.pc.hardware.video/CIwBRIX9Spw/YQIsql5GwAYJ.

Allen, B., T. Hanley, B. Rokers, and C. Shawn Green. 2016. Visual 3D motion acuity predicts discomfort in 3D stereoscopic environments. *Entertainment Computing* 13: 1–9.

Andersen, G. J. and M. L. Braunstein. 1985. Induced self-motion in central vision. *Journal of Experimental Psychology: Human Perception and Performance* 11(2): 122–132.

Artaud, A. 1958. *The Theatre and Its Double: Essays.* Translated by Mary Caroline Richards. New York: Gross Press.

Doulin, A. 2016. Virtual reality development tips. *Gamasutra: The Art & Business of Making Games.* Last modified June 14, 2016, accessed April 11, 2017. http://www.gamasutra.com/blogs/AlistairDoulin/20160614/274884/Virtual_Reality_Development_Tips.php.

Evarts, H. 2016. *Fighting Virtual Reality Sickness.* The Fu Foundation School of Engineering & Applied Science, Columbia University. Last modified June 14, 2016, accessed April 11, 2017. http://engineering.columbia.edu/fighting-virtual-reality-sickness.

Fernandes, A. S. and S. K. Feiner. 2016. Combating VR sickness through subtle dynamic. *2016 IEEE Symposium on 3D User Interfaces (3DUI).* Greenville, SC, 201–210.

Hall, C. 2016. Sony to devs: If you drop below 60 fps in VR we will not certify your game. *Polygon.* March 17. Accessed December 12, 2016. http://www.polygon.com/2016/3/17/11256142/sony-framerate-60fps-vr-certification.

Hurd, D. and E. Reidland. 2016. 'Lucky's Tale': The unexpected delight of third-person virtual reality, a technical postmortem. Video. Accessed on April 11, 2017. http://www.gdcvault.com /play/1023666/-Lucky-s-Tale-The.

Kisner, J. 2015. Rain is Sizzling Bacon, Cars are Lions Roaring: The Art of Sound in Movies. *The Guardian.* July 22. Accessed December 12, 2016. https://www.theguardian.com/film/2015/jul/22/rain-is-sizzling-bacon-cars-lions-roaring-art-of-sound-in-movies?utm_source=nextdraft&utm_medium=email.

Kolansinski, E. M. 1995. *Simulator Sickness in Virtual Reality.* Technical Report, Alexandria, VA: United States Army Research Institute for the Behavioral and Social Sciences.

Kolasinski, E. M. 1996. *Prediction of Simulator Sickness in a Virtual Environment.* Dissertation, Orlando, FL: University of Central Florida.

Kramida, G. 2016. Resolving the vergence-accommodation conflict in head-mounted displays. *IEEE Transactions on Visualization and Computer Graphics* 22(7): 1912–1931. doi:10.1109/tvcg.2015.2473855.

Lang, B. 2016. Touch and Vive Roomscale Dimensions Visualized. Road to VR. December 5. Accessed December 12, 2016. http://www.roadtovr.com/oculus-touch-and-htc-vive-roomscale-dimensions-compared-versus-vs-visualized/.

Lanman, D. and D. Luebke. 2013. Near-eye light field displays. *ACM Transactions on Graphics (TOG)* 32(6). doi:10.1145/2508363.2508366.

Murray, J. W. 2014. *C# Game Programming Cookbook for Unity 3D.* Boca Raton, FL: CRC Press.

Sell, M. A., W. Sell, and C. Van Pelt. 2000. *View-Master Memories.* Cincinnati, OH: M.A. & W. Sell.

Statista. 2016. Virtual Reality (VR)—Statistics & Facts. *statista.* Accessed December 12, 2016. https://www.statista.com/topics/2532/virtual-reality-vr/.

Venere, E. 2015. 'Virtual nose' may reduce simulator sickness in video games. Purdue University. Last modified March 24, 2015, accessed April 11, 2017. http://www.purdue.edu/newsroom/releases/2015/Q1/virtual-nose-may-reduce-simulator-sickness-in-videogames.html.

Weinbaum, S. G. 1949. *A Martian Odyssey: And Others.* Reading, PA: Fantasy Press.

Wikipedia, "Binary Tree," *Wikipedia, The Free Encyclopedia.* Last modified April 15, 2017. https://en.wikipedia.org/w/index.php?title=Binary_tree&oldid=773837683.

Index